MARK TWAIN:
A Sumptuous Variety

27.

MARK TWAIN:
A Sumptuous Variety

edited by
Robert Giddings

VISION
and
BARNES & NOBLE

Vision Press Limited
Fulham Wharf
Townmead Road
London SW6 2SB

and

Barnes & Noble Books
81 Adams Drive
Totowa, NJ 07512

ISBN (UK) 0 85478 006 8
ISBN (US) 0 389 20541 9

Printed and bound in Great Britain by
Unwin Brothers Ltd.,
Old Woking, Surrey.
Phototypeset by Galleon Photosetting,
Ipswich, Suffolk.
MCMLXXXV

Contents

Introduction

by ROBERT GIDDINGS

> He had the Southwestern, the Lincolnian, the Elizabethan
> breadth of parlance, and I was often hiding away . . . the letters
> in which he had loosed his bold fancy to stoop on rank
> suggestion; I could not bear to burn them, and I could not, after
> the first reading, quite bear to look at them.
> —William Dean Howells (1837–1920) on Mark Twain's letters

1

Mark Twain is a resounding genius whose brilliant light has
been hidden behind the bushel of his own reputation. The
Missouri Vacation Guide, published by the Missouri Division of
tourism, in Jefferson City, the capital of the state which
proudly claims Twain as its native son, devotes several highly
colourful pages to the 'Mark Twain Region'. And what a jolly
legacy the old fellow seems to have left us:

> From a famous whitewashed fence, a scenic skylift and the
> homes of distinguished soldiers to fine hunting, caves, beaches
> and covered bridges, the Mark Twain region of Northwest
> Missouri offers fun for the whole family. The author and
> humourist who gave the region its name was a native of the
> Hannibal area. Born in Florida, Missouri, where his birthplace
> is preserved, Samuel Clemens moved to nearby Hannibal and
> spent his boyhood years in this Mississippi River town. His
> boyhood home is now a free museum honouring the youngster
> who grew up to become Mark Twain, one of the best loved
> writers of all time. At Twain's boyhood home is the famous
> board fence that Tom Sawyer got his friends to whitewash and
> across the street is the home of Becky Thatcher. Just down the
> Mississippi is Mark Twain Cave, open to visitors, where Twain
> went exploring as a youth. . . .[1]

The association of Twain with the past, with boyhood, innocence and wholesome fun is altogether characteristic. In some ways it is relevant, in ways unsuspected by those who wish to promote tourism in the state of Missouri. There *is* an important element of the child in Mark Twain. Elinor Glyn met him in New York in 1907 and recorded:

> He is a dear old man with a halo of white silky hair and a fresh face, and the eyes of a child which look out on life with that infinite air of wisdom one sees peeping sometimes from a young pure soul. To find such eyes in an aged face proves many things as to the hidden beauties of his character. . . .[2]

But there are serious qualifications to be made. Bearing in mind Dumas's famous comment—'Why is it that children are so intelligent and adults so stupid? It must be education that does it . . .'—we need to focus attention on certain aspects of Twain child-like qualities.[3]

To be sure there is the sense of fun. The fun is frequently to be located in Twain's way of looking at things, in his recognition of the essential daftness of life. His work is rich in such examples. This is bound to be the case, as it seems basic to his perceptions. From the myriad possible passages, take any one of those seemingly casual pieces of jokey narrative in *Tom Sawyer*. You can open this masterpiece anywhere and find them. There is his description of the system which allows Tom—of all boys—to win a prize Bible. This is possible because the prize is awarded on the basis of accumulating tickets of varying colours for learning verses by heart.

This is silly enough, but a genius like Twain does not have it in him to leave it at that:

> . . . each got his reward in small blue tickets, each with a passage of scripture on it; each blue ticket was pay for two verses of the recitation. Ten blue tickets equalled a red one, and could be exchanged for it; ten red tickets equalled a yellow one; for ten yellow tickets the Superintendent gave a very plainly bound Bible (worth forty cents in those easy times) to the pupil. How many of my readers would have the industry and the application to memorize two thousand verses, even for a Doré Bible? And yet Mary had acquired two Bibles in this way; it was the patient work of two years; and a boy of German parentage had won four or five. He once recited three thousand

verses without stopping; but the strain upon his mental faculties was too great, and he was little better than an idiot from that day forth—a grievous misfortune for the school, for on great occasions before company the Superintendent (as Tom expressed it) had always made this boy come out and 'spread himself'. Only the older pupils managed to keep their tickets and stick to their tedious work long enough to get a Bible, and so the delivery of one of these prizes was a rare and noteworthy circumstance; the successful pupil was so great and conspicuous for that day that on the spot every scholar's breast was fired with a fresh ambition that often lasted a couple of weeks. . . .[4]

Here we have the viewpoint of one who clearly refuses to take the world on its own terms. The very system which supports the functioning of the community—albeit in this case only a provincial school—is perceived as utterly unreasonable. The prize offered is worth only forty cents in real money, but the ceremonies and rituals in which the whole matter has been dressed up ensures that many strive to achieve it. Not only that, but the very means of earning the prize—learning scripture by rote—successfully devalues the true worth of the prize, as it renders the scriptures merely stored data in the striver's retrieval system which is transformed into meaningless mumbo-jumbo in the very act of memorizing. In spite of this, the silly system has been so successfully socially constructed that many compete and several by their determined efforts win several of these worthless prizes. Given this treatment, far from providing divine light and guidance, the scriptures have driven beings mad. This is a shame because the school (that is to say, the system) liked to show off its more successful contestants.

Twain's very way of telling you these things makes you willynilly a partner of his particular perspective. It is assumed that neither Mark Twain nor the reader in whom he is confiding would be able to manage these feats of memory, or would even bother to manage them, though the prize might be a 'Doré Bible'. There is a wholly characteristic 'knowingness' which Twain communicates to you as you read the words on the page. This turns you into a sharer of Twain's worldview without your realizing it.

9

The viewpoint crystallizes a particular way of looking at the world, not accepting the world's self-estimate, and answering 'Oh yeah?' to each and every one of the world's basic assumptions. Comedy, in the hands of Mark Twain, becomes chief amongst the weaponry by which to resist received opinion and the seeming permanence of the social order. Much of Twain's humour may easily be seen as part of a long and respectable tradition. As Eric Mottram wrote:

> His world-wide reputation was based on a gift for mixing boyish rascality and innocence in a naïve, vernacular vision, one complicated, however, by his darkening, bitter view of man as hypocrite, victim and self-deceiver.[5]

It is a fact that much of Twain's humour seemingly belongs in the context of a tradition which proudly includes among its ornaments such geniuses as W. C. Fields and Groucho Marx.[6] Max Sennett once said revealingly of a brilliant sketch by Fields: 'I had the notion that he had settled several old scores known only to himself.'[7] There is an element of getting-your-own-back which is basic to all humour. It is often quite strongly to be sensed in Twain, but its obviousness is masked by artistry.

In Twain the technique is infallible. Here is his reaction when granted a sight of a manuscript by the greatest epic poet of Augustan Rome, annotated in the handwriting of one of Italy's most celebrated poets:

> We saw a manuscript of Vergil, with annotations in the handwriting of Petrarch, the gentleman who loved another man's Laura and lavished upon her all through life a love which was a clear waste of the raw material. It was sound sentiment, but bad judgement. It brought both parties fame and created a fountain of commiseration for them in sentimental breasts that is running yet. But who says a word in behalf of poor Mr. Laura? (I do not know his other name.) Who glorifies him? Who bedews him with tears? Who writes poetry about him? Nobody. How do you suppose *he* liked the state of things that has given the world so much pleasure? How did he enjoy having another man following his wife everywhere and making her name a familiar word in every garlic-exterminating mouth in Italy with his sonnets to her preempted eyebrows? They got fame and sympathy—he got neither. This is a peculiarly

felicitous instance of what is called poetical justice. It is all very
one-sided—too ungenerous. Let the world go on fretting about
Laura and Petrarch if it will; but as for me, my tears and my
lamentations shall be lavished upon the defendant.[8]

The essence of the humour lies in Twain's eccentric
rejection of received opinion. He comes at us as a completely
honest man, directly reacting to what he sees. His opinions are
wholly uncluttered by the débris of academic fustian or
classical learning. He is speaking as a man among men, and as
a man directly to the reader. This was a manner which he took
great pains to achieve. Twain once told William Dean
Howells: 'I amend dialect stuff by talking and talking it till it
sounds right.' Obviously connected with this tendency in his
art is his notorious detestation of Sir Walter Scott and James
Fenimore Cooper. Twain's was the art which hides art. This
apparently easeful vernacular delivery was not created by
anything less than the most harsh apprenticeship, involving
much toil. He advised an amateur in 1884: 'You write as a
man *talks* and very few can reach that height of excellence.'[9]
His handling of language was a quality singled out for praise
by H. L. Mencken:

> Mark was not only a great artist; he was pre-eminently a great
> American artist. No other writer that we have produced has
> ever been more extravagantly national. Whitman dreamed of
> an America that never was and never will be; Poe was a
> foreigner in every line he wrote; even Emerson was no more
> than an American spigot for European, and especially German,
> ideas. But Mark was wholly of the soil. His humour was
> American. His incurable philistinism was American. His very
> English was American. . . .[10]

In a later essay, *American Language* published in 1930,
Mencken claimed that Twain had deliberately engrafted the
American West's 'greater liberty and more fluent idiom upon
the stem of English, and so lent the dignity of his high
achievement to a dialect that was as unmistakably American
as the point of view underlying it'.[11] To which we might in all
fairness add the plea that the great American humourist and
author had also assimilated the influence of a fair amount of
European literature and the English classics in particular, and

that he was well steeped in our eighteenth-century masters, especially Swift, Goldsmith and Smollett, and that the mark of Thomas Paine should also be acknowledged as formative and beneficial.[12]

Twain's years of experience as a popular lecturer obviously aided the shaping of his truly oral use of American English. But it is not just a matter of vocabulary and syntax which is of importance here. It is also the relationship between Twain and his reader, and Twain and his listening audience. That typically American institution, the oral tale, in which not only the story but the way of telling it is so vital, is central in Twain's art. He must have cultivated the poker face, the deadpan delivery, during his career as a public speaker. One reviewer describes him performing:

> The aggrieved way in which he gazes with tilted chin over the convulsed faces of his audience, as much as to say—'Why are you laughing?'—is irresistible in the extreme. . . . His face is immovable while his hearers laugh, and as he waits for the merriment to subside, his right hand plays with his chin. . . . These characteristics agree so well with his description of himself in his books—Innocence victimized by the world, flesh and Devil—that one cannot fail to establish the resemblance and laugh at the grotesque image.[13]

In his own words:

> I do not claim that I can tell a story as it ought to be told. I only claim to know how a story ought to be told, for I have been almost daily in the company of the most expert story tellers for many years.
>
> There are several kinds of stories, but only one difficult kind—the humorous. . . . The humorous story is American, the comic story is English, the witty story is French. The humorous story depends for its effect upon the *manner* of the telling; the comic story and the witty story upon the matter. . . .[14]

According to Twain, a humorous story may be spun out and wander about at will, whereas comic and witty stories have to be brief. Humorous stories simply bubble along, the others burst. He recognizes the high art involed in humorous story-telling. Comic and witty stories can be told by anyone: 'The humorous story is told gravely; the teller does his best to conceal the fact that he even dimly suspects that there is anything funny about it. . . .'[15]

The humorous story, according to Twain, was created in America, and has remained at home. This may well be true. But as far as Mark Twain was concerned, it was America at a particular stage of its development.

2

Samuel Langhorne Clemens was born in Florida, Missouri, on 30 November 1835. Halley's Comet appeared at the time. In 1910, as he lay dying, the Comet was again seen in the sky. His lifespan was appropriately outlined in heavenly brilliance.

Samuel's father was a carefree lawyer and storekeeper who originally came from Tennessee. He was locally known as 'Judge' Clemens. When the boy was 4 years old the family moved to Hannibal, Missouri. He died when Samuel was 12. The family was left on the breadline and young Samuel had precious little formal education, but was to enjoy the benefit— of which he made overwhelming use—of two significant influences. One was the life and lore of the Mississippi river town, frontier life and the vast oral traditions he absorbed almost as the air he breathed. The other was his early acquaintance with publishing, the world of print and journalism. Twain's art is a dazzling example of the fusion of the creative imagination with the technology of the means of production and distribution.[16]

Sam became a printer's apprentice and a few years later was a printer for his elder brother, Orion, on the *Hannibal Journal*. He was later to say, with reference to his qualifications as a novelist: 'I surely have the equipment, a wide culture and all of it real, none of it artificial, for I don't know anything about books.'

His childhood made a lasting impression on him, and provided a reservoir of experience he was able to draw on all his life as a writer. He was to find developments in America which he saw all around him far less congenial, and this creates a marked tension in his world, between the present and the past, a tension between idyll and nightmare, which becomes a characteristic of his cast of mind. In some significant respects Samuel was a child of his time. He was growing to maturity in the West where there was unquestionably the feeling that a new society was in the making, and it was the Civil War (in which Twain was to play so curious a part) which gave the U.S.A. the imprimatur of nationhood. In 1845 a company of 160 emigrants set out from Independence, Missouri, for Oregon and California. Lansford W. Hastings, who went with them, recorded on 16 May 1845:

> Now, all was high glee, jocular hilarity, and happy anticipation, as we thus darted forward into the wild expanse, of the untrodden regions of the 'western world'. The harmony of feeling, the sameness of purpose, and the identity of interest, which here existed, seemed to indicate nothing but continued order, harmony and peace, amid all the trying scenes incident to our long and toilsome journey. But we had proceeded only a few days travel, from our native land of order and security, when the 'American character' was fully exhibited. All appeared to be determined to govern, but not to be governed. Here we were, without law, without order, and without restraint; in a state of nature, amid the confused, revolving, fragments of elementary society! Some were sad, while others were merry; and while the brave doubted, the timid trembled! Amid this confusion, it was suggested by our captain, that we 'call a halt', and pitch our tents, for the purpose of enacting a code of laws, for the future government of the company. The suggestion was promptly complied with, when all were required to appear in the legislative capacities.[17]

As Daniel J. Boorstin comments on this passage, the point is that the nation was actually forming itself before men's eyes, and the very formation of its nationhood was in the air:

> The nation was beginning not at one time or place, but again and again, under men's very eyes. Americans were forming new communities all over the wild expanse of the western world. Within less than a century after the American Revolution— even before the Civil War—the fringe of colonial settlements, ocean-bound to their mother countries, would become a continent-nation.[18]

The Civil War and the railways, forces which were foremost in the creation of America's nationhood, were the very forces which destroyed the river-town and river-traffic idyll which

14

Twain's imagination was so happy to haunt. The past was the price sacrificed to make the present and urge the construction of the future. Charles Francis Adams, Jr. commented on the impact of the transcontinental railroad in 1868:

> Here is an enormous, an incalculable force . . . let loose suddenly upon mankind; exercising all sorts of influences, social, moral, and political; precipitating upon us novel problems which demand immediate solution; banishing the old, before the new is half matured to replace it; bringing the nations into close contact before yet the antipathies of race have begun to be eradicated; giving us a history full of changing fortunes and rich in dramatic episodes. Yet, with the curious hardness of a material age, we rarely regard this new power otherwise than as a money-getting and time-saving machine. . . . not many of those . . . who fondly believe they control it, ever stop to think of it as . . . the most tremendous and far-reaching engine of social change which has ever either blessed or cursed mankind. . . . Perhaps if the existing community would take now and then the trouble to pass in review the changes it has already witnessed it would be less astounded at the revolutions which continually do and continually must flash before it; perhaps also it might with more grace accept the inevitable, and cease from useless attempts at making a wholly new world conform itself to the rules and theories of a bygone civilization.[19]

Powerful social and economic forces were at work long before the Civil War. The extension of the western frontier was an essential ingredient in the fulfilment of the Jeffersonian dream of a land-owning democratic society. Strong support was articulated by the *New York Tribune*, edited by Horace Greeley, by the Free Soil Party, by the Democratic Party and finally by the Republican Party.[20] The result was the Homestead Act, which was approved on 20 May 1862: 'An Act to secure Homesteads to actual Settlers on the Public Domain'. Technically the land was free, any citizen who settled on a vacant lot and made improvements on it within five years got a grant of 160 acres, paying only the slight fees required to record applications. Before the end of the Civil War 26,552 entries were made. There was a rush for claims after the War. In 1866 the number of recorded settlements was 15,355 but in 1871 it was 39,768 and by 1902 there were 98,829 entries. The extension westward was further encouraged by the Timber Culture Act of 1873 and the Desert Land Act of 1877.[21]

In 1883 Mark Twain looked back on his formative years in the little river town, and this is what he saw clearly through the intervening years:

> Once a day a cheap, gaudy packet arrived upward from St. Louis, and another downward from Koekuck. Before these events, the day was glorious with expectancy; after them, the day was a dead and empty thing. . . . After all these years I can picture that old time to myself now . . . the white town drowsing in the sunshine of a summer's morning; the streets empty, or pretty nearly so; one, or two clerks sitting in front of the Water Street stores, with their splint-bottomed chairs tilted back against the wall, chins on breasts, hats slouched over their faces, asleep—with shingle shavings enough around to show what broke them down; a sow and a litter of pigs loafing along the sidewalk, doing a good business in watermelon rinds and seeds; two or three lonely little freight piles scattered about the 'levee'; a pile of 'skids' on the slope of the stone-paved wharf, and the fragrant town drunkard asleep in the shadow of them; two or three wood flats at the head of the wharf, but nobody to listen to the peaceful lapping of the wavelets against them; the great Mississippi, the majestic, the magnificent Mississippi, rolling its mile-wide tide along, shining in the sun; the dense forest away on the other side. . . .[22]

Here Twain seems to have finalized a powerful graphic American image, a logo of the national soul which recurs in American culture in so many of its manifestations both élitist and popular, epitomized in the river steam-boat, which he exploits for all it is worth:

> . . . a film of dark smoke appears. . . . instantly a Negro drayman, famous for his quick eye and prodigious voice, lifts up the cry, 'S-t-e-a-m-boat a-comin'!' and the scene changes! The town drunkard stirs, the clerks wake up, a furious clatter of drays follows, every house and store pours out a human contribution, and all in a twinking the dead town is alive and moving. Drays, carts, men, boys, all go hurrying from many quarters to a common center, the wharf. Assembled there, the people fasten their eyes upon the coming boat as upon a wonder they are seeing for the first time. And the boat *is* rather a

16

handsome sight, too. She is long and sharp and trim and pretty; she has two tall, fancy-topped chimneys, with a gilded device of some kind swung between them; a fanciful pilothouse, all glass and 'ginerbread', perched on top of the 'texas' deck behind them; the paddle boxes are gorgeous with a picture or with gilded rays above the boat's name. . . .[23]

This scene, once read, stamps itself indelibly on the mind, but the moment Twain describes—the sleepy river town briefly brought to life by the glamorous glittering floating palace of the steam-powered paddlesteamer—is a recurring configuration of experience in the American experience; it crops up time and again and it never fails to exert its strange power, in Currier and Ives prints, in *Showboat*, Walter Mitty, the labels on bottles of Southern Comfort, *The Music Man*, *The Foxes of Harrow* and numorous films and stage shows. It even works when transplanted to another location—witness the success of the Australian television serial version of *All the Rivers Run*. Its denotive and connotive power must never be undervalued. It denotes small-town western American life at a particular stage of its historical development, and it connotes the perfect, colourful, endlessly sun-dappled and harmonious old world America, when mankind stood a chance of attaining happiness in a simple kind of civilization, which was totally erased by the Civil War, the coming of the railways, the opening of the west, the development of American industrial capitalism, militarism and imperialism.

3

Samuel Clemens left the peaceful, dreamy world of the river town as a journeyman-printer, which craft took him eastwards to New York and Philadelphia before he was 19. He came back in 1857 to become appenticed to the famous Horace E. Bixby, pilot of the *Paul Jones*. Sam had already published humorous sketches in various journals and newspapers, and kept notes of his journeys and eventually became a licensed pilot himself in September 1858.

During the early days of the Civil War he served with a unit of Confederate irregulars, although officially his was a Union state.[24] His military service, in which he fired not a single shot, became the subject of *The Private History of a Campaign that Failed*. When this unit disintegrated Sam yielded his part in the great national struggle and went west with his brother Orion, who had been appointed Lieutenant-Governor of Nevada (he had a friend in Lincoln's cabinet). These experiences, including the account of his brief (and unsuccessful) career as a goldminer, Sam turned into *Roughing It* (1872). It is a classic record of that particular moment of the pioneering epoch in the West. He had intended to stay only three months, but his adventures around the Carson City area took him seven years. As he says at the end of the book: 'However, I usually miss my calculations further than that.'

He next worked as a journalist on the *Virginia City Territorial Enterprise*, where he first used the name 'Mark Twain'—a call used on the Mississippi in taking soundings. His next move was to San Francisco, where he associated with a group of wits which included Artemus Ward and Bret Harte. He supported himself by freelance writing. Then, in 1865, came the moment of the famous 'jumping frog'—which was published as a story in the *Saturday Press*, New York, and in 1867 as a small book with the title, *The Celebrated Jumping Frog of Calaveras County*.

Although Twain was not impressed with its sales, this little story has a central place in his career as a writer, and indeed, in the creation of 'Mark Twain'. In form, it is a story within a story. The narrator, Mark Twain, is asked by a friend back East to enquire from a certain Simon Wheeler if he has any information about a certain Rev. Leonidas W. Smiley. Twain finds Simon Wheeler, and asks him. Wheeler seems to know nothing about any Leonidas Smiley, but he does recall the famous betting man, Jim Smiley. He then proceeds to narrate the humorous tale of the betting contest between Smiley and a stranger. Smiley would bet on anything, it was in his blood and he couldn't help it. He had a pet frog which he patiently trained to jump. He carried the frog with him in a little box.

Jim Smiley loses the bet as the cunning stranger secretly fills the famous jumping frog of Calaveras County with lead shot and he simply can't take off. The point is not in the story, but in the manner of its telling. The same may be said—to its everlasting glory—of *Huckleberry Finn*. And there is an important connection to be stressed between this gem of a

18

short story and the massively complex narrative which makes up *Huckleberry Finn*. The connection is in the voice of Twain— the prose of *The Celebrated Jumping Frog* captures in cold print the very tone and voice of the West, and begins a new literature—which we now recognize as classical American literature. When Hemingway said 'All modern American literature comes from one book by Mark Twain called *Huckleberry Finn*', he was not indulging in the hyperbole, but the tone of *Huckleberry Finn* was already prefigured to a noticeable extent in *The Celebrated Jumping Frog*. It is here, in this story, that the real, true and original voice of Mark Twain first emerged. Here for the first time he displays that mastery of deadpan narrative, and establishes that special relationship with the reader. We *overhear* Wheeler tell the story of the frog-jumping contest, and we relish the story which Twain, in recounting to us, seems so seriously to undervalue. But that is the point of the story. It is essentially populist art—we in the audience get the point which the narrator fails to notice. The obvious comparison, for narrative technique, would be with *Citizen Kane*, where the journalist who has striven throughout the film to grasp the meaning of Kane's final word— 'Rosebud'—fails to unravel the mystery, while we, in the cinema seats, see the burning sledge and the word 'Rosebud' on the woodwork as it is consumed forever by the flames. This was the solution to the whole mystery of Charles Foster Kane.[25]

We should note Twain's detailed description of the manner in which Wheeler tells the story to him:

> He never smiled, he never frowned, he never changed his voice from the gentle-flowing key to which he tuned his initial sentence, he never betrayed the slightest suspicion of enthusiasm; but all through the interminable narrative there ran a vein of impressive earnestness and sincerity, which showed me plainly that, so far from his imagining that there was anything ridiculous or funny about his story, he regarded it as a really important matter, and admired its two heroes as men of transcendent genius in *finesse*. I let him go on in his way, and never interrupted him once.[26]

The story made him famous and he went to New York. Here he gave his lecture on the Sandwich Islands at Cooper

Institute. The San Francisco *Alta California* commissioned him to travel with a party embarking on the steamship *Quaker City* for a tour of the Mediterranean. He was to cover the tour in a series of letters. These later became *The Innocents Abroad*, which he published in 1869. He was now the most widely read writer in America. He married and set up house in Hartford. A string of masterpieces followed—*Roughing It* (1872), *The Adventures of Tom Sawyer* (1875), *A Tramp Abroad* (1880), *Life on the Mississippi* (1883), *The Adventures of Huckleberry Finn* (1885), *A Connecticut Yankee in King Arthur's Court* (1889) and *Pudd'nhead Wilson* (1894).

The story of his life, with its financial vicissitudes, hopes, follies, ambitions, business ventures and failures, lectures, public acclaim and international honours, reads like one of his novels. His life also seems to shadow in outline the development of the very society which produced him—quiet early life in the Mississippi river town, engagement in the Civil War, the expansion westward, business interests and torment of conscience make him uniquely the voice of his country, if not the keeper of its conscience. His attachment to his country and his times was always ambiguous, and this tension gives his work one of its strangest and strongest attractions. He is so very American, but his admiration for his nation is certainly not unqualified. He seemed in step with the idea of progress and the modern, yet the strain of nostalgia in his work is very strong. Early in his marriage he wrote to one of his friends from Hannibal days:

> The old life has swept before me like a panorama; the old days have trooped by in their old glory again; the old faces have looked out of the mists of the past; old footsteps have sounded in my listening ears; old hands have clasped mine, and the songs I loved ages and ages ago have come wailing down the centuries.[27]

The *Connecticut Yankee* concerns a man going back in time, but may also be read as a satire of modern history. The 'medieval England' that Twain portrays, with its aristocratic knights supported by a feudal economy, might well stand for the gentlefolks of the old slave-owning South. Here Twain brilliantly reworked ideas latent in American thinking of his own day, as apologists for the slave-owning economy were fond of making the comparison between the happy South and 'Merrie England'. The notorious George Fitzhugh asserted that slavery and Christianity brought about lasting peace, and that pauperism and beggary were unknown in Feudal times, before 'the vassals and villeins' were liberated by the doctrines of *laissez faire*.[28] Hank's political plans for Britain may be seen as a parody of the Reconstruction after the War.[29] Hank's military masterpiece, the Battle of the Sand Belt, may be read as a portrait of the horrors of the U.S. Civil War, the first war of modern times, fought with the pitiless technology of destruction made possible by 'progress'.

In some ways it is clear that Twain did not like the nineteenth century, which his more optimistic contemporaries regarded as the true adulthood of human civilization. In many ways Mark Twain regretted growing up. Towards the end of his life he wrote in a letter to the widow of one of his boyhood friends: 'I should greatly like to relive my youth . . . and be as we were, and make holiday until fifteen, then all drown together.' Revealing comments like this compel one to read the conclusion of *Tom Sawyer* with fresh eyes: 'So endeth this chronicle. It being strictly a history of a boy, it must stop here; the story could not go much further without becoming the history of a man.' The episode, central in the novel both in narrative as well as symbolic terms, of the boys' 'drowning' (Ch. 15) and relishing their return to watch their own funeral, therefore takes on a much greater significance than might seem at first sight.

It is a fact that childhood seems to have been invented in the nineteenth century, and that in its literary treatment it is endowed either with mystical/quasi-religious qualities as in Wordsworth, or with nostalgia and romance as in Dickens— but there is something very special about Mark Twain's treatment of boyhood. It is wrapped up with feelings of loss at the end of innocence, the loss of Eden, the end of the dream. This was true not only personally for Samuel Clemens, who had to lose his boyhood as the price for becoming a writer, lecturer, inventor and ultimately a celebrity parading the streets in his famous and recognizable white suit, as much as for his country, which made further steps towards becoming a nation as a result of civil war, built railways, hoofed the indigenous native population off the plains, extended itself westwards and became an industrial and imperial power. This is only part of the story, though the sense of loss is powerful in Twain's writing. Anthony Burgess once wrote of the American experience:

> When Europe, after millenia of war, rapine, slavery, famine, intolerance, had sunk to the level of a sewer, America became the golden dream, the Eden where innocence could be recovered. Original sin was the monopoly of that dirty continent over there; in America man could glow in an aura of natural goodness, driven along his shining path by divine reason. The Declaration of Independence itself is a monument to reason. Progress was possible, and the wrongs committed against the Indians, the wildlife, the land itself, could be explained away in terms of the national control of environment necessary for the building of a New Jerusalem. Right and wrong made up the moral dichotomy; evil—that great eternal inextirpable entity—had no place in America.[30]

But Twain was always aware of the evil and the violence in humanity; Tom and Huck constantly encounter it and are threatened by it. Twain went on observing all his life. Elinor Glyn was right, he had the eyes of a child, and his vision and perceptions were just as uncompromisingly ruthless as a child's. In some ways it seems reasonable that, like that other great satirist, Jonathan Swift, whom in some fundamental respects he resembles, Twain's work is sometimes taken as written for young audiences, whereas it ranks amongst the most adult literature ever written. For the essence of Twain we must look beyond the cosmetic nostalgia of Norman Rockwell and the *Reader's Digest*,[31] far deeper than all that Jerome Kern and steamboat chic.[32] It is a mistake to argue that his work grew more pessimistic as he matured and that his later years were marred by incurable misanthropy. His perceptions remained as crystalline as ever, but his vision and understanding matured with his growing command of expression. What seems to be darker, more gloomy Twain, is really more powerful Twain. *The Mysterious Stranger* belongs to the same authorship as *Huckleberry Finn*, and shares the same infinite air of wisdom. Twain watched the hard-fought presidential campaign between Stephen Grover Cleveland and James Gillespie Blaine, and a century ago—on 21 August 1884—he wrote in a letter to William Dean Howells:

Introduction

This presidential campaign is too delicious for anything. *Isn't* human nature the most consummate sham and lie that was ever invented? Isn't man a creature to be ashamed of in pretty much all his aspects? Man, 'know thyself'—and then thou wilt despise thyself, to a dead moral certainty. . . .

Surely in the light of the stale hubbub of party politics in Britain, and the media razzmatazz of the U.S. presidential campaign a century after Twain wrote that letter, there is little need to revise his opinion. Isn't the world still a Twainian place?

NOTES

1. *Missouri Vacation Guide* (Missouri Division of Tourism, Jefferson City, Missouri, 1976), p. 8.
2. Anthony Glyn, *Elinor Glyn: A Biography* (Hutchinson, London, 1955), p. 143.
3. There are those who consider that Twain suffered from the despair of arrested development—see Richard Altick, 'Mark Twain's Despair: An Explanation' in the *South Atlantic Quarterly* (1935), and C. O. Parsons, 'The Devil and Samuel Clemens' in the *Virginia Quarterly Review* (1947). Cf. Dixon Wecter, *Sam Clemens of Hannibal* (1952), Chs. 13 and 19.
4. Mark Twain, *Tom Sawyer* (1876; Penguin, Harmondsworth, 1963), pp. 30–1.
5. *The Penguin Companion to Literature: United States and Latin America*, edited by Malcolm Bradbury, Eric Mottram and Jean Franco (Penguin, Harmondsworth, 1971), p. 255.
6. See Marcus Cunliffe, *The Literature of the United States* (Penguin, Harmondsworth, 1971), pp. 166–77.
7. Robert Lewis Taylor, *W. C. Fields: His Follies and Fortunes* (New American Library, New York, 1967), p. 187.
8. Mark Twain, *The Innocents Abroad* (1869; Airmont Publishing Company, New York, 1967), p. 119.
9. For evidence of his careful consideration of the nature of language, what language does and how it does it, see *The Awful German Language*, from *A Tramp Abroad*, in *The Complete Humorous Sketches and Tales of Mark Twain*, edited by Charles Neider (Doubleday, New York, 1961), pp. 439–55, and *Concerning the American Language* (1882), op. cit., pp. 495–98.
10. H. L. Mencken, *Mark Twain's Americanism* (1917), in *The Young Mencken: The Best of his Work*, edited by Carl Bode (The Dial Press, New York, 1973), p. 563.
11. Cf. Kenneth Lynn, *Mark Twain and Southwestern Humor* (1959).

12. See Harold Aspiz, *Mark Twain's Reading*, unpublished doctoral dissertation, University of California at Los Angeles, 1950 and M. M. Brasher,
Mark Twain: Son of Missouri (1964).
13. Quoted in Cleanth Brooks, R. W. B. Lewis and Robert Penn Warren
(eds.), *American Literature: The Makers and the Making 1861–1914* (St.
Martin's Press, New York, 1974), pp. 1265–266.
14. Mark Twain, *How to Tell a Story* (1895), in *The Complete Essays of Mark
Twain*, edited by Charles Neider (Doubleday, New York, 1963), p. 155.
15. Ibid., p. 156.
16. Twain's early life is very interestingly discussed in Van Wyck Brooks,
The Ordeal of Mark Twain, first published in 1920, but revised in 1933.
The controversial thesis of this book, that Twain was a genius whose
fulfilment was restricted by his hick background and money-grubbing
society, was answered in 1932 in Bernard de Voto's book, *Mark Twain's
America: An Essay in the Correction of Ideas.*
17. Journal of Lansford W. Hastings, quoted as 'New Beginnings' at the
opening of Daniel Boorstin, *The Americans: The National Experience*
(Vintage Books, New York, 1965).
18. Daniel Boorstin, ibid.
19. Charles Francis Adams, Jr., quoted as 'Changes' at the opening of
Daniel Boorstin, *The Americans: The Democratic Experience* (Vintage Books,
New York, 1974). Cf. R. W. B. Lewis, *The American Adam: Innocence,
Tragedy and Tradition in the Nineteenth Century* (University of Chicago Press,
1955), pp. 2–10.
20. The Democrats, a Southern dominated party during the presidency of
Franklin Pierce between 1853–57, were opposed to the western extension
of the frontier. Democratic policies at this time divided the Party and led
to the election of Lincoln and the success of the Republicans in 1860.
21. See *An American Primer*, edited by Daniel Boorstin (New American
Library, University of Chicago Press, 1966), pp. 405–11.
22. Mark Twain, *Life on the Mississippi* (1883; Airmont Publishing Company,
New York, 1965), p. 33.
23. Ibid.
24. Harry Hanson, *The Civil War* (New American Library, New York, 1961),
pp. 93–7.
25. See Keith Reader, *Cultures on Celluloid* (Quartet Books, London, 1981),
pp. 65–8.
26. Mark Twain, *The Celebrated Jumping Frog of Calaveras County*, in Cleanth
Brooks *et al.*, op. cit., *American Literature: The Makers and the Making
1861–1914*, p. 1295. Twain's discussion and demonstration of the art of
story-telling in this example is very revealing, cf. *The Jumping Frog: In
English Then in French. Then Clawed Back into a Civilized Language Once More
by Patient, Unremunerated Toil*, in *The Complete Humorous Sketches and Tales of
Mark Twain*, edited by Charles Neider (Doubleday, New York, 1961),
pp. 261–76.
27. Quoted in Cleanth Brooks, op. cit., p. 1269.
28. George Fitzhugh: *Sociology for the South: Or the Failure of Free Society*,
published in Richmond, Virginia in 1854. See Harvey Wish, *Ante-Bellum:*

Writings of George Fitzhugh and Hinton Rowan Helper on Slavery (Capricorn Books, New York, 1960), pp. 47 and following.

29. See James S. Allen, *Reconstruction: The Battle for Democracy* (International Publishers, New York, 1970), pp. 36–42.

30. Anthony Burgess, 'Is America Falling Apart?' in *New York Times Magazine*, 7 November 1971, reprinted in *The Norton Reader: An Anthology of Expository Prose*, edited by Arthur M. Eastman (W. W. Norton and Co., New York, 1973), p. 427.

31. One of the supreme ironies of modern mass communications must surely be the *Reader's Digest* production of *Tom Sawyer* in De Luxe Panavision in 1973, replete with songs and real Mississippi locations—a reverential confection in which the integrity of the original is totally evaporated.

32. For this splendid phrase I am indebted to A. Robert Lee, of the University of Kent at Canterbury.

1

Sport on the River and the Science of Play

by PHILIP MELLING

Twain had a keen feeling for costume, as Howells tells us, and a lifelong fascination with games and entertainment.[1] Yet recent criticism has tended to emphasize Twain's concern with the dark side of play and with the spoiling of innocence by acts of make-believe. Judith Fetterley has suggested that 'the portrait of the entertainer that emerges from Mark Twain's fiction is a negative one: it is a portrait flooded with anxiety, rage, contempt, and disavowal.'[2] While many of Twain's books are filled with aggressive entertainers who are engaged in acts of hostility toward an audience,[3] there is a danger involved in describing the behaviour of those who are concerned with the possibilities of play as cruel and puerile. Twain was aware of this and in his autobiographical work he explored the idea that entertainment might be integral to the creative self. As Justin Kaplan and Fred Lorch have demonstrated[4] Twain was highly self-conscious about the art of public performance, more so than he was about the art of writing. Often sloppy when it came to revising manuscripts, he would spend hours polishing a lecture or analysing a per-formance down to the last detail, and 'How to Tell A Story' is perhaps his major aesthetic document. The art of public performance was more than a mode of concealment to Twain. His non-fiction prose work—speeches, letters, autobiographi-cal dictations in particular—indicate his belief that the craft of the performer withheld the possibility of meticulous enterprise.

In spite of his darkening vision of American life many of Twain's reflections on sport and performance are accompanied by feelings of exhilaration and unfettered personal delight. Twain's fascination with billiards can be traced to his experiences in Nevada and California in the 1860s, while his interest in steamboat racing began as a child on the banks of the Mississippi in Hannibal, Missouri. Both the steamboat pilot and the billiards player provided Twain throughout his career with a model of physical control and imaginative excellence; they seemed to offer him a stylish demonstration of timing, co-ordination and poise, an artistic statement which was at least the equivalent of that offered by the man of letters to his own audience. Yet in Twain's estimation, the wit and purpose of the pilot in the wheelhouse was not somehow separate from the serious purposes of life on the river. Nor were the mannerisms of the pilot distilled into a set of apocryphal gestures or a gleefully showy and unfathomable etiquette when he took to the water on race days. In what he regarded as his 'finest' book,[5] *Life on the Mississippi*, Twain gave no hint that the essential or knowledgeable self of the pilot was at any point obscured when the purposes of work were displaced by the purposes of play. Sport, for the pilot of a steamboat, was anything but child's play, especially steamboat racing. Recent criticism which extends the use of sociological reference and 'a game model gloss' to Twain's theories of entertainment has tended, therefore, to go amiss. Twain did not look upon the game, especially the steamboat race, as a 'gloss upon the self', an abstract formulation essentially remote from the 'serious' business of living; nor did he use the sport to superimpose upon life an 'analytical concept' which is merely 'useful' in the study of 'social behaviour'.[6]

Twain's view of sport and spectacle is much more dynamic than such a presentation allows for. For him the game does not stand in 'marked contrast' to the occurrences of everyday life nor does it work as a formal obstruction in the realization of 'serious' pursuits.[7] The methods of a game may allow for only a momentary expression of the self but they do not create, of necessity, a separate and phenomenal territory where the rules of everyday life are suspended and the 'serious' business of living is discarded. Twain's views on sport are not restricted to a particular activity. As a boy and young man in Hannibal and Virginia City he loved swimming, skating and fencing (which makes nonsense of the claim that he, Twain, 'had no great interest' in games and 'was much too fond of his ease to be attracted to sports').[8] Nor are his interests prescribed by a particular landscape or a fixed historical view of the world. Just as the methods of sport and work are seen to be inter-changeable, so sport can be capable of adopting itself to the changing conditions of American life. Neither the context within which the game is set nor the tools which are used are absolute referents for legitimate action. Billiards can be played as it is by Texas Tom in Jackass Gulch—a man of 'almost superhuman skill'[9]—with limited facilities and defective equipment. Yet steamboat racing, which also requires a certain touch and skill, is far more dependent on technological support. Only on occasion is technology an absolute. On the Mississippi river sport is possible with a raft and with a steamboat; it is geared neither to the rhythms and principles of engineering nor is it moved by the spirit of the garden. Its worth depends upon the work of the player and not the particularities of landscape or setting. Sport which is organized, therefore, does not of itself violate the purity of authentic play. It can be ruined by the etiquette of the garden as easily as it can by the statements and waywardness of science. It is not surprising, therefore, that neither the pastoral nor the mechanical in themselves are able to claim supremacy over Twain's affections such is the complexity of his personal and public vision of the world.

This is particularly true in *Life on the Mississippi* where the genius of sport is writ large in the comments which Twain makes about those activities which transcend the social and geographic boundaries of American life. Sport when played in a southern state is no less vital an activity than when it is played outside that state, since the Mississippi river, which bisects the Mason-Dixon, makes all sport possible and all locations accessible. The democracy of sport is made possible by the river but also by technology which uses the river. If Twain had wished to indicate that sport and technology were not compatible, that the genius of play was captured best by the spirit of the primitive, then he would not have been willing to look upon sport as a mode of activity able to accommodate itself to the ravages of fast change on the river; *Life on the Mississippi* is not only concerned with the life of the keelboatman, it is also devoted to examining, without prejudice, the habits of the pilot who displaced the keelboatman.

In his book *Sport and the Spirit of Play in American Fiction*[10] Christian Messenger has argued against this and suggested that what is presented in *Life on the Mississippi* is a vision of heroic obsolescence in America. Messenger believes that Twain's view of American history is neatly symbolized by the degenerative character of American sport and its tendency towards a spiritless uniformity. Sport, says Messenger, provides us with an accurate historical record of Twain's cynicism, and a graph on which can be registered his increasing disillusion with the manners of American life. Sport achieves its apotheosis in the mind of Mark Twain, says Messenger, in the virtuoso performances of the keelboatman and steamboatman—men of unaffected genius who travelled the Mississippi before the Civil War. Thus in the 'Old Times' section, in which Twain looks back to the days of his youth as a cub pilot, sport is a pre-technological activity: a mode of expression in which pilots and raftsmen reigned supreme as performing artists and asserted their dominance over a potentially debilitating technology. A pilot like Horace Bixby is 'a modern athletic hero', idolized for his power, authority, glamour and salary, says Messenger. On racing days 'the machine as the nominal hero is dominated by the smoothly working team of deckhands and mates, all of whom are at the command of the pilot'. After the Civil War, says Messenger, and in the later sections of *Life on the Mississippi*, Twain makes clear that 'free prowess heroes' are redundant on the river and that any opportunities for self-expression are increasingly limited by the methods of modern industry. Spectator sport controlled by businessmen and built on the principles of profit and loss, replaces the spontaneity of frontier and river sport; the sportsman becomes the poodle of the entrepreneur and the sensational nature of the sportsman's antics merely underline the gimmicks which are thought necessary to stimulate the appetite of a jaded and war-weary public. For Twain the modern sportsman lacks authority; he is, says Messenger, the antithesis of both the keelboatman with his 'physical strength and freedom' and the steamboatman with his 'feats of memory and control'. Consequently, the 'Old Times' section in which Twain looks back to the past reads like a lament for a lost heroism, a despairing statement on the mastery and initiative of men who 'caught the craft of steamboating at its highest moment, turned its deepest secrets into a metaphor of artistic control, and transformed the power of both river and pilot to images of majesty and mastery'. The tragedy says Messenger, is that the pilot's self-mastery and artistic control are dashed by Twain's conclusion of the 'Old Times' section and the explosion on board the Pennsylvania where his brother, Henry, is scalded to death. Not only does the pilot's freedom fall prey to technological error (the explosion) and technological advance (the growth of the railroads); it is also undermined by a trend toward collectivism as evidenced by the growth in pilots' associations and a consequent decline in pilot autonomy. With these events and expressions, says Messenger, 'Twain suggests an abrupt end to a brief but expressive tradition of work and competition built on the life of the river.' Authentic activity ceases to exist with industrial expansion. 'The power of the keelboatman or his more complex brother, the steamboat pilot, was nowhere to be found during Twain's 1882 trip down the river.'

This thesis, which is largely derived from the presentations made by Kenneth Lynn and James Cox, is premised on the idea that there is a structural 'break' in Mark Twain's imagination at the conclusion of the 'Old Times'. The concluding events of this section symbolize, says Messenger, the end of an integrated sporting life on the frontier. 'The functionalism of rifle, horse, and keelboat/steamboat could no longer coexist with their use in sport.' For the most part, therefore, 'Old Times' is little more than a 'romantic remembrance', a 'eulogy' in which Twain balks at the prospect of the new technology that looms ahead of him.[11]

Such an argument does little to rescue the text from the charge of sentimentality nor does it consider the possibility that any 'break' there might be in Twain's imagination is far less obvious at the end of Chapter XX than it is in the chapters that appear after the Huckleberry Finn interlude. To suggest that what 'Old Times' provides us with is a glimpse of a lost pastoralism is to ignore the abrupt change of theme and emphasis that occurs in Chapter IV, 'The Boy's Ambition', where the text moves away from the jokiness and spontaneity of keelboat life and begins to consider the style and 'grandeur' of steamboat society. This is an important consideration. In the company of the pilot we enter a private, more enclosed world where the noise and swirl of 'river rat' society gives way to a mode of laconic expression, where the smell and chatter of the man on a raft is obscured by the smoke that swirls around the 'texas' deck and the clashing of gears in the engine room. The steamboat does not provide us with an image of serenity or peace. It creates a highly charged dramatic atmosphere. To the young Twain on the river bank in Hannibal, Missouri, the steamboat is stylish and colourful. With its 'gorgeous' fittings and handsome trim it is a visually exciting and 'imposing' piece of machinery which registers its presence in 'great volumes of the blackest smoke . . . rolling and tumbling out of the chimneys'.[12] This initial description of the steamboat as an object which combines decorative effect with industrial power is a far cry from the idyllic privitivism which Messenger associates with the 'Old Times' section.

As we proceed through the early chapters it becomes clear that the pilot in the wheelhouse, 'all glass and "gingerbread" ' on the 'texas' deck (22), is a dominant figure in Twain's imagination. He it is who occupies 'the grandest position of all', for unlike the driftboatman—whose work is oblivious to the momentum of history—the pilot is responsive to his surroundings. The pilot is mechanic, navigator and naturalist and the nature of his craft demands an intelligence and a level of feeling which those previous picaresque adventurers on the river did not possess. For the pilot, play can never legitimately occur as a diversion to work nor can it be separated from the skills he has learned in the wheelhouse. The pilot must, by the very nature of his task, be responsive to the influences of nature as well as the demands of man and machinery. His must be the ear that hears the cry of the leadsman, the eye that watches for the snags and reefs and shoaling water, the hand on the wheel that offers articulate expression to the play of the senses as the paddleboat is guided with 'the marvelous precision' that is 'required' in almost complete silence through a 'murky waste of water' (38). Although his voice may be used to give vent to anger (as it is in his clashes with the unlit trading scows) the pilot's actions must always speak loudest. As a man of action the pilot does not pull himself out of the main current of American Life in order that he might drift with his cronies in some quiet backwater and play to the gallery. His play is both tuitional—offered as it might be for the benefit of the cub—and intuitional—offered as it is one night to a group of awe-struck spectators who watch him with fascination as he navigates by touch on a particularly dangerous stretch of river. The play of the pilot is that of an educationalist, but it is also the play of a modernist and a pragmatist. Those pilots who work in the wheel-house of the *R. E. Lee*, *A. E. Shotwell* and *Eclipse*, have sense enough to realize that a consequence of their play—especially their prowess at steamboat racing—is the forming of judgements by those who observe them. Play means pace and pace means trade for the business interests whom the pilot represents. Steamboat racing is not only fun; it is a natural extension of that daily competition that occurs between power-driven traffic on the Mississippi river for the custom of the country and for those substantial revenues that can be earned from the speedy transportation of freight.

Through Horace Bixby, Twain extolls the virtues of the American democrat, a man who must know his times and serve in the places where the times are acted out fully. Bixby is a man of passion and a man of knowledge; he is deeply immersed in the manufacture of his age; yet Twain is quite clear that in order to succeed at his task he must not be dismissive of the landscape that surrounds him. Like Emmerson's American scholar Bixby is neither timid, imitative nor afraid; he is a man of eclectic individualism whose style is a mode of involvement, a thrust into the society and psychology of his times. Bixby is a man implicated in his age, deeply immersed in its mind and manufacture. He does not fight a rearguard action in defiance of the possibilities of industrial progress. On the contrary he accepts the danger of supervising, as best he can, a potentially lethal technology even though that technology eventually destroys his status on the river. In *The Liberal Imagination* Lional Trilling points out that 'in any culture there are likely to be certain artists who contain a large part of the dialectic within themselves . . . the very essence . . . the yes and no of their culture.'[13] The pilot, as Twain describes him in *Life on the Mississippi* has become such an artist; he incorporates within his work a central 'dialectic' in nineteenth-century American life: the imprint of the pastoral and the promise of the industrial. In the person of Horace Bixby the dramatic amalgam is released into art. Bixby lives at the crossroads of American culture, the point at which the machine is beginning to assert itself and make incursions into the territory of the garden. Bixby allows himself to be pulled in two directions—he is devoted to understanding nature as phenomenon at the same time that he is committed to the celebration of hard, technological realities. As a pilot Bixby is not the shrill prophet of either party; there is in him neither an inchoate longing for a more 'natural' environment nor a prosaic worship of industrial progress. Bixby observes the behaviour of nature because it is pleasing to him and because the information which it gives him is necessary if he is to achieve safe passage for his craft. For a brief transitional moment on the river 'Two Kingdoms of Force'[14] (Leo Marx's phrase), briefly co-exist in his work. The pilot is able to accept the benefits of technology yet he dedicates himself to a personal acquaintance with the ancient requirements of navigation on the river. In the dualistic world of the pilot the steamboat and the river are seen to fulfil each other, to mutually support each other in a relationship of opposites. The pilot makes an effort to maintain this partnership, he is the resolvent faculty—the artist as mechanic, the artist as naturalist—and he strives to keep the boat on an even keel in spite of the river's potential for anarchism. At work and at play he is equally responsive to cog and current. For him sport is not a 'gloss' upon the self—an extracurricular or diversionary activity—but a subtle merger of style and skill which exists at that point where the play of the river and the play of machinery intersect. The pilot is the great co-ordinator of unfocused energies—wilderness energies, industrial energies. Through him America is able to make sense of itself, to manage its own momentum.

What the pilot recommends to others who wish to do as he does is summarized in the following remarks:

> 'Now watch her; watch her like a cat, or she'll get away from you. When she fights strong and the tiller slips a little, in a jerky, greasy sort of way, let up on her a trifle; it is the way she tells you at night that the water is too shoal; but keep edging her up, little by little, toward the point. You are well up on the bar now; there is a bar under every point, because the water that comes down around it forms an eddy and allows the sediment to sink. Do you see those fine lines on the face of the water that branch out like the ribs of a fan? Well, those are little reefs; you want to just miss the ends of them, but run them pretty close. Now look out—look out! Don't you crowd that slick, greasy-looking place; there ain't nine feet there; she won't stand it. She begins to smell it; look sharp, I tell you! Oh, blazes, there you go! Stop the starboard wheel! Quick! Ship up to back! Set her back!' (45)

Bixby has learned what Ishmael must learn on the masthead of the *Pequod*, lulled into listlessness by the wash of waves on the ocean floor below him. Because he is sensitive to the unpredictability of nature and because his awareness is based upon practical understanding and tactile response, Bixby is able to negotiate the river. He is also able to make sense of the rise and fall of the water after a flood, the movement of shadows, sunlight and fog, the shapes of snags and shoals and the deposits of silt. The importance to him of scanning the river quickly and intelligently is underlined by the energetic, impassioned manner in which Bixby gives his advice to the cub. The cub is having his first lesson on 'water-reading' (44) and what Bixby strives for in this lesson is an immediacy of feeling, a mode of expression which argues the need for spontaneous knowledge and intuitive understanding. On other occasions Bixby is more reticent and he will express an opinion with a cool and stylish wit. Sometimes he might prefer to be a silent witness to the cub's mistakes or he will affirm his position by denying the value of verbal tuition altogether. In commenting on the differences between wind reefs and bluff reefs he says:

> I can't tell you. It is an instinct. By and by you will just naturally know one from the other but you will never be able to explain why or how you know them apart. (47)

The belief in a knowledge which is wordlessly attained, the idea of an 'instinct' sustained by hard work and the mystical energies of the environment, is endemic to nineteenth-century American thinking. The pilot represents in his remarks the American's sense of himself as a latter-day Adam in an Edenic Garden of the World, free to rise and favoured by a perfect and completely open environment, untrammelled by the taint of original sin or the heritage of the past. The pilot also represents the belief that knowledge can be discovered by those who allow their imaginations to be nourished by the hard technological realities of life, by the material facts which provide in themselves a visible symbol of the philosophy of progress. By the 1840s the machine had captured the public imagination; it had become, as Leo Marx tells us, 'the embodiment of the age'. In his comments (1840) on Tocqueville's *Democracy in America*,[15] John Stuart Mill argues that machine technology inculcates its message imagistically and wordlessly. A locomotive, he says, is a perfect symbol because its meaning need not be attached to it by a poet; it is inherent in its physical attributes. To see a powerful, efficient machine in the landscape is to know the superiority of the present to the past. 'The more visible fruits of scientific progress', says Mill, 'The mechanical improvements, the steam engines, the railroads, carry the feeling of admiration for modern and disrespect for ancient times, down even to the wholly uneducated classes.'[16] During the nineteenth century, therefore, no one needs to spell out the idea of progress to Americans. They can see it, hear it and feel it as the idea of history most nearly analogous to the rising tempo of life. To look at a steamboat, as Leo Marx tells us, is to see the sublime progress of the race. The awe and reverence once reserved for God and bestowed by philosophers upon the visible landscape is now directed toward the technological conquest of matter. In the period between 1830 and 1860 popular discussions of technological progress assumed that inventors were uncovering the ultimate structural principals of the universe. The inventor accordingly is often considered the intellectual hero of the age. As a magazine writer put it in 1840:

> It is a happy privilege we enjoy of living in an age, which for its inventions and discoveries, its improvements in intelligence and

virtue, stands without a rival in the history of the world. . . .
Look at our splendid steamboats.[17]

Hart Crane has said that 'unless poetry can absorb the
machine . . . [it] has failed of its full contemporary function.'[18]
In 1841 and 1844 in his essays on 'Art' and 'The Poet'
Emerson was urging American intellectuals to conquer the
new territory being opened up by industrialization. Technology, he stressed, was not of itself anti-poetic. If technology
was the creation of man, who is the product of nature, then
how could the machine in a landscape be thought to represent
an unresolvable conflict? It was to the poet to recognize that
there was nothing inherently ugly about factories and railroads and it was incumbent upon him to dispel the ideas of
ugliness which surrounded the new technology. Artists had a
special responsibility to incorporate into their work such 'new
and necessary facts' as the shop, mill and railroad. Such artists
who perceived relations hidden from other men, disclosed the
underlying unit of experience and so helped to direct the
course of events. A great poet not only asserted but exemplified the possibility of harmony. When he assimilated new and
seemingly artifical facts into the texture of a poem, he
provided an example for all men. What he achieved in art they
could achieve in life.

Like Emerson's poet the riverboat pilot is able to reconcile
the facts of nature with the facts of science and give each its
'proper place in the human scale' of things.[19] Twain points us
to the creative tension that is a hallmark of the pilot's work,
what Scott Fitzgerald refers to as 'the ability to hold two
opposed ideas in the mind at the same time, and still retain the
ability to function'.[20] What is at once a crucial ambiguity at
the heart of the American experience becomes a source of
creative strength for Bixby, a way of establishing a line of
control. If Bixby never fully articulates the precise nature of
this ambiguity, he does at least overcome the dilemma of his
age. His knowledge of the river matches that of a naturalist
like Henry Thoreau, and he combines this knowledge with an
appreciation of machinery and modernist travel that anticipates a pilot like Charles Lindbergh. Twain refers us to the
continual dialogue that goes on in Bixby's mind between the

'language' (48) of the river and the movement of the boat. The act of navigation is the art of coherent statement, the making of a play within and without two modes of civilization, the making of forms that can retain their shape in spite of the ruinous horseplay of the river and the potential for anarchism within the machine.

In resolving the tension that emanates from the play of the river and the play of the boat the pilot is a teacher and dramatist. The 'texas house' is a theatre and a school which the cub must attend to learn the techniques of navigation. Sometimes the cub is forced to play the rôle of patsy to the pilot's straight man for the obligatory 'audience' that assembles on the hurricane deck. But the reason for such a play is never recreational and the pilot will only make sport of his cub in order to teach his apprentice the virtue of grace under pressure. The cub may find it difficult to bear up under the weight of scrutiny. When he panics at the wheel in Chapter IX Bixby hides theatrically behind a chimney and then reappears 'blandly and sweetly' to rescue the ship and offer a few words of 'sarcasm' (46). After a particularly 'humiliating experience' where Bixby derides his cub for panicking at the sight of 'shoal water', Twain concludes: 'It was a good enough lesson but pretty hardly learned' (70). Such lessons are often given by Bixby in almost complete silence. The pilot is in the tradition of the *mimus*, he is 'a performer of wordless skills' for whom 'Theatre is always more than mere language.' While linguistic extravagance is the ploy of the driftsman, what Bixby strives for is a much more abstract, theatrical effect which draws its resources from improvised play and the ancient traditions of *commedia dell'arte*. On occasion possibilities for tuition are extended into the realm of the dream play and fantasia. When the somnambulist boatman is said to have steered his craft in a dream he is performing for himself and for the crew what Apuleus refers to as the *mimus hallucinatus*, the play of the visionary.[21]

What the pilot does not countenance is play for the sake of it. Sport that exists independently of the self in action and is merely 'entertaining' (31) is a pointless extravagance to Bixby. Steamboat racing is legitimate because it is an expression of competence at work. The competitions of the driftsmen, of the kind that we see in the Huck Finn interlude, represent little more than a cult of braggadocio, play without the necessary Protestant virtues of diligence and sober effort. Twain's book highlights the distinctions between the pilot and driftsman without approving of the pilot's prejudice. Where the pilot is a 'solitary mister propp'd between trees and water' in the wheelhouse of his boat, the driftsman is a member of a theatre collective—a drifting, carousing crowd at play, whose tales Huck listens to in fascination on the raft. While the pilot is a believer in the 'science' (70) of play the keelboatman is committed to the spontaneity of play—a sociable encounter of gregarious types. Except for his watch the driftsman concentrates his energies and attentions at night on the art of verbal jousting, on a narrative style in which the telling of a story in a histrionic manner allows an opportunity for a wordy largesse. Where the driftsman is all yells and blather the pilot (for much, though tragically, not all of the time) is able to demonstrate coolness and etiquette. His primary responsibility is to his crew, his craft and the freight he is carrying. On duty the pilot is a man with a mission who cannot afford any of those recreational pursuits that might interfere with his understanding of the river or the technology at his disposal. The game of the driftsman, on the other hand is show without knowledge, a 'bluff' encounter which obscures concentration and can lead to the destruction of a craft. It is the cub who tells us what is wrong with such behaviour:

> I did not know that he was hiding behind a chimney to see how I would perform. I went gaily along, getting prowder, for he had never left the boat in my sole charge such a length of time before. I even got to 'setting her' and letting the wheel go entirely, while I vaingloriously turned my back and inspected the stern marks and hummed a tune, a sort of early indifference which I had prodigiously admired in Bixby and other great pilots. Once I inspected rather long, and when I faced to the front again my heart flew into my mouth so suddenly that if I hadn't clapped my teeth together I should have lost it. (45–6)

The art of navigation does not seem to concern the driftsman. The style which he is renowned for is one of free invention: wit, horseplay, random expressiveness. As Marion Montgomery tells us, his is 'the Mike Fink tradition which is really the

Gawain tradition, the fights in both being more verbal than physical'.[22] The driftsman is a pure entertainer; he is the barbarous braggart of the west, the archetypal bully and roustabout who rose to prominence in the popular culture of the nineteenth century. His world is that of the frontier and backwoods, a region which teased out the inherent theatricality of the American adventurer, born of that precipitous fate which came from living an experimental life. His style of braggadocio was a means of ridiculing the inhospitable wilderness, of converting terror into *joie de vivre* and helplessness into an exhilarating sense of power. The backwoodsman, in competition with other fellow travellers on the trail, was in desperate search of an audience to play to. The style of his performance, which tended toward swaggering self-assertion, whimsicality and bombast, was a common feature of his life and it made his efforts to root out an audience a highly ritualized and combative affair. 'The tall tales' of the backwoodsman, strolling actor and keelboatman 'were often like wrestling machines', says Constance Rourke, and the fantastic fictions of the showmen-entertainers (like Mike Fink and Sam Patch) which the west threw up have much to do with that desperate need for dramatization, that urgent quest to supervise the attention of a captive audience, which life in the backwoods regions encouraged.[23]

The era of Mike Fink and his athletic mates was dashed by the invention of the steamboat. The keelboat began to disappear during the 'flush times' of steamboating that Twain puts between 1811 and 1842. At first the boatmen poled down the river to return home as deck passengers on a steamboat, ultimately becoming mere deckhands or mates, their bodies ageing, their skills irrelevant. Victims of fast change on the river, the keelboatman was only a memory by the late 1850s when Twain was a cub pilot in 'Old Times'. The death of the rollicking boatman had been T. B. Thorpe's lament through Mike Fink's rueful nostalgia for the fun of the river, and the telling of 'The Big Bear of Arkansas' ominously takes place on the steamboat Invincible. What Twain recognizes in *Life on the Mississippi* is the part which the steamboat played in the disappearance of the keelboat. 'But after a while the steamboats so increased in number and in speed that they were able to absorb the entire commerce; and then keelboating died a permanent death' (10). At the same time if the natural world could be mastered by the steamboat, it could also be mastered by more than the steamboat. Just back from an excursion on a new section of railroad, the editor of the *Cincinnati Enquirer* reported in 1846 that 'steam is annihilating space. . . . Travelling is changed from an isolated pilgrimage to a kind of triumphal procession. . . .'[24] If people were travelling on water—rising and falling 'on the bosom of the deep'—they were also gliding 'over cultivated acres on rods of iron'. By the 1840s the locomotive, perhaps much more than the steamboat, had begun to testify to the nation's fascination with power machinery. The typical American, said Michael Chevalier, 'has a perfect passion for railroads; he loves them . . . as a lover loves his mistress'. In the words of another Frenchman, Guillaume Poussin, 'the railroad animated by its powerful locomotive, appears to be the personification of the American.'[25] As many commentators noticed, mechanism was taking possession of mind and the march of science appeared relentless. If the steamboat, as Twain remarks, displaced 'the old-fashioned keelboating by reducing the freight trip to New Orleans to less than a week', then the railroad 'killed the steamboat passenger traffic by doing in two or three days what the steamboats consumed a week in doing' (115). There is no bitterness from Twain when he makes the announcement that steamboat traffic as a mode of transportation is 'Out of the question'. So powerful it seems is Twain's recognition of the connection between the advancement of machinery and the development of life in America that he has no difficulty in reconciling his belief in the virtue of machinery with his faith in progress and democratic advancement.

The ultimate tragedy of the pilot is that he is overrun by that very technology which makes his presence on the river a possibility and in whose service he is employed. His life of fast travel on the Mississippi river is dependent not only upon an alliance between the skills of the wheelhouse and the energies of the boilerhouse but also upon the continued relevance of the trade he has chosen. In 1839 one French commentator was so impressed by the American passion for travel in riverboats and locomotives that he thought either would be a suitable emblem for the American people.[26] By 1860 the choice was a clear one and the locomotive had superseded the steamboat in the national consciousness as the most powerful symbol of American buoyancy. Where the pilot had been the earliest beneficiary of the transportation revolution, by the 1860s he had fallen victim to massive technological change and to a passion for speed greater on land than on water. As the nineteenth century progressed, movement up and down the Mississippi river did not remain as central to the demographic and commercial life of the nation as it had once been. If Americans travelled for the sake of travel between 1835 and 1860, they also travelled for the sake of new land. Territorial expansion meant the westward movement of people and during this period the geographic centre of the population shifted from western Virginia to Ohio.

In *Life on the Mississippi* the momentum of machinery and the lure of the utilitarian reduce the spiritual capacity of the pilot and impair his facility as an artist on the river. Bixby who rides forth on the shirt tails of a burgeoning technology becomes a prisoner of history and whilst, in a broad sense, we are meant to view him as a cultural hero of the decade in which he serves, his demise is a tragic one. The origins of this demise are implicit within the task which the pilot has set himself.[27]

As an artist in the making the pilot is a translator of signs, an analyst who must master 'the language' (48) of the river and the various inflexions of its dialect. The pilot must correctly translate the statements of the river, root out its most 'cherished secrets' (47)—the figures in the carpet that lie along the surface of the water and on the river bed. Yet Art is not made, says Twain, on the basis of investigative analysis alone. Art is an offering from the world of imagination—in part it is a free, pointless and phenomenal exercise. For the navigator with a trained eye what the river offers is not the challenge of the unknowable but the challenge of fact; what it offers is 'the grimmest and most dead-earnest of reading-matter', a sombre parade of documentary evidence which the pilot must use for the purpose of calculation. This style of 'reading' in which nature is a commodity to be mined for evidence can limit the territory of aesthetic feeling. It can force the pilot to degenerate into a scientist with a want of imagination, a man in search of things which are relevant only to the world of the mathematical. In straining to read only the runes of the navigable river the pilot may take no delight in the merely illustrational. He may ignore those images of pastoral felicity, those 'pictures' 'painted by the sun and shaded by the clouds' (48) which only appeal to the untrained eye of the tourist. The pilot in the wheelhouse, therefore, may come to lack an empathy for nature, a facility for wonder which Nick Carraway describes for us in *The Great Gatsby* in his portrait of the Dutch sailors as they glimpse for the first time the 'fresh green breast of the new world'.[28] The mood of the visionary, says Twain, can easily be lost in that 'earnest' quest for reading material, in that piling up of merely useful information.

> Now when I had mastered the language of this water, and had come to know every trifling feature that bordered the great river as familiarly as I knew the letters of the alphabet, I had made a valuable acquisition. But I had lost something, too. I had lost something which could never be restored to me whilst I lived. All the grace, the beauty, the poetry, had gone out of the majestic river! . . . All the value any feature of it had for me now was the amount of usefulness it could furnish toward compassing the safe piloting of a steamboat. (48–9)

That delicate balance between secular needs and poetic ideals is rent asunder if the pilot is to work as the mere servant of the real. If in the very act of becoming accomplished he loses his faith in the phenomenal world, then at that very moment—the moment he achieves safe passage for his craft—he no longer stands as the embodiment of his culture, as an artist for America. What science offers him are dreams of megalomania, anticipations of future power. The pilot who accepts the possibility of power becomes not merely a custodian of mechanical energy but a scientist who is working to discover the order and organization of the universe, a player playing a game against the arch enemy, disorganization. Herman Melville recognized the dangers in a letter to Hawthorne in the summer of 1851. He wrote: 'the reason the mass of men fear God, and at the bottom dislike Him, is because they rather distrust His heart, and fancy Him all

43

brain like a watch.'[29] To Huckleberry Finn the pilot's singlemindedness, his dedication to the cause of mastering the river, makes him just like a 'watch', all brain and no heart. Huck's encounter with a steamboat is a portentous event and it creates within him both awe and terror and a sense of powerlessness.

> . . . all of a sudden she bulged out, big and scary, with a long row of wide-open furnace doors shining like red-hot teeth, and her monstrous bows and guards hanging right over us. There was a yell at us, and a jingling of bells to stop the engines, a pow-wow of cussing, and whistling of steam—and as Jim went overboard on one side and I on the other, she came smashing straight through the raft.

The pilot, who is 'like a watch', is uncaring, dismissive and unmindful of watching others, says Huck; '. . . that boat started her engines again ten seconds after she stopped them, for they never cared much for raftsmen . . .'[30] The pilot has become a mere timekeeper and the craft of piloting at this level has deteriorated into a display of Nietzschean arrogance.

As an artist the craft of this particular pilot may be said to lack a Jamesian facility for life. For James art was an act of the moral imagination and James's elaborations on and experiments in fictional method were conscious exercises in the possibilities and even the modes of moral experience. In his preface to *The Portrait of a Lady* James saw a 'perfect dependence of the "moral" sense of a work of art on the amount of felt life concerned in producing it'. We must ask he says, 'is it valid, is it genuine, is it sincere, the result of some direct impression or perception of life?'[31] The steamboat pilot who smashes Huck's raft and who spares only a moment's thought for its occupants suffers from a want of moral imagination. He looks as does little Miss Barrace (in her commentary on Waymarsh) in *The Ambassadors* 'too much to the eye'; he accepts too easily the representational style of the raft on the river—its lack of mechanical power—as the determining factor in the degree of consideration he chooses to give it. His becomes a remote perception of life from the ivory tower of the 'texas house', one that is influenced by a concept of might unmindful of lesser forms of energy. The art of his navigation can only exist, therefore, at the expense of the art of the raftsman; it is not the result of a 'direct' Jamesian perception of life and its consequence is an abuse of power.

As early as 1862 Henry Adams had told his brother Charles:

> You may think all this nonesense, but I tell you these are great times. Man has mounted science and is now run away with. I firmly believe that before many centuries more, science will be the master of man. The engines he will have invented will be beyond his strength to control. Some day science may have the existence of mankind in its power, and the human race commit suicide by blowing up the world.[32]

If the tempo of technology can regulate compassion it can also ruin the composure of those who rely on its energies. Occasional glimpses of the pilot in action in *Life on the Mississippi* confirm this impression. Brown and Bixby appear to lose heart—as if they are a type toppled by their own expertise and by the workings of a machinery that does not love them or respect their energies. Intimations of apocalypse are a part of the very fabric of the 'Old Times' section. The spinning wheels on which the paddles are fixed smash the steering oar of a trading scow to matchwood; they destroy in a second the ship's own 'sounding boat' and kill two of the ship's crew. At such moments the pilot appears to be helpless within the grip of a reductive technology, a technology which finally goes out of control on board the *Pennsylvania* and kills Twain's brother, Henry. In this respect Twain's nostalgia for the river and piloting has perhaps been taken too literally. The idyllic and the tormented aspects of life on the river are two facets of the same reality, and the steamboat incorporates this particular reality. The idea that the raft is a happy island of peace while the steamboat is simply a force of destruction is not the equation we ought to be seeking. When it comes to heavenly places, none can surpass Jackson's Island as a paradise, and on one occasion Huck and Jim find themselves completely reconciled in a beautiful but dark vision of the island.

> I rose up and there was Jackson's Island, about two miles and a half down stream, heavy-timbered and standing up out of the middle of the river, but dark and solid, like a steamboat without any lights.[33]

In the dark recesses of Mark Twain's mind, the river is an ambiguous god and tormentor and the key to Mark Twain's work may well be this double vision of the world. Twain believed himself the victim of some 'mysterious stranger' and also the killer of his own ghost—like William Wilson. From the beginning his paradise was lost, and even before the images of despair became the core of his fiction in later years, his major works already contained an ambivalent picture of the world that was both heaven and hell to him.

Moments of redemption are sometimes available, however, and the transcendent hope which Mark Twain's love of sport makes possible shines through even in the bitterest years. In Twain's personal recollections and occasionally in his fictional work sport is seen to evolve and adapt itself to the new conditions of American life: to the new modes of fast travel on the Mississippi river, to new areas of expertise, and to new patterns of expression. In spite of the tragedy that befalls the pilot his memory lives on and his moment of achievement is a source of lasting exhilaration to Twain. Horace Bixby is the victim of a necessary technology, yet for Twain he remains a figure of heroic grandeur and a source of hope for the future sportsmen of America. If the steamboat disappears from the river as a carrier of freight after the Civil War, this does not prevent Twain from suggesting the idea of a steamboat race as a worthwhile attraction to David Rowland Francis, president of the corporation promoting the Saint Louis World's Fair. The letter which appeared in the *New York Times* in 1903 proposed that the race should be a 'genuine reproduction of the old-time race' but that modern 'six-day boats' be used rather than the conventional short distance ones. Twain gave his reason thus:

> Then you have a continuous six-day world advertisement, for you would have wireless operators and Associated Press representatives on both boats, and they would report the positions of the contestants hourly, day and night, and describe the succeeding or failing jockeyings and stratagems of the pilots. This would be an innovation and dreadfully modern, but the value of it would condone it. It would keep the boats quite vividly in sight straight along a stretch of 1400 miles, and for the first time the world would see a six-day boat race from start to finish.[34]

The argument that organized sport is intrinsically offensive to Mark Twain is difficult to support, therefore. As the above letter indicates, sport, in Twain's view, could be the beneficiary of an improved technology; it need not be degraded, as some critics have suggested, by the modern 'availability of capital, developments of communication and a growing transportation network'.[35]

Twain knew that the steamboat had always been linked with commercial practices; that its economic functions aided the use of organized sport by carrying horse racing and prize-fight crews up and down the Mississippi Valley before the telegraph network was fully developed in the 1840s. He knew that steamboats also transported racing thoroughbreds as well as their patrons to all turf centres. In terms of creature comfort Twain looked upon the steamboat as a deserving beneficiary of industrial enterprise and a worthy advertisement for consumer capitalism. Twain regarded those boats that were blessed with the latest fittings as having a distinct advantage over their competitors. The décor of one steamboat in New Orleans, for example, is described with almost Dreiserian lavishness and a fascination that befits a committed member of the Gilded Age.

> There was a sumptuous glass temple; room enough to have a dance in; showy red and gold window-curtains; an imposing sofa; leather cushions and a back to the high bench where visiting pilots sit, to spin yarns and 'look at the river'; bright, fanciful 'cuspidores.' instead of a broad wooden box filled with sawdust; nice new oilcloth on the floor; a hospitable big stove for winter; a wheel as high as my head, costly with inlaid work; a wire tiller-rope; bright brass knobs for the bells; a tidy, white-aproned, black 'texas-tender', to bring up tarts and ices and coffee during mid-watch, day and night.

The description ends with an affirmation of faith in this 'great steamer'. Here Twain extends his capacity for wonder from the spectacle of the ship's finery to the Promethean brilliance of its mechanical engineering. Whether it be ship's fittings or ship's engines Twain is inspired by the flair and invention which the steamboat encourages. 'The fires were fiercely glaring from a long row of furnaces, and over them were eight huge boilers! This was unutterable pomp. The mighty engines . . .' (33).

On race days the engines can drive the steamboat along at phenomenal speed. 'Racing Days', in which Twain records the race speed with the care of a statistician, is principally a chapter about boats not pilots, the 'stripped' sleek hulls of ships like the *Eclipse, A. E. Shotwell, R. E. Lee* with their fittings and fixtures pared down to minimize all wind resistance. The scene which Twain presents us with as these ships prepare for their races is one of 'consuming excitement', a spectatorial occasion with the combatants locked in battle on the river and the audience at a distance watching from the shoreline. The event is dominated by the noise and smell of industrial machinery, the massive crowds, the hard-working crews, a feeling which is both urban and cinematic. It is as if the restlessness and zest of the factory gates has found its way into the American garden. At a steamboat 'race' the romantic adventurer has no real need to 'light out for the territory'; he can perform for an audience on the deck of his machine. The fan, similarly, is not lost in the wilderness, a disinterested bystander at an impromptu game; he is a person who plans his activities 'several weeks in advance' (86) and comes together with other fans in an organized way to give his support to a particular boat or crew. Steamboat races, therefore, are not spontaneous or informal affairs—they are contrived and well rehearsed events which reflect the growth of a new industrial society. With the steam and smoke from the coal flats and wood flats America is experiencing an urban invasion in the image of its own salvation. Yet curiously, for Twain, there is little cause for concern. The sight of steamboats with their burning rosin and pitchpine makes a 'picturesque spectacle . . . some two or three miles long, of tall, ascending columns of coal-black smoke' (85). The 'black-smoke' of the steamers as they move in procession up river from New Orleans adds colour and drama to a festive occasion. Smoke is necessary to make the right impression on the spectator. Twain tells us that as a young boy in Hannibal he was most fascinated by the black smoke which the steamboat 'created with a bit of pitch-pine just before arriving at a town' (22). At a later point in the book, where he is discussing mule racing and cockfighting in New Orleans, Twain returns to his preferred sport of steamboat racing with a further reference to the fascination of smoke.

Two red-hot steamboats racing along, neck-and-neck, straining every nerve—that is to say, every rivet in the boilers—quaking and shaking and groaning from stem to stern, spouting white steam from the pipes, pouring black smoke from the chimneys, raining down sparks, parting the river into long breaks of hissing foam—this is sport that makes a body's very liver curl with enjoyment. A horse-race is pretty tame and colourless in comparison. (217)

The raw vigour of the steamboat can degenerate into aimless and unbridled power or it can aspire to fabulous standards of achievement. Twain's interest in 'Racing Days' in the times which the fastest craft have recorded on their various journeys indicates his belief in the measurement of those standards by the use of statistics. In spite of the disaster that befalls the *Pennsylvania* Twain does not beat on against the current, borne back ceaselessly into the past. His fascination with practical science, with instrument mechanics and precision tooling, is a counterbalance to the 'abstruse science' (138) of the River Commission that Twain finds so abhorrent in 1882. Such a fascination also displaces his concern with the dark pastoralism of the Mississippi settlements and the cruel joking of the shore-based children who cause Dutchy's death. Though not always consistent Twain, on occasion, does reject the relics of 'antiquity' that the settlements rely upon. He refers us to the benefits of steam power that improve the lowering of the stage from the derrick and the wisdom of using speaking tubes to transmit the sound of the engine bells. ('It was another good contrivance which ought to have been invented half a century sooner' (118).) Even his comments on the restrictive practices and closed shop politics of the pilots association and the collusion between captains and owners in the fixing of wages are tempered by his belief that piloting has become a much safer and more humane occupation since welfare benefits were provided.

In a curious passage in his chapter on Twain, Christian Messenger describes the crew of the early steamboat as 'a lionized team of smoothly functioning players, much as early baseball players travelling the urban circuit would be only a few decades later'.[36] The equation between pilot, fireman and baseball player is unfortunate since elsewhere Messenger

49

refers to baseball—or rather, Twain's opinion of it—as a modern, 'homogenized' and 'spectatorial' activity.[37] Messenger's ideas on baseball derive from a speech which Twain gave at a testimonial dinner on 8 April 1889, at Delmonico's Restaurant in New York City. The dinner was in honour of Albert G. Spalding the sports goods entrepreneur and owner of the Chicago White Stockings, and the major league all-star players who had just returned from a six months round-the-world trip. One of the ports of call for the Chicago White Stockings had been the Sandwich Islands that Twain had visited in 1867. In his speech Twain marvelled that baseball had been played in 'that far-off home of profound repose, and soft indolence, and dreamy solitude'. And, he continued, 'these boys have played baseball there!—baseball which is the very symbol, the outward and visible expression of the drive and push of the raging, tearing booming nineteenth century.' Yet the playing of baseball in the Sandwich Islands does not seem to noticeably offend Twain. His speech affirms the mood of the evening and lends support to a jingoistic celebration of play and patriotism. Nor does Twain use the occasion, in spite of what Christian Messenger implies, to make sport of what might be considered American social imperialism. On the contrary he looks upon the ingenuity of those Americans who perform for an audience in far-off parts, however un-American, with fascination and pride.[38] As he says about the baseball match in *A Connecticut Yankee*: 'the first public game would certainly draw fifty thousand people; and for solid fun would be worth going around the World to see.'[39]

Mark Twain had an eye for burgeoning industries and heroic young capitalists of the popular culture at the same time that he feared their precision and power. In the 1880s he was in the full flush of hope for his monumental investment in the Paige type-setting machine into which he would pour hundreds of thousands of dollars between 1880 and 1894. After his bankruptcy he had no pangs of conscience when he closed his eyes to the evils of capitalism and clung to the coat-tails of Standard Oil tycoon H. H. Rogers. As a financier Mark Twain almost made a fortune, and, in his mining days, he almost 'struck it rich'. There was a time when everything he touched turned into gold; but in the same breath, he added that he was frightened of his own prosperity. Rightly so, because it did not last. This anguish about a found and lost treasure is an aspect of Mark Twain's fundamental ambivalence, a source of wild enthusiasm and torment which greatly influenced his writing. He served on the staff of the Golden era, but was meant to become an unfortunate hero of the Gilded Age.

Nevertheless, because of his experiences, Twain was unwilling to argue against those for whom sport was a profession: the riverboat gamblers, the baseball players whom he saw in Hartford and, at the end, in Bermuda, boxers like Corbett whose skills impressed him and billiard players like Hoppe, Schaeffer and Sutton whose exhibition games Twain attended at Madison Square Garden. While celebrating history's progress in sport as an ideal Twain could not wholly accept all its ramifications. He embraced the progressivist position but he could not prevent himself from having some doubts about it—doubts eventually to explode in his face in *A Connecticut Yankee* and the later fictions. In the *Autobiography* Twain's fondest memories are reserved for those who have triumphed over adversity and whose acts of play are an integral expression of the self. He remembers the 'marooned miners' of Jackass Gulch, a played-out mining town in California, in whose 'ruined and rickety bar' the ingenious people of the West devote themselves to perfection at billiards. 'The balls were chipped' says Twain, 'the cloth was darned and patched, the table's surface was undulating and the cues were headless and had the curve of a parenthesis.' But the miners displayed, in spite of this, an 'art and science' which was 'a wonder to see'. 'Once I saw Texas Tom', says Twain, 'make a string of seven points in a single inning!—all calculated shots and not a fluke or a scratch among them.'[40] For Twain, Texas Tom is a man of brilliance and audacity, he compels admiration in the way he manages his genius and in the way he transcends the limited resources at his disposal. Texas Tom is the pilot as primitivist and the pilot as westerner; he is a performer whose work is an expression of almost 'super human skill' which the playing of a game makes possible.

The nostalgia which Twain seems to thrive on in the *Autobiography* is not so apparent in the earlier reminiscences in *Life on the Mississippi*. But it does exist. The idea that there is 'rest and healing in the contemplation of antiquities' appears in Chapter XXII in his description of the Southern Hotel and Bogard's saloon in St. Louis. Twain's nostalgia is almost inconsolable when he discovers, on his return, that the steamboat crowd with their 'swell airs and graces' (112) have gone for good from the billiard rooms. This feeling of loss became more acute in the later years as Twain turned in upon himself in response to the personal and public tragedies that he encountered. As Dwight Macdonald tells us, the 'note of baffled despair sounds more and more' in the published fiction, and Twain's belief in the value of public entertainment becomes one of 'neurotic bitterness'.[41] In *The Mysterious Stranger* entertainment is a cosmic weapon for Satan who exhorts the human race to laugh and by so doing to blow the world to bits. Yet the fascination remains. If Twain is willing to use the figure of the public entertainer to express his feelings of despair, he is also prepared to continue his activities as a private performer to gain some protection from a world he mistrusts.

Just as baseball became popular in the Civil War camps, providing soldiers with an involvement in coherent patterns of competition that did not seem present in the war itself, so Clemens, after the death of his wife and children, turned to billiards as an ordering point for his own life. He would play for hour after hour, inventing new games, solipsistically obsessed with protecting his mind against the random incursions of a too-vivid reality. In the playing of billiards Twain appeared as a pastiche version of his hero Horace Bixby: a man steering just for the hell of it, a pilot without an audience in the comfort of his parlour, playing a game to safeguard his mind against the arbitrary expressions of an unfathomable world.

At the end billiards for Twain is what pool is for Krebs, the battle-scarred victim of Ernest Hemingway's short story 'Soldier's Home'. In a world of corrupt glory Krebs achieves his peace in the coolness and silence of the small-town pool hall. For him the pool hall is a place of refuge, a bulwark against the pain and unpredictability of a world which is far too senseless to encounter through 'the intrigue and the politics' of an unnecessary language. What Krebs resists in the playing of pool is the exploitation of personal feeling at a moment of crisis. As Hemingway tells us: 'He [Krebs] did not want any consequences ever again. He wanted to live along without consequences.'[42] What Krebs prefers are the simple, visual patterns that he can look at from a distance, those which the girls in the street provide him with in their sweaters and shirts and Dutch collars and bobbed hair. What he prefers is a place of retreat where he can escape the glaring heat of the day and the crowds. Twain, likewise, whose only real stability was the binding love of his family, retreated into the sanctuary of the billiards room after the death of Livy his wife in 1904 and Jean his youngest daughter in 1909. For Dwight Macdonald, Twain's refusal to accept 'any consequences' in the later years shows up in his billiards-playing where he was 'always willing to postpone his re-entry into reality for "just one more game" '.[43] In the playing of such a game Twain was able to invent a singular and necessary status for himself, an alternative identity in which he could resist the relentless pressure of the public performer—a rôle which, throughout his life, he had so conspicuously embraced. In billiards Twain was refusing a right of entry to a world he had invented, he was protecting himself with a mode of expression in which passive calculation and limited action appeared to make sense in an absurd world. In observing the colours and the clean formation of the pool balls on the baize, Twain was presenting himself with an image of pictorial felicity, a spectacle in which form and colour were transcendent modes.

Twain was able to discover in the playing of billiards at the end of his life a sense of sequence and procedure in a world which appeared random and chaotic. The ability to perceive the ball in its true relationship to the pocket, to control the cue and exert the correct pressure—these things required from the player a specific kind of effort and a specific definition of task. On the framed world of the billiard table there were no 'consequences' for Twain. The game could be played at his own pace and on his own terms. Accidents might happen but contingency plans could be set in motion. The balls that struck each other unexpectedly would come to rest and the outcome of the game could be reconsidered. Personal control might not be abandoned entirely. The science of play—the resurrection of a mode that Twain had believed in from the beginning—could, for a moment anyway, make things seem all right.

Mark Twain: A Sumptuous Variety

NOTES

1. William Dean Howells, *My Mark Twain: Reminiscences and Criticism* (New York, 1910), pp. 4–5. Biographies of Mark Twain make much of this fascination, of Twain's delight in making up new games, in acting out children's fantasies, in poker and billiards, in wild costumes and cake-walks, impersonations, jokes, toys, pranks, puzzles, riddles, newspaper hoaxes, children's games. Numerous examples of these tastes can be found in Albert B. Paine, *Mark Twain: A Biography*, 3 vols. (New York, 1912); and Paul Fatout, *Mark Twain in Virginia City* (Bloomington, 1964). Edward Wagenknecht nicely summarizes Twain's play obsession in *Mark Twain: The Man and his Work* (Norman, 1962), pp. 123–25.
2. Judith Fetterley, 'Mark Twain and The Age of Anxiety', *Georgia Review*, 33 (1979), 382–91. See also Bruce Michelson, 'Huck Finn and the Games of the World', *American Literary Realism*, 13 (1980), 108–21; Bruce Michelson, 'Deus Ludens: The Shaping of Mark Twain's Mysterious Stranger', *Novel*, 14 (1980), 44–56; Jerry Shear 'Games People Play in Huck Finn', *Midwest Quarterly*, 20 (1979), 378–93.
3. The returned crusader of the spoof on legends in *Innocents Abroad* who enters the castle disguised as a harlequin and exterminates his audience; Tom Sawyer whose staging of his own funeral involves the potential humiliation of all of St. Petersburg; the Duke and the King whose Royal Nonesuch denigrates that craving for entertainment in an audience; Hank Morgan whose entertainments cause his audience to collapse by platoons; Dave 'Pudd'nhead' Wilson who enters his world with a hostile joke whose intention he ultimately fulfils by killing his half of the social dog; Philip Traum, a divine Player, cavorting through the human amusement park and amusing himself recklessly at the world's expense.
4. See Fred W. Lorch, *The Trouble Begins at Eight: Mark Twain's Lecture Tours* (Iowa City, 1968); and Paul Fatout, *Mark Twain on the Lecture Circuit* (Bloomington, 1960).
5. Howells, *My Mark Twain*, p. 20.
6. Stanford W. Gregory and Jerry M. Lewis, '*Huck Finn and The Game Model Gloss*', *Qualitative Societée Sociology*, 3 (1980), 136–51; see especially 136, 140, 141.
7. Ibid.
8. Wagenknecht, p. 123.
9. *The Autobiography of Mark Twain*, intro. by Charles Neider (London, 1960), p. 135.
10. Christian Messenger, 'Sport and the Spirit of Play' in *American Fiction: Hawthorne to Faulkner* (New York), 1981.
11. Ibid., 86–90.
12. Mark Twain, *Life on the Mississippi* (New York, 1963), p. 22. All subsequent references to *Life on the Mississippi* are to this edition. Page references appear after quotations.
13. Lionel Trilling, *The Liberal Imagination* (New York, 1953), p. 7.
14. Leo Marx, *The Machine in the Garden: Technology and the Pastoral Ideal in America* (New York, 1967).

15. Ibid., p. 191.

16. 'M. de Tocqueville on Democracy in America', *Edinburgh Review*, October 1840, in *Dissertations and Discussions: Political, Philosophical, and Historical* (Boston, 1865), 11, 148.

17. 'The Utility and Pleasures of Science', *Scientific American* 11 (August 1847), 381.

18. Hart Crane, 'Modern Poetry', reprinted in *The Collected Poems of Hart Crane*, ed. Waldo Frank (New York, 1946), p. 177.

19. *The Selected Writings of Ralph Waldo Emerson*, ed. Brooks Atkinson (New York, 1950), pp. 305–15, 319–41.

20. F. Scott Fitzgerald, *The Crack-Up and Other Pieces and Stories* (Harmondsworth, 1965), p. 39.

21. Martin Esslin, *The Theatre of the Absurd* (New York, 1961), pp. 321–32.

22. Marion Montgomery, 'Mark Twain's Dilemma in *Life on the Mississippi*', *Mississippi Quarterly*, 11 (1958), 79.

23. Constance Rourke, *American Humour: A Study of the Natural Character* (New York, 1953), pp. 47, 49.

24. Quoted in Leo Marx, *The Machine in the Garden*, p. 196.

25. Ibid., p. 208.

26. Michael Chevalier, *Society, Manners and Politics in the United States* (1839), quoted in Fred Somkin, *Unquiet Eagle: Memory and Desire in the Idea of American Freedom 1815–60* (Ithaca, 1967), p. 84.

27. Christian Messenger ignores the essential complexity of the problem. He believes the pilot, without reservation, is able to control his boat the way in which an artist controls his novel. For Messenger, Bixby is the presiding consciousness, the voice of authority to whom all information is given and through whom all information is translated into action. For Messenger the pilot is a lucid reflector whose various deputies—mate, leadsman, boilerman, cub—are strategically placed around the boat to give help whenever they are called upon and to offer whatever comment is necessary. His argument, therefore, makes light of the compulsions that affect the pilot and flaw his art. It ignores the idea that any sustained comparison between the pilot's rôle and the processes of art can only make sense if the nature of the pilot's craft is not dismissive of the craft of others. In fact what Messenger's argument ignores are those moments of ecstasy and anger which the pilot finds difficult to negotiate when the processes of art and the perceptions of the artist become subordinate to certain technical concerns.

28. F. Scott Fitzgerald, *The Great Gatsby* (New York, 1953), p. 182.

29. Melville to Hawthorne, June 1 (?), 1851, *The Letters of Herman Melville*, eds. Merrill R. David and William H. Gillman (New Haven, 1960), pp. 126–31.

30. S. L. Clemens, *Adventures of Huckleberry Finn* (Scranton, 1962), p. 130.

31. Henry James, *The Portrait of a Lady* (Harmondsworth, 1976), p. 8.

32. Henry to Charles F. Adams, Jr., quoted in Ernest Samuels, *The Young Henry Adams* (Cambridge, Mass., 1948), p. 130.

33. *Huckleberry Finn*, p. 60.

34. Letter to *New York Times*, 31 March 1903 in Paul Fatout, *Mark Twain*

Speaks For Himself (West Lafayette, 1978), p. 176.

35. Messenger, p. 89.
36. Ibid., p. 87.
37. Ibid., p. 89.
38. Twain, 'Welcome Home', *Mark Twain's Speeches* (New York, 1923), p. 145.
39. Mark Twain, *A Connecticut Yankee in King Arthur's Court* (New York, 1899), p. 367.
40. Twain, *Autobiography*, p. 135.
41. Dwight MacDonald, *Against the American Grain* (New York, 1962), p. 86.
42. *The Essential Hemingway* (Harmondsworth, 1972), p. 313.
43. MacDonald, p. 94.

2

Kids' Stuff: Mark Twain's Boys

by JOHN S. WHITLEY

In his famous introduction to *Huckleberry Finn*, T. S. Eliot remarks that he first read *Tom Sawyer* and *Huckleberry Finn* in the order of their publication: '*Tom Sawyer* did not prepare me for what I was to find its sequel to be. *Tom Sawyer* seems to me to be a boy's book, and a very good one.'[1] Twain himself *seems* to have changed his mind about the kind of book he was writing. In a letter to William Dean Howells in July 1875 he explains why he had not taken up an earlier hint of his friend's, that Tom should be taken forward into maturity:

> If I went on, now, and took him into manhood, he would just be like all the one-horse men in literature and the reader would conceive a hearty contempt for him. It is *not* a boy's book, at all. It will only be read by adults. It is only written for adults.[2]

This has sometimes been taken to imply that the novel is only ostensibly about a boy but is actually a social satire, a serious study of innocence confronting experience and, according to Albert E. Stone, 'a full-dress study of personality, community, and the anatomy of social evil'.[3]

Yet a remark in Twain's notebook a quarter of a century after *Tom Sawyer* was first published helps to put his earlier remark in perspective: 'I have never written a book for boys; I write for grown-ups who have *been* boys.'[4] It is a novel for adults only in the sense that its third-person narration knowingly plays to adult nostalgia ('. . . the reader probably remembers how to do it, if he has ever been a boy' (I)) and also pokes fun at the absurdities of that nostalgia by showing how the tale we would all like to have told about our child-hoods can only be told by a studious avoidance of conflict, compromise, sexuality, pain and guilt; all those aspects necessary, in various permutations, to the fictional representa-tion of a truly adult world. Such a reading of Twain's remark goes far to explain his rapid agreement with an apparently opposite view stated by Howells in November 1875:

> It's altogether the best boy's story I have ever read. It will be an immense success. But I think you ought to treat it explicitly *as* a boy's story. Grown-ups will enjoy it as much as you do; and if you put it forth as a study of boy character from a grown-up point of view, you'd give the wrong key to it.[5]

Twain replied immediately, concurring with this judgement: 'Mrs. Clemens decides with you that the book should issue as a book for boys, pure and simple—and so do I. It is surely the correct idea.'[6] Stone sees this as a complete capitulation on Twain's part: 'His respect for Howell's judgement was great, and likely to weigh heavily against his own unproven preferences'[7]; but this is surely to assert too great a lack of authorial confidence, even in such an entrepreneurily inclined writer as Twain. The study of boy character from a grown-up point of view was to follow in *Huckleberry Finn*. That is, the point of view which places the boy character in an adult world of slavery, feuds, confidence-tricksters and murder and lets him get on with the task of making sense of it all. The world of *Tom Sawyer*, by contrast, is an hermetically sealed world which allows the boy's sense of fiction to govern the narrative. It is a specifically and wryly self-conscious wish-fulfilment narrative in that the adventures the boy wishes to have are granted to him, not in ironic juxtaposition to 'real life', but in a manner which validates the enclosures developed in his imagination through his reading of Hugo, Dumas, Scott and their much lesser imitators. *Tom Sawyer* conforms to a number of the desiderata listed by a recent commentator on children's fiction, such as a play element not only presented but also reflected in the form and texture of a story; the ability of characters to improvise; 'archetypal threats and promises' which reflect the fears and hopes of the child; the *vicarious* experience of danger; mischievous behaviour which is never seriously punished and a simple, humorous attitude to adults 'especially where this tends to cut them down nearer to child-size'.[8]

The differences between *Tom Sawyer* and *Huckleberry Finn* can first of all be indicated in terms of narrative point of view. Stephen Crane, in his marvellous short story, 'The Open Boat', points to one of the crucial problems of the American realist: how to maintain a balance between an olympian naturalistic/deterministic view of human behaviour and a closer, more humanized view of that behaviour; how to use fictional techniques both for theoretical comment on society and life and for the depiction of human motive and action which, if not noble, is at least psychologically explicable and capable of being sympathetically understood. Crane balances a view from a 'balcony' which sees the situation of four men crammed into a tiny boat in a tempestuous sea as 'wierdly picturesque',[9] with a view of the sea and human companionship through the eyes of these very men. Twain is not writing naturalistic fiction in *Tom Sawyer*, but he can be said to balance a view from the balcony in that novel with a view from the boat (raft) in the first-person narrative of *Huckleberry Finn*. The olympian narrative view in the earlier novel is, of course, more affable and positive than Crane's, but it is amused, patronizing and totally in control. The narrative voice ranges from an almost deliberate nostalgic banality:

> The locust trees were in bloom and the fragrance of the blossoms filled the air. Cardiff Hill, beyond the village and above it, was green with vegetation, and it lay just far enough away to seem a Delectable Land, dreamy, reposeful, and inviting. (II)

(note the giveaway capitals for 'Delectable Land'): through a very literary sentimentality ('Gradually their talk died out and drowsiness began to steal upon the eyelids of the little waifs' (XIII)), unnecessary explanations ('the theatrical gorgeousness of the thing appealed strongly to his nature' (XV)), lengthy comments on education in Chapter XXI, and moments of ostentatious irony:

> It might have seemed to him a waste of pomp and
> ammunition to kill a bug with a battery of artillery, but there
> seemed nothing incongruous about the getting up such an
> expensive thunderstorm as this to knock the turf from under an
> insect like himself. (XXII)[10]

There are, indeed, occasions when the narrator makes
sardonic comments on the limitations of St. Petersburg
society, being that of a 'poor shabby little village' (I).
Remarking on the speed with which news of the murder of Dr.
Robinson ran through the village, he notes, 'Of course the
schoolmaster gave holiday for that afternoon; the town would
have thought strangely of him if he had not' (XI). Later, after
Tom has told the truth and proved Muff Potter's innocence:

> As usual, the fickle, unreasoning world took Muff to its
> bosom and fondled him as lavishly as it had abused him before.
> But that sort of conduct is to the world's credit; therefore it is
> not well to find fault with it. (XXIV)

This last quotation has *almost* the crispness of one of
Puddn'head Wilson's maxims but in that novel the maxims
summarize the moral squalor of St. Petersburg's first cousin,
Dawson's Landing. In *Tom Sawyer*, the need of the narrator to
assert that the world of St. Petersburg is 'fickle' and
'unreasoning' points to a process of telling rather than
showing. The society which surrounds Tom is supportive
because its adult denizens are children writ large. The
repetition of human experience is insisted upon in the first
chapter:

> Within two minutes, or even less, he had forgotten all his
> troubles. Not because his troubles were one wit less heavy and
> bitter to him than a man's are to a man, but because a new and
> powerful interest bore them down and drove them out of his
> mind for the time—just as men's misfortunes are forgotten in
> the excitement of new enterprises

and it is the concept of similarity between youth and age,
rather than dislocation, which governs the novel. Tom's
attempts to 'show off' in front of the Thatchers are mirrored by
the activities of all the inhabitants of the Sunday School,
including the adults.[11] If there is a juvenile pariah, Huckleberry Finn, he is matched by an adult pariah, Muff Potter.

Both are forgiven and clasped to the bosom of the community. If Tom's return to life at his own funeral impresses him with its theatricality, that is what also impresses the members of the congregation: 'As the "sold" congregation trooped out they said they would almost be willing to be made ridiculous again to hear Old Hundred sung like that once more' (XVII). When Tom and Huck discover and keep their treasure, their adult fellow-citizens, albeit for rather different motives, replicate the boys' activities:

> Every "haunted" house in St. Petersburg and the neighbouring villages was dissected, plank by plank, and its foundations dug up and ransacked for hidden treasure—and not by boys, but men—pretty grave, unromantic men, too, some of them. (XXXIV)

This replication of experience makes it difficult to take seriously the contention that there is a dark side of St. Petersburg. Stone talks about 'the pervasive presence of evil' and suggests that there is an ironic juxtaposition of the play deaths which Tom invents and the real deaths of Dr. Robinson and Injun Joe[12] and Robert Regan feels that St. Petersburg is being criticized because it is 'benign' by day and 'sinister' by night.[13] Yet this is to ignore the extreme melodrama of these dark aspects, a melodrama totally in keeping with the plots of popular blood-and-thunder novels like those offered to Laura Hawkins at the bookstore in Twain and Warner's, *The Gilded Age*.[14] Tom is one of many characters in late nineteenth-century American fiction whose lives are seriously affected by persistent contact with popular culture. Laura's own crime of murder is seen as partly the result of too much early reading of romantic trash, just as Maggie's repeated visits to the popular theatre in Stephen Crane's *Maggie: A Girl of the Streets* point to the absurd ease with which she can make false, romantic interpretations of the hideous reality around her. One should also note that the way in which Tom is 'taken in' by what he reads is cleverly paralleled by Aunt Polly's naïve faith in patent medicines: 'She was a subscriber for all the 'Health' periodicals and phrenological frauds; and the solemn ignorance they were inflated with was breath to her nostrils' (XII). Mystery, blood and death erupt like travelling theatre into

Tom's world, validating his own lurid, boyish imagination. Twain recognized this many years later when he wrote, in his *Autobiography*: 'I think that in *Tom Sawyer* I starved Injun Joe to death in the cave. But that may have been to meet the exigencies of romantic literature.'[15] Death and the principal villain are introduced in Chapter IX but in the heading to that chapter Twain cannot resist a joke ('Grave Subjects Introduced'). Tom's imagination, whilst he is lying in bed, prepares for what happens:

> Old beams began to crack mysteriously. The stars creaked faintly. Evidently spirits were abroad. . . . Next the ghostly ticking of a deathwatch in the wall at the bed's head made Tom shudder—it meant that somebody's days were numbered. (IX)

When Tom gets out of bed and accompanies Huck to the graveyard, the scene plays on the same kind of childhood fears: 'A faint wind moaned through the trees, and Tom feared it might be the spirits of the dead, complaining at being disturbed' (IX). The 'spirits' who do appear are like demons of melodrama. Dr. Robinson *is* a citizen of the village, but one engaged in the ghoulish practice of grave-robbing, and Injun Joe is a standard melodramatic villain whose 'social' reason for murdering the doctor hardly constitutes a criticism of the community since the reader will believe that any right-thinking man would turn such a creature from his door. The murder itself ('. . . the half-breed saw his chance and drove the knife to the hilt in the young man's breast' (IX)) is later and easily transmuted into boyish fantasy:

> They made an imposing adventure of it, saying, 'Hist!' every now and then, and suddenly halting with finger on lip; moving with hands on imaginary dagger hilts; and giving orders in dismal whispers that if 'the foe' stirred, to 'let him have it to the hilt', because 'dead men tell no tales.' (XIII)

It is surely difficult to believe in the nocturnal side of St. Petersburg society when the murder in a graveyard one and a half miles from town is committed by a figure who has so little connection with the community. James M. Cox has commented on the wealth of types in *Tom Sawyer*: even with Tom we are unsure of his age and have no clear idea what he looks like.[16] Wallace Hildick has noted that in children's fiction adults tend to illustrate single aspects of personality, such as greed and bravery, because they operate

> in a world that is none the less valid because it is a dream world, for it is in effect the world of the subconscious and therefore an important part of human experience, and the trimming down of characters to single facets of personality, single humours or traits, is itself a reflection of the dream mechanism, a replica of the myth-making, symbolizing way in which the subconscious seems often to operate[17]

and no character in *Tom Sawyer* is a stronger example of type than Injun Joe. His origins lie in the seventeenth-century New England conception of the Indian as anti-Christ, in the use of Indians as Gothic demons in such early American novelists as Charles Brockden Brown[18] and in the later nineteenth-century shift of villainy (*Tom Sawyer* appeared only half a decade before Helen Hunt Jackson's *A Century of Dishonour*) to the figure of the half-breed, the Cain-like wanderer in a waste borderland who belongs to neither whites nor Indians but who manages to acquire the worst characteristics of both races. Francis Parkman, in *The Oregon Trail*, defined the half-breed, 'According to the common saying half Indian, half white man, and half devil,' and in John Esten Cooke's *Lord Fairfax*, published eight years before Twain's book, the half-breed villain is truly a creature of nightmare:

> His forehead was scarcely an inch in height; his small eyes, as cunning and cruel as a serpent's, rolled beneath bushy brows; his nose was crooked like a hawk's bill, and the hideous mouth, stretching almost from ear to ear, was disfigured with protruding tusks like those of a wild boar.[19]

When on the run, Joe disguises himself as another outsider, a deaf and dumb Spaniard. He is a figure of children's bad dreams who is encountered in graveyards and labyrinths and not in the daylight world. He represents the usual view of the child that the terrors he/she will have to face are always 'out there' and grotesque rather than internal and endemic to human nature.[20] In *Huckleberry Finn* the darkness of human nature is not simply transferred to such types. The Grangerfords are kind and loving but their attempts to validate the sickly romanticism of their culture, demonstrated brilliantly in the artefacts of their home as seen by Huck's bemused eyes, are imaged in the feud which senselessly kills off members of their family.

Tom Sawyer is, more than anything, a boys' book because its hero can always go home again. In Chapter XXXIII, Tom and Huck discuss the advantages of being robbers: ' "Why, its real bully Tom. I b'lieve its better'n to be a pirate." "Yes, it's better in some ways, because it's close to home and circuses and all that." ' Like the diminutive heroes and heroines of the many books by Enid Blyton, he can enjoy the most outrageous adventures and then go back home to tea and buns. Because both St. Petersburg society and the structure of the novel follow Tom's romantic inclinations he is never in any danger of expulsion from the community. He can turn work into play (the famous whitewashing scene) and death into life (when he attends his own funeral). He can even find his way out of the labyrinth of caves, whereas Injun Joe, once in there, is utterly doomed because he has no home to which he can return:

> Injun Joe lay stretched upon the ground, dead, with his face close to the crock of the door, as if his longing eyes had been fixed, to the latest moment, upon the light and the cheer of the free world outside. (XXXIII)

He dies as he had lived. When Tom goes off to his 'pirate' camp, 'It was but a small strain on his imagination to remove Jackson's Island beyond eyeshot of the village' (XIII); yet the Island is always close to home, so that Tom can nip back to St. Petersburg and hear Aunt Polly bewailing his death. He is like one of those small rubber balls attached, by a length of elastic, to a wooden bat. No matter how hard the ball is hit it still returns. Huck seems to find a home by the end of *Tom Sawyer*, but in *Huckleberry Finn* someone cuts the elastic. In the later novel, Jackson's Island is but a way stage on an inevitable and final journey away from home.

The final chapter of *Tom Sawyer* does serve, in a minor key, as a transition from the world of St. Petersburg to the world of the raft. Tom's own evaluation of himself as a hero, signalled by his emergence from the caves and his acquiring such a large sum of money, is vindicated by Judge Thatcher's comparison of the boy with the young George Washington and his determination to secure a great military/legal career for Tom. Tom's play rebellions are all now comfortably subsumed into the possibility of an Horatio Alger-like 'rags-to-riches' happy ending. Huck, by contrast, is made unhappy by the respectability which wealth has conferred upon him, a respectability defined in terms which playfully echo major social problems of post-Civil War America. Tom's 'freedom' occurs strictly within civilized society; Huck loses his freedom amid the 'bars and shackles of civilization'. He sees the Widow Douglas's protection solely in terms of confinement, a confinement brought about by money and imaged by a regularity like that of recent industrializing processes: 'The widder eats by a bell; she goes to bed by a bell; she gets up by a bell—everything's so awful regular a body can't stand it.' Tom is able to persuade Huck to postpone his true rebellion in favour of a play rebellion: a robber gang in which, significantly, all the members must be respectable because, in romantic literature, robbers are frequently 'dukes and such' and they swear to 'kill anybody and all his family that hurts one of the gang'. Huck cannot join this gang unless he returns home to live with the Widow Douglas. There *Tom Sawyer* ends, but that ending prepares us for its greater sequel where Huck and Jim do constitute a gang headed by a King and a Duke and where the Grangerford family *is* being destroyed by a romantic (that is, non-explainable) feud.

Before that happened, Twain published a novel half-way between enchanted confinement and appallingly difficult freedom, *The Prince and Pauper*. Tom Sawyer's dreams of power and fame had stopped short of royalty. He dreamed of being an outlaw, a pirate and a treasure-seeker. His last dream, in the manner of much of the novel, comes true when he and Huck discover the huge fortune of 12,000 dollars. One of the heroes of *The Prince and the Pauper* is also called Tom, Tom Canty, and, lying on the floor of his family hovel, he persistently dreams of being a prince. Like Tom Sawyer, he can persuade his playmates of the validity of his dreams and can duly create the central parts:

> Daily the mock prince was received with elaborate ceremonials borrowed by Tom from his romantic readings; daily the great

affairs of the mimic kingdom were discussed in the royal
council; and daily his mimic highness issued decrees to his
imaginary armies, navies and viceroyalties. (II)

Very early in the novel Tom Canty transfers from dream to
reality when he inadvertently changes places with his look-
alike, Edward the Prince of Wales. Both, following this, feel
that they are in a dream-state and both are thought by their
respective fathers to be mad. Both, like Huck, have bad fathers
(there is mutual affection between Henry and Edward but,
nationally, the King is known as a 'grim tyrant' (XII)) and
both, like Huck, have to move from the confinements of the
romantic to a harsher reality. Tom moves from his dream of
royalty to the less acceptable realities of power, realities which
seem imprisoning: 'And turn where he would, he seemed to
see floating in the air the severed head and the remembered
face of the great Duke of Norfolk, the eyes fixed on him
reproachfully' (V). Edward moves out into the bustling world
beyond the palace gates, a world of cruelty and pursuit where
he continually feels lost. 'The houseless prince, the homeless
heir to the throne of England, still moved on, drifting deeper
into the maze of squalid alleys' (IV). The solitariness of both
boys is persistently emphasized. Tom is to be crowned head of
a nation divided sharply into the overwhelmingly rich few and
the miserably poor many; Edward is 'crowned' by the Ruffler
and his gang, not now the pirates and banditti of Tom Sawyer's
imagination but a miserable band of thieves for whom
violence, treachery and licentiousness have become a way of
life and whose stories suggest, unlike Injun Joe's, an alternative society forced into existence by the harsh laws of Tudor
England. Both boys gain humanity and courage through their
experiences, experiences which seem more realistic than those
of *Tom Sawyer* because they are given greater social and
historical weight.

Both these heroes, therefore, look forward to Huck far more
than they look back to Tom, particularly in suggesting a
version of the Wordsworthian notion that the child is father to
the man. Just as Huck is to show a sensitivity and wisdom
beyond both his years and the very limited adults who
surround him, so the two boys put most of their elders to

shame because they have acquired an experience of the 'two nations' which none of the adults (except Miles Hendon) possesses. Even while thinking them mad, the adults recognize this quality in the boys. Yet the terrible freedom granted to Huck is circumscribed here by Twain's sentimentality and careful use of a romance plot. Although both boys have tyrannical fathers, Tom Canty has a loving mother and sisters:

> the young girls crept to where the prince lay and covered him tenderly from the cold with straw and rags; and their mother crept to him also, and stroked his hair, and cried over him, whispering broken words of comfort and compassion in his ear the while. (X)

whom he comes close to renouncing when his love of power and majesty becomes too strong at the coronation. In the end he is reunited with them; he returns 'home'. Edward, too, returns home from the Underworld, but principally because he has a helper, Miles Hendon, who is also trying to return home and prove his identity. Hendon has been correctly described by Stone as 'a small boy's dream of a father-protector'[21] (though he thinks of himself instinctively as 'his elder brother' (XII)). He is the ideal protector because he is himself in quest for a re-established identity and has all the necessary skills to make his way through the turmoil of Tudor England. He is introduced as '. . . tall, trim-built, muscular . . .' (XI) and, when the mob lays its hands on Edward, '. . . the stranger's long sword was out and the meddler went to the earth under a sounding thump with the flat of it' (XI). In this introduction an interesting comparison is made, for it is said of Hendon that '. . . his swaggering carriage marked him at once as a ruffler of the camp' (XI). According to John Awdeley,

> a ruffler goeth with a weapon to seek service, saying he has been a servitor in the wars, and beggeth for his relief. But his chiefest trade is to rob the poor wayfaring men and market-women . . .[22]

and, according to Thomas Harman, the ruffler '. . . weary of well-doing, shaking off all pain doth choose him this idle life, and wretchedly wanders about the most shires of this realm'.[23] Hendon has seen service abroad, been imprisoned and is wretchedly poor, though far from being criminal. Like some members of the Ruffler's gang, he has been the victim of a gross injustice, occurring within his family rather than the 'family' of England. He is at home in both nations and is therefore an ideal wish fulfilment father/brother/protector. From the moment he enters the novel the reader can foresee everybody going home to a happy ending. No such protector ever appears to aid Huck. His father is worthless; the Grangerfords are being killed off by the Shepherdsons; the King and the Duke use him for their own ends. His one genuine relationship, with Jim, does not provide him with a protector because Jim is a frightened slave whose level of education and knowledge of the world leaves him in need of Huck's protection. The child is, again, father of the man. Small wonder that Huck, trying desperately to make sense of the bloodshed and mendacity that surround him, should acquiesce in Tom's absurd games at the Phelps Farm. Tom has always been the leader, the initiator of the action, and Huck is relieved to have the burden of his responsibility lightened. Throughout his journey Huck has used Tom as a Yardstick for measuring his actions and plans. Leaving a false trail before starting for Jackson's Island, Huck laments 'I did wish Tom Sawyer was there . . .' (VII) and, urging Jim to help 'rummage' the wrecked steamboat, he argues, 'Do you reckon Tom Sawyer would ever go by this thing?' (XII). Much later, trying to work out the Wilks family problems, he pats himself on the back: '. . . I judged I had done it pretty neat—I reckoned Tom Sawyer couldn't a done it no neater himself' (XXVIII). Now, at Phelps Farm, with consummate irony, Tom appears as Huck's saviour (and Jim's):

> What a head for just a boy to have! If I had Tom Sawyer's head, I wouldn't trade it off to be a duke, nor mate of a steamboat, nor clown in a circus, nor nothing I can think of. (XXXIV)

Huckleberry Finn begins his story surrounded by fictions which have a greater social resonance than those in the earlier novel and so prod the reader at a very early point into a revaluation of the superstition and moral blinkeredness of the Missouri small town. Miss Watson's view of heaven ('She said all a body would have to do there was to go around all day long with a harp and sing, forever and ever' (I)) is matched by

Tom's boook-learning ('Don't you reckon that the people that made the books knows what's the correct thing to do?' (II)) which transforms a Sunday school picnic into a crowd of Spaniards and A-rabs and leads Huck, at the end of Chapter III, to unite, in his contempt, these two kinds of fiction ('It had all the marks of a Sunday school'). Aunt Polly acts as a proper parent to Tom, a representative of comfort and home. Just as Huck rejects his surrogate parent, the Widow Douglas, he also rejects his real parent whose reality is that of the thing itself, almost primeval in its awfulness, but decidedly and anciently human ('A body would have thought he was Adam, he was just all mud' (VI)) and, seen through the keenly sensitive eyes and sharply accurate descriptive powers of Huck, no longer a type ('. . . not like another man's white, but a white to make a body sick, a white to make a body's flesh crawl—a tree-toad white, a fish-belly white' (V)).

From then on, the reality of Huck's journey is chronicled both by the truth of the innocent vision and by persistently setting that vision against reminders of Tom's adherence to a popular, debased romantic view. The quality of Huck's truth-telling can be illustrated by two comparisons. Here is Huck describing a view along the river:

> The first thing to see, looking away over the water, was a kind of dull line—that was the woods on t'other side—you couldn't make nothing else out; then a pale place in the sky; then more paleness, spreading around; then the river softened up, away off, and waren't black anymore, but gray; you could see little dark spots drifting along, ever so far away—trading scows, and such things; and long black streaks—rafts: (XIX)

where the vagueness of the uneducated vocabulary is tempered by a marvellous sense of the process of the human eye identifying changes in its surroundings; the whole passage becoming a description of seeing as much as the seen.[24] Against that, here is a typical passage from *Tom Sawyer*:

> It was a cool gray dawn, and there was a delicious sense of repose and peace in the deep pervading calm and silence of the woods. Not a leaf stirred; not a sound intruded upon great Nature's meditation. (XIV)

The vagueness of this description has nothing to do with the process of seeing but is deliberately platitudinous in order to remind the reader of an adult memory which idealizes and deserts observation. In the social realm, descriptions of people in *Tom Sawyer* are suitably typological:

> The superintendent was a slim creature of thirty-five, with a sandy goatee and short sandy hair; he wore a stiff standing collar whose upper edge almost reached his ears and whose sharp points curved forward abreast the corners of his mouth—a fence that compelled a straight lookout ahead. . . . (IV)

The amusing assumption of exceedingly minor authority is transmitted, in a gently Dickensian manner, through the stiff pomposity of his dress, a Sunday get-up which imprisons adults and children alike. Compare this with Huck's description of the undertaker at the Wilks funeral:

> When the place was packed full, the undertaker he slid around in his black gloves with his softy soothering ways, putting on the last touches, and getting people and things all shipshape and comfortable, and making no more sound than a cat. He never spoke; he moved people around, he squeezed in late ones, he opened up passage-ways, and done it all with nods, and signs with his hands. Then he took his place over against the wall. He was the softest, glidingest, stealthiest man I ever see; and there warn't no more smile to him than there is to a ham. (XXVII)

The sibilant alliteration captures beautifully both the movement and the attitude of this man and the 'black gloves', instead of being merely a part of the typology of reification, enforce his activity, where people and things are treated indiscriminately. The basic lack of compassion, despite the professional silence, is emphasized by the final flat sound of 'ham' and serves to make the undertaker an emblem of the society he serves. In other words he exists as an index of the society in which Huck moves and as an individualized figure caught, however briefly, in the full light of Huck's honesty.

Romanticism, as many critics have commented, gets exceedingly short shrift in *Huckleberry Finn*. On the reality of the river, steamboats sink, especially if they are called the 'Walter Scott' (whom Twain blamed for the American Civil

War) or the 'Lally Rook' (a lengthy exercise in romantic orientalism by Thomas Moore, who had some very disparaging remarks to make about American democracy). The Grangerford's refusal to see the horror of their feud is indicated by the grossly sentimental visions of death painted by their late daughter,[25] visions condemned by both Huck's genuine if brief farewell to Buck and by the relative casualness with which death is discovered and discarded early in the journey:

> He went and bent down and looked, and says: 'It's a dead man. Yes, indeedy; naked, too. He's ben shot in de back. I reckon he's ben dead two er three days. Come in, Huck, but doan' look at his face—it's too gashly.' I didn't look at him at all. Jim throwed some old rags over him, but he needn't done it; I didn't want to see him. (IX)

One measure of the distance we have travelled from *Tom Sawyer* is the astonishing amount of violence and death that occurs in *Huckleberry Finn*, and the grisliness of death is here underlined by its manifestation as a sight which cannot deter Huck and Jim from their looting and by its difference from the nocturnal child's nightmare of death that occurs in the earlier novel. The death in *Tom Sawyer* was that of the grave-robbing Dr. Robinson and a Dr. Robinson appears in *Huckleberry Finn*, but now an upstanding, intelligent citizen who immediately sees through the King and the Duke. Miss Watson's (and the Sunday school's) vision of heaven is counterbalanced by the 'natural' religion which emerges on the raft. Huck kneels to pray, unencumbered by the restrictions of social, sentimental piety and finds, in this one-to-one relationship with God, that, 'You can't pray a lie' (XXXI) and so decides, in the most momentous decision of the book, that he will go to Hell. The power of this decision, vested as it is in the fully-developed relationship between the hero and the runaway slave, is heavily supported by a memory of the St. Petersburg fiction of heaven. Huck never believed in that but he truly believes in the torments of Hell to which he freely decides he will be subjected. As Huck says of one of his adventures on the river; '. . . it wor'nt no time to be sentimentering' (XIII). Finally, of course, the process of Huck's education down river is viciously counterpointed by the return of Tom, still full of Hugo and Dumas, determined to reduce Jim to a comic object of his literary games, to impose his pattern of play on a situation which has grown too complex and serious to be so contained. To the end Tom remains resolutely himself. Not even the misfortune of being shot can stem the babble of his fantasies of control, and in the last paragraph he is shown fetishizing the bullet, hanging it round his neck as a watch-guard and constantly looking to see what the time is, that time which should tick him towards a maturity he can never have. Since Huck, as we have seen, looks plaintively to Tom, throughout the novel, as a measure of his success in dealing with the world, it is ironic that, when mistaken for Tom at Phelps Farm, he at last believes he has an identity: 'But if they was joyful, it wor'nt nothing to what I was; for it was like being born again, I was so glad to find out who I was' (XXXII). The moral divide between Tom and Huck has now become unbridgeable. Tom is a 'flat' character; he cannot surprise us. Huck is 'round' because he has learned and changed; even if, at Phelps Farm, he cannot find the courage to repudiate Tom's games.

Problems of identity bring us back to the theme of 'home'. Huck repudiates any concept of a home in St. Petersburg and succeeds in making a home with Jim, both on Jackson's Island and on the raft. Despite feeling lonely once he has arrived at Jackson's Island, Huck makes himself a 'nice camp' there and, unlike the boys in *Tom Sawyer*, does not continue to think of the life he has left behind. It is no longer a pirates' lair, but his new home: 'I was boss of it; it all belonged to me, so to say, and I wanted to know all about it' (VIII). Even after he meets Jim he remarks, 'I wouldn't want to be nowhere else but here' (IX), and after they see the dead man on the boat, he ends Chapter IX with the words, 'We got home all safe.' After exchanging Jackson's Island for the raft he similarly makes himself comfortable: 'We said there wor'nt no home like a raft, after all' (XVIII). Yet Twain never falls into a simplistic river-versus-land polarization. The raft steadily takes Huck and Jim deeper into slave-holding territory; it is continually threatened by the hidden dangers of the river (which is presented as 'natural', that is to say, both good and bad) and it is not free from the duplicities of adult life. The raft is taken over by the King and the Duke, grotesques who use romantic, aristocratic identities to defraud the gullible river communities. As with the Grangerfords, their moral vacuity is matched by the vacuity of their culture. The Duke's Shakespearian soliloquy is a monstrously funny, magpie affair, without any continuous sense. Huck quickly recognizes the rogues for what they are but, as a realistically timid boy, does not want any trouble:

> It didn't take me long to make up my mind that these liars worn't no kings nor dukes, at all, but just low-down humbugs and frauds. But I never said nothing, never let on; kept it to myself; it's the best way; then you don't have no quarrels, and don't get into no trouble. If they wanted us to call them kings and dukes, I hadn't no objections, 'long as it would keep peace in the family. . . . (XIX)

A 'family' is created on the raft 'home' but it is an utterly bogus one which both points up the frailty of that home and speeds its destruction. The inadequacy of this family is further emphasized by the participation of the King and the Duke, in bogus identities, as mourners at the family funeral of the Wilkses: pretending to be family in order to exploit family.

Huck's frequent changes of identity both spotlight the difficulties of finding a proper family and home, and his abiding wish to do so. The bogus identity he gives himself usually involves him in lying descriptions of his family, but the families, in these sagas, seem destined to suffer disaster, disintegration and death: 'Pa's luck didn't hold out; a steamboat run over the forrard corner of the raft, one night, and we all went overboard and dove under the wheel' (XX). Moreover, his fake identities are never safe because he is such an incompetent liar. His disguise of a young girl is quickly penetrated and his attempted rôle in the Wilks episode is equally untalented: ' "I reckon you ain't used to lying, it don't seem to come handy; what you want is practice. You do it pretty awkward" ' (XXIX). It is Huck's moral salvation and social damnation that he *is* a bad liar. For the novel has shown him arduously working his way to true relationships with God, Jim, the river, Mary Jane, and to true compassion when he sees the tarred and feathered figures of the King and the Duke. Yet his vision of the truth prevents him joining any family permanently or finding more than a temporary home. In the final pages Tom recovers his Aunt Polly, and Huck at last learns that his miserable father is dead. He also learns that Tom's adventure has been one huge lie, for Jim has been a free man all along. Tom wants again to be a hero, but now his heroism is shown to be as bogus as the culture of the South-West which supports his fantasies. Tom is the hero of Twain's Gilded Age, an era which Twain had already described as false and possessing an almost Jonsonian capacity for corrupting the truth. Huck is a mythic, timeless American hero, making that ever-recurrent, endlessly hopeful and desperate move West.

Twain later told a little more of the story of Tom Sawyer (leaving aside the utterly insignificant *Tom Sawyer Abroad* and *Tom Sawyer, Detective*: puny attempts at literary embalming). In *A Connecticut Yankee in King Arthur's Court* the central figure, Hank Mogan, is a practical man, a 'Yankee of the Yankees', who professes to be no poet but whose closest affinity is with his mortal enemy, Merlin. For Hank is a nineteenth-century, Gilded Age, necromancer: a Barnum-like figure whose 'modern' improvements in Camelot are mostly tricks to gain control of that world, to make it conform to his private ethic, as Tom had done in St. Petersburg. Unfortunately, sixth-century England proves less tractable than he had thought. Now the bullets cannot end as watch-guards; for Hank, the superintendent of the fire-arms factory, brings the Gatling gun to Malory's world and creates a holocaust which is appallingly prophetic of the carnage of modern warfare:

> The thirteen gatlings began to vomit death into the fated ten thousand. They halted, they stood their ground a moment against that withering deluge of fire, then they broke, faced about and swept toward the ditch like chaff before a gale. (XLIII)

Tom's play mischief has become real. If, as Lyall Powers suggests, Tom Sawyer is an image of that best of all possible

American heroes, the non-conforming natural man who conforms all the time,[26] then Twain may even have been prophetic about the 'innocent' imperialist drive which began to plague American foreign policy at the end of the century.

In Twain's grimly funny and last American novel, *Puddn'head Wilson*, written in one of the most harrowing periods of his life, there is another Tom, Tom Driscoll, who is now very much the villain of the piece. Liar, thief, coward and murderer, he is also discovered to be one thirty-second black and, Dawson's Landing being an obvious first cousin to St. Petersburg, he is promptly sold down river. Perhaps, at the last, Twain balanced the books, repaying Tom for all Jim's indignities.

NOTES

1. T. S. Eliot, 'Introduction', *The Adventures of Huckleberry Finn* (London: The Cresset Press, 1950), p. viii.
2. Henry Nash Smith and William M. Gibson (eds.), *Mark Twain-Howells Letters* (Cambridge, Massachusetts: Harvard University Press, 1960), p. 91.
3. Albert E. Stone, Jr., *The Innocent Eye: Childhood in Mark Twain's Imagination* (New Haven: Yale University Press, 1961), p. 63.
4. Ibid., p. 60.
5. *Twain-Howells Letters*, pp. 110–11.
6. Ibid., p. 112.
7. Stone, p. 59.
8. Wallace Hildick, *Children and Fiction* (London: Evans, 1974), p. 29.
9. Stephen Crane, *Works*, Vol. V (Charlottesville: University of Virginia Press, 1970), p. 69.
10. Hildick remarks that one of the desiderata of fiction for children is 'Irony—but only when properly announced.' Hildick, p. 29.
11. I am indebted here, as elsewhere, to James M. Cox, *Mark Twain: The Fate of Humour* (Princeton: Princeton University Press, 1966), pp. 141–49.
12. Stone, pp. 80–2.
13. Robert Regan, *Unpromising Heroes* (Berkeley and Los Angeles: University of California Press, 1966), p. 124. See also William C. Spengemann, *Mark Twain and the Backwoods Angel* (Kent, Ohio: Kent State University Press, 1966), pp. 41–7.
14. Mark Twain and Charles Dudley Warner, *The Gilded Age* (New York: Harper, 1915), Vol. 11, Ch. V.
15. Charles Neider (ed.), *The Autobiography of Mark Twain* (New York: Harper, 1959), p. 68.

16. Cox, pp. 133–34.
17. Hildick, p. 8.
18. Particularly in *Edgar Huntly* (1799). It is entirely in keeping with the nature of *Tom Sawyer* that the citizens of St. Petersburg should believe in the tricks of Gothic fiction: 'Injun Joe helped to raise the body of the murdered man and put it in a wagon for removal; and it was whispered through the shuddering crowd that the wound bled a little!' (XI). Of course, the reader is asked to consider believing it, too.
19. See Louise K. Barnett, *The Ignoble Savage: American Literary Racism, 1790–1890* (Westport, Connecticut: Greenwood, 1975), pp. 120–28.
20. A view thoroughly overturned by William Golding in *Lord of the Flies*. There is a useful comparison to be made with the graveyard scene which opens *Great Expectations*. There Pip, alone in a country churchyard, feels lonely and frightened, and the appearance of the escaped convict, Magwitch, is, one feels, almost dreamed up by the boy out of his nightmares. Dickens, however, does not leave it at that, for *Great Expectations* validates Pip's view (and denies it) in far more ways than are open to Twain in *Tom Sawyer*. Magwitch holds Pip upside down: just as he is to turn Pip's whole life upside down. He seems like an ogre but also turns out to be the nearest approach to a father Pip ever has. He is an outcast whose outcast nature has many important things to say about the society which cast him out.
21. Stone, p. 121.
22. G. Salgado (ed.), *Cony-Catchers and Bawdy Baskets* (Harmondsworth: Penguin, 1972), p. 63.
23. Ibid., p. 89.
24. Tony Tanner puts the matter well: 'Rather as though he had just taken Whitman's "first step" Huck absorbs the totality of things unsieved'—Tony Tanner, *The Reign of Wonder* (Cambridge: Cambridge University Press, 1965), p. 124.
25. Not according to Bradley, Beatty and Long, who say: 'The two chapters devoted to the Grangerford episode contrast the idyllic and picturesque description of the family and their home with the hideous and vainglorious inhumanity of the feud, which even Huck's experience has not prepared him to stomach'—Sculley Bradley, Richard Croom Beatty, E. Hudson Long (eds.), *Adventures of Huckleberry Finn* (New York: Norton, 1962), p. 95.
26. Lyall Powers, 'The Sweet Success of Twain's Tom', *Dalhousie Review*, Volume 53, No. 2, pp. 310–24.

3

The Comedic Stance: Sam Clemens, His Masquerade

by WILLIAM KAUFMAN

'The Germans have a word', says Albert Goldman, '*Todlachen.*
Laugh till it kills you.' He uses the word to describe the effect
upon an audience of one Joe Ancis, a Jewish comedian from
New York, and mentor of Lenny Bruce. Joe is an amateur, he
has never set foot on a stage; but when he, Lenny and
company gather in a group on the street corners of a Brooklyn
Saturday night, he incapacitates his listeners with a comic
delivery that is 'demonic':

> Laugh till it kills you. That's the way he likes to make them
> laugh. . . . He gets this mad glint in his eye and starts working like
> a Jewish rhythm 'n' blues act. A seizure, a paroxysm. Such restless
> tickling, twitching, hair patting, collar pulling, throat clearing,
> finger popping, hand slapping, knee bending, with elbows into
> the gut, shoulders up around the ears, bent from the waist.
> You're caught in this terrible double-bind. You're loving it.
> It's killing you! You can't bear to miss a single word. When he
> sees you're on the ropes, going down, he works twice as hard to
> kill you. Zooms in close to your face, locks on to the rhythms of
> your body, lasers and razors you till finally you tear yourself
> away. Then he stands up straight and laughs. He wants to
> laugh you out of existence.
> (Albert Goldman, *Ladies and Gentlemen . . . Lenny Bruce!!*
> (London: W. H. Allen, 1975), p. 106)

Then the comedian might walk away, noting with relish his success in reducing a stone-faced, immovable listener to convulsions of laughter mixed with tears: 'I fetched him! I broke him up utterly!' 'I knew I could lick him. I shook him up like dynamite.' 'Wracked all the bones of his body apart.' '. . . knocked out of his iron serenity.'[1] These are not the words of Joe Ancis; they are those of Samuel Clemens, after having vanquished the 'Iron General' Ulysses S. Grant at a banquet in his honour, before the eyes of the entire Army of the Tennessee. The Commander of the Union forces—bested by a failed Confederate deserter. The hero defeated by the anti-hero. The weapons are words, the wounds are laughter, and they are delivered from behind the mask of a meek, confused, shuffling, taunting, self-effacing Missourian named Mark Twain. His delivery is not as maniacal as that of Ancis; if anything, it is the opposite—he has been accused of quietly d-r-a-w-l-i-n-g out his words to the rate of three per minute. And while Ancis punctuates the recognition of his victory with his *own* laughter, Mark Twain only looks around with an expression of bewilderment at the interruptions of laughter that he himself has engendered. He seems to be unaware that anything is funny, or could be. Yet when he leaves the stage, to shed the mask of Mark Twain in private, he may then look in the mirror and rub his hands with glee. Another audience annihilated; the best of them, this time.

It is possible that Sam Clemens was one of the most violent men to ever have refrained from using his fists in anger, discounting one youthful intervention in a fight on his younger brother's behalf. His writings in fact depict a pervading abhorrence of physical violence, especially his own participation in it; as he says in his own 'Burlesque Biography', he is one of 'a succession of soldiers—noble, high-spirited fellows, who always went into battle singing, right behind the army, and always went out a-whooping, right ahead of it'. His disgust over atrocities in America and abroad was known to the readers of every newspaper that quoted him; and he was an avowed anti-vivisectionist. Yet he says this of his alter ego's fictional ancestor, Augustus Twain, in the same 'Burlesque Biography':

The Comedic Stance: Sam Clemens, His Masquerade

> He was as full of fun as he could be, and used to take his old saber and sharpen it up, and get in a convenient place on a dark night, and stick it through people as they went by, to see them jump. He was a born humorist.

An anti-vivisectionist, slicing his targets to ribbons. His targets are the sacred cows of his contemporaries—blind patriotism, religious convention, overbearing technology—yet he still needs welcome, depends on the acceptance and support of his audience, must eat. He is, in Kurt Vonnegut's words, 'Lincolnesque, and Quixotic, too, in his wish to please crowds without lying to them':

> If I am right about this, then every present day comedian who says after mocking something supposedly sacred, 'But I'm only kidding, folks', is following in the footsteps of Samuel Clemens, of the uxorious, Victorian American gentleman, diligent in business and often depressed, who became a world citizen while necessarily disguised as Mark Twain. .
>
> ('Opening Remarks', *The Unabridged Mark Twain*, edited by Lawrence Teacher, Volume I, p. xv)

On 3 February 1863, the day Clemens first signed his name in public as 'Mark Twain'—which he would often refer to as his 'nom de guerre'—there began for him the life-long trauma of leading a double existence. With the appearance of the pseudonym below a travel letter in the Virginia City *Territorial Enterprise*, Clemens established himself with the commitment of becoming and remaining a professional humorist. As it has so often been noted, the decision to confine his art to the restricted identity of Mark Twain caused him to wrestle with his self-imposed limitations in a battle to extend the scope of the American humorist's expression farther than had hitherto been attempted. Clemens assigned to Mark Twain the task of invading, as James Cox called it, 'the very citadel of seriousness, transforming it into humor with each encroachment'. Yet Mark Twain was never permitted overtly to reveal the serious inspirations—and the frequent accompanying rage—of Samuel Clemens. With varying degrees of calculation and success, Clemens effected his often violent encroachments under the guise of a complete humorist, an artist who in the immediate analysis—but rarely in the latter—was 'only kidding, folks'.

A study of Samuel Clemens and Mark Twain is one of

conflict between a living being arbitrarily thrust into life in a century and country whose attributes he simultaneously admired and despised, and the artistically moulded being who depended on both the artist's motivation and the acceptance of an audience often opposed to that motivation. Mark Twain's precarious position was in part caused by the ambivalence of his creator, who must both criticize and placate to the point of laughter the representatives of his culture.[2] Often his gestures went so far beyond placation as to amount to conscious and unconscious approbation or emulation of those he chose to criticize; but even more notably, in his later life, Clemens's disgust with what he called 'the damned human race' affected his art of comic impersonation in variously crippling degrees.[3] The primary requisite of his art as a comedian lay in convincing his audience that his words were in jest in spite of the underlying awareness that the opposite was true; this is the comedian's confidence-game, his masquerade, and in maintaining it Clemens walked a tight rope through his creative life, balancing his rage on one hand with the playfulness of Mark Twain on the other.

The comedian was recurrently frustrated in his efforts to maintain the masquerade; one reason for this was the nature of that conflict between the artist who must publicly and commercially comment on the conditions that have put him, in Mark Twain's own words, 'in eruption'. The conflict was further exacerbated by collisions within Clemens, and between Clemens and the image of Mark Twain: provincial *vs*. world traveller; hack journalist *vs*. serious author; artist *vs*. businessman; Presbyterian *vs*. God-hater; outsider *vs*. joiner; philosopher *vs*. clown.[4]

A clue to the comic success of Mark Twain's written works can be seen in an examination of his art as a lecturer. 'It was the personal appearances, I am sure', says Vonnegut,

> that persuaded his fellow-citizens that the holder of often-monstrous opinions was not a monster after all. As Twain presented himself in lecture halls, in fact, he was an utterly winsome sort of teddy bear, in need of all the love he could get.[5]

The success of his delivery also depended on his famous deadpan expression, which permitted the humour while betraying no recognition of it. The delivery was based on the tension between the compulsion to make fun and the repeated disillusionment of the artist, often amounting to anger, horror and disgust. The comedian's compulsion to treat his horrors comedically amounts to a built-in, though excusable, irreverence which is a fundamental element of his personality.[6] Such irreverence is permitted because it is offered through a multiple shield—a mask. Onstage, it is, in Stephen Leacock's words, the voice of 'discomfiture in the first person'; in print it is the same, as it exists, for instance, in the voice of a semi-literate, ignorant boy, from the pen of an 'adventure' writer.

One might consider the fury of Samuel Clemens when being charmed by the straight-faced soliloquy of Huck Finn. I do not propose that a given incident had a direct bearing on a given passage, but to understand just how mitigating a shield is the juvenile voice of Huck Finn, one might think of the shame of his creator at the hands of the Langdon family throughout his courtship. Clemens, newly arrived in New York with the influences of five years of roughing it in the West, sees in Olivia Langdon a reason for earnest self-improvement. He is no doubt insulted by her mother's launching of a character investigation based on her conviction that his status as a Christian worthy of her daughter is in doubt. Clemens, who only a few years before so questioned his own worth that he actually put a pistol to his head, must swallow a bitter pill when he sees the standards by which Mrs. Langdon measures improvement. When his best efforts at accommodation and promises of a better Christian deportment are placed before her, she meets them with the cynical question:

> From what standard of conduct, from what habitual life, did this change, or improvement, or reformation, commence? Does this change, so desirably commenced, make of an immoral man a moral man, as the world looks at men?[7]

Clemens, certainly wondering how to draw blood from a stone, can only respond with a protest of exasperation: 'I do not live backwards! God does not ask of the returning sinner what he *has* been.' And when all his demonstrations of forbearance and temperance are dismissed as worthless, it is only an example of utter fabrication and hypocrisy that finally softens Mrs.

Langdon towards him. In a last-ditch effort to woo her approbation, he resorts to writing a flatulent, gaudy essay on the Nativity, as a demonstration of his Christian awareness. He thus depicts a glorious, idyllic Bethlehem which, during the writing of *The Innocents Abroad*, he had seen and reported to be a leprous, stinking slum.[8]

These shameful, self-effacing steps that Clemens was forced to take in order to marry the woman he loved provided one example for him of the manner in which some of the professedly pious can be so swayed by pretension, yet so unmoved by honest endeavour. In *Huckleberry Finn*, the same conclusion is presented, softened, as the Socratic internal debate of a confused, precocious child:

> I says to myself, if a body can get anything they pray for, why don't Deacon Wynn get back the money he lost on pork? Why can't the widow get back her silver snuff box that was stole? Why can't Miss Watson fat up? No, I says to myself, there ain't nothing in it. . . . Sometimes the widow would take me one side and talk about Providence in a way to make a body's mouth water; but maybe next day Miss Watson would take hold and knock it all down again. I judged I could see that there was two Providences, and a poor chap would stand considerable show with the widow's Providence, but if Miss Watson's got him there warn't no help for him anymore. I thought it all out, and reckoned I would belong to the widow's, if he wanted me, though I couldn't make out how he was agoing to be any better off then what he was before, seeing I was so ignorant and so kind of low-down and ornery.

Huck's final self-denigration is more than the comedian's ancient tactic of attacking himself to ward off criticism; it is a demonstration that Clemens recognized the crippling effects of conventional Christianity's unbalanced preoccupation with outward appearance and pretence. In *Huckleberry Finn*, Mark Twain is patient and creative enough to propose that there must be two Providences—one for show, and one for true conviction—without explicitly saying that few pay attention to the latter. In his final tale, *The Mysterious Stranger*, he would betray the conclusion that the latter does not even exist. Satan tells the narrator:

'It is true, that which I have revealed to you: there is no God, no universe, no human race, no earthly life, no heaven, no hell. It is all a Dream, a grotesque and foolish dream. Nothing exists but You. And You are but a *Thought*—a vagrant Thought, a useless Thought, a homeless Thought, wandering forlorn among the empty eternities!'

He vanished, and left me appalled; for I knew, and realized, that all he had said was true.

THE END

As Vonnegut says of the closing pages of *A Connecticut Yankee*: 'What a funny ending.'

The Mysterious Stranger is an example of Clemens's inability to disguise the annihilation of his targets with the mask of Mark Twain. The adoption of the mask as a coating of sugar was a recognized necessity expressed by Aristotle, who wrote in the *Poetics* that 'the comic mask is ugly and distorted, but does not cause pain.' Perhaps his statement might be modified to say that the comic mask prevents *immediate* pain, and allows the *immediate* reception and expenditure of laughter. The adoption of the mask is the comedian's lie, defined by the word 'play'. Max Eastman gives as the first law of humour:

> Things can be funny only when we're in fun. There may be a serious thought or motive lurking underneath our humor. We may be only 'half in fun' and still funny. But when we are not in fun at all, when we are 'in dead earnest', humor is the thing that is dead.

Wondering aloud how many articulate and thoughtful people must have been despised because they failed to get it across that they were 'only kidding', Eastman cites as the crux of the masquerade the cowboy's response to an insult: 'Smile when you say that.'[9]

Gregory Bateson notes that, even in animals, such as a pair of rough-housing dogs, signals are sent between them to assure each other that the play combat really *is* play. The failure to interpret the signal 'this is play' can have dire consequences, as in a custom of the Adaman Islanders, through which peace is concluded between warring parties with each side given the symbolic freedom to strike the other. If the ceremonial blows are somehow mistaken for real, the peacemaking ceremony turns into another battle.[10] A similar failure to communicate was experienced by Clemens at a dinner in honour of Whittier; his verbal caricatures of Holmes, Emerson and Longfellow produced such a chilled reception from the Brahmins of Boston that he spent the months following in pathetic apology. Likewise, as a young newspaper editor in California, he so thinly disguised his printed attacks on a rival editor that he awoke one morning to the challenge of a duel.

Johan Huizinga once delineated a theory of play which, with its particular relevance to the understanding of comedic success, deserves to be related in full:

> All play has its rules. They determine what 'holds' in the temporary world circumscribed by play. . . . The player who trespasses against the rules or ignores them is a 'spoil sport'. The spoil-sport is not the same as the false player, the cheat; for the latter pretends to be playing the game and, on the face of it, still acknowledges the magic circle. It is curious to note how much more lenient society is to the cheat than to the spoil-sport. This is because the spoil-sport shatters the play-world itself. By withdrawing from the game he reveals the relativity and fragility of the play-world in which he had temporarily shut himself with others. He robs play of its *illusion*—a pregnant word which means literally 'in play'. . . . Therefore he must be cast out, for he threatens the existence of the play community.
>
> (Johan Huizinga, *Homo Ludens* (London: Routledge and Kegan Paul, 1949), p. 11)

In light of this, the comedian cannot be a spoil-sport; he must be a false player, and 'pretend to play the game, on the face of it'. He must convince his audience that he is not a rule-breaker, that any impression they might hold of him as a heretic or cabbalist is immediately subordinated to their impression of him as a game player. The comedian requires the consent of his victims in creating and manipulating their belief; his technique is a ritualization of human intercourse, a transfer of trust between the audience and himself, utilizing accepted conventions of thought and communication—or so it seems.[11] As Huizinga says, 'the cheat's dishonesty does not destroy the game'—thus he need not believe in the rules in order to play by them; he may think them conventional or ridiculous, or think the game is meaningless, but if he dismisses the game and refuses to play it, he is a nihilist, a spoil-sport, an outlaw.

It would be an outlaw comedian who would write sceptically to his friend,

> I suspect that to you there is still dignity in human life, and that Man is not a joke—a poor joke—the poorest that was ever contrived—an April fool joke, played by a malicious Creator with nothing better to waste his time upon.[12]

So he writes *What Is Man?*, unable, in his own words, to treat his subject 'gaily' or 'praisefully'—and publishes it anonymously, copyrighted under another name. In the preface he explains his reticence in exposing such pages of undisguised doom and contempt:

> Every thought in them has been thought (and accepted as unassailable truth) by millions of men—and concealed, kept private. Why did they not speak out? Because they dreaded (*and could not bear*) the disapproval of the people around them. Why have I not published? The same reason has restrained me, I think. I can find no other.

Yet the outlaw is in Clemens from the beginning, when he first signs the name 'Mark Twain'. An aspiring journalist in the West who has failed at every mining and prospecting enterprise that has brought the society together, he is a pen-pusher among what he describes in *Roughing It* as 'a driving, vigorous, restless population':

> It was an assemblage of two hundred thousand *young* men—not simpering, dainty, kid-glove weaklings, but stalwart, muscular, dauntless young braves, brimful of push and energy, and royally endowed with every attribute that goes to make up a peerless and magnificent manhood—the very pick and choice of the world's glorious ones.

He is living in a society where the noblest reputation meant having 'killed your man'—he, who so abhors violence and physical disturbances that he instinctively recoils from practical jokes, let alone duels and murders. Yet the jokes of Mark Twain allow him to play by the rules of his violent frontier society; as Van Wyck Brooks notes, his early humour is 'knee deep in the blood of chambermaids, barbers, lightning-rod men, watchmakers, and other perpetrators of the small harassments of life'. Through Mark Twain, Clemens could vent those aggressions which in less cultivated men resulted in the violent explosions of lawlessness in the streets and saloons. As Brooks notes:

> By means of ferocious jokes—and most of Mark Twain's early jokes are ferocious to a degree that will hardly be believed by anyone who has not examined them critically—he could vent his hatred of pioneer life and all its conditions, those conditions that were thwarting his creative life; he could, in this vicarious manner, appease the artist in him, while at the same time keeping on the safe side of public opinion, since the very act of transferring his aggressions into jokes rendered them innocuous.
> (Van Wyck Brooks, *The Ordeal of Mark Twain* (New York: Meridian, 1955), p. 200)

In his practice, Clemens was following in the footsteps of the Southwestern humorists whose traditions he inherited. They, for the most part, were like him in that they were sensitive, cultivated individuals who were loath to participate in the violence of their surroundings, were aware of the dangers, yet who were also humans with the necessity of discharging aggression. Southwestern humour was to become a definitive brand of American literary humour, with its beginnings in countless obscure journals and backwoods newspapers, and culminating in the full-scale books of Mark Twain, who introduced it to the world.

The Southwestern humorists operated creatively under two masks: the identity of the comedian—the funny man—and the pseudonym. The general identity of the comedian allowed both reader and writer to benefit from the saving grace of laughter which made bearable the overhanging terror of the frontier. Humorous creation was a means of coping and respite, dynamically balancing the 'sense of horror' with the 'sense of humour' needed to survive in an environment constantly threatening annihilation.[13] Thus Augustus Baldwin Longstreet, one of the earliest Southwestern humorists, wrote the sketches collected in 1835 as *Georgia Scenes*, in which 'men writhe in agony to the tune of raucous laughter' amid frontier violence, cruelty, and the dog-eat-dog ethics of the backwoods.[14] One of the first reviews of Longstreet's book was written by Edgar

Allan Poe. In describing the various rough-and-tumble scenes, fights, eye-gougings, and 'gander pullings'—contests of cruelty wherein ragamuffins on horseback attempt to pull the head off a live greased gander—Poe says of Longstreet,

> To be sure, our Georgian . . . is learned in all things pertaining to the biped without feathers. In regard, especially, to that class of southwestern mammalia who come under the generic appellation of 'savagerous wild cats', he is a very Theophrastus in duodecimo.

Yet in spite of the raw, frequently inhuman nature of the material, Poe could say without hesitation:

> Seldom—perhaps never in our lives—have we laughed as immoderately over any book as over the one now before us. If these *scenes* have produced such effect upon *our* cachinnatory nerves—upon *us* who are not 'of the merry mood', and, moreover, have not been used to the perusal of somewhat similar things—we are at no loss to imagine what a hubbub they would occasion in the uninitiated regions of Cocaigne.
>
> (*The Selected Writings of Edgar Allan Poe*, edited by David Galloway (Harmondsworth: Penguin, 1980), p. 306)

The second mask adopted in the creations of Southwestern humour was the pseudonym invariably taken by any given author. Being earthy realists in an age when romantic fiction ruled, hundreds of still unidentified pseudonymous authors published their stories in such papers as *The Spirit*, the St. Louis *Reveille*, and the New Orleans *Picayune* and *Delta*. As the authors were often professionals with reputations to protect—Longstreet, for instance, was a Yale graduate, lawyer, editor, minister, and college president—they did not wish to be accused of vulgar levity or association with the vernacular characters who gave them their raw material.[15] The predecessors and contemporaries of Mark Twain in the school of Southwestern humour went by such names as Johnson J. Hooper, Thomas Bangs Thorpe, Artemus Ward, John Phoenix, and Petroleum V. Nasby. Although some of their techniques of dialect and caricature were later employed by Mark Twain, they differed from him in that they designated themselves as particular characters, personalities marked by and confined to special identifying eccentricities. For instance,

Petroleum V. Nasby, Artemus Ward, and Josh Billings depended for their individuality on an orthography that gave oral and regional identity to their characters.[16] Thus, Josh Billings:

> The Duk iz a kind ov short legged hen.
> They kan sale on the water as natral and eazy as a grease spot.
> Duks hav a broad bill which enables them tew eat their food without enny spoon.
> Thare aint any room on the outside of a Duk for enny more feathers.
> The duk don't kro like a rooster, but quaks like a duk.
> (Quoted in Max Eastman, *Enjoyment of Laughter*, p. 175)

The chosen names of these humorists were indelibly linked with the comic, and predominantly verbal, identities which they had created. In choosing his pseudonym, Clemens followed the tradition without limiting himself to such narrow boundaries of identification. But the name 'Mark Twain', though more plausible than such lunacies as Petroleum V. Nasby and Orpheus C. Kerr, was nevertheless a comic pseudonym; Clemens established Mark Twain first as a humorist, and it was to this fate he committed himself throughout his creative life. This initiated severe conflicts in Clemens, evidenced in his recurrent attempts to obliterate the comic personality of Mark Twain in favour of 'nobler' contributions to art and culture. Such attempts were *The Prince and the Pauper*, a 'grave and stately work', he called it, 'considered by the world to be above my proper level'; and *What Is Man?*, which he published anonymously; and *Joan of Arc*, which he published under the conspicuous authorship of Samuel L. Clemens—not Mark Twain. Clemens was aware that the identity of Mark Twain was a commitment to humour itself. As James Cox has noted, although Clemens did not have to write humorously, Mark Twain did; he cites such awareness as the reason for Dickens's abandonment of the pseudonym in the transformation into a credible novelist: 'Boz' could not have written *David Copperfield*.[17]

Clemens, on the other hand, was to cut off the source of his creative genius when he denied Mark Twain, and in spite of his various attempts to do so, he seems to have sensed that knowledge early. In his address to the Society of California Pioneers in 1869, he said that he had worked

> at all the different trades and professions known to the catalogues. I have been everything from a newspaper editor down to a cowcatcher on a locomotive, and I am encouraged to believe that if there had been a few more occupations to experiment on, I might have made a dazzling success at last, and found out what mysterious designs Providence had in creating me.[18]

But he already knew, as he had written to his brother from California, after completing the 'Jumping Frog' story that launched his career:

> I have had a 'call' to literature of a low order—i.e. humorous. It is nothing to be proud of, but it is my strongest suit, and if I were to listen to that maxim of stern *duty* which says that to do right you *must* multiply the one or the two or the three talents which the Almighty entrusts to your keeping, I would long ago have ceased to meddle with things for which I was by nature unfitted, and turned my attention to seriously scribbling to excite the *laughter* of God's creatures. Poor, pitiful business.
> (Quoted in James Cox, *Mark Twain: The Fate of Humor*, p. 33)

To scribble 'seriously' represents the paradox of an artist who grew into world renown as a comedian at a time when Matthew Arnold was deriding America's foolish preoccupation with 'funny men' and men of low distinction, like Abraham Lincoln. The comedian as outlaw: he would sail into the East and settle amongst the finery of New York, Elmira, Hartford and Boston, where people's first reactions would be arched eyebrows and the question, 'Is there anything of Mr. Clemens except his humor?' The comedian must negotiate the good intentions of censorious women friends who say, 'I want the public, who know him now only as "the wild humorist of the Pacific Slope", to know something of his deeper, larger nature.' The comedian is about to marry a woman of whom he says, 'Poor girl, anybody who could convince her that I was not a humorist would secure her eternal gratitude! She thinks a humorist is something pretty awful.'[19] The comedian storms into the wings from the lecture platform, crying aloud, 'I am demeaning myself. I am allowing myself to be a mere buffoon. It's ghastly. I can't endure it any longer.'[20] The literary comedian breathes a sigh of relief to the editor of the journal to which he contributes: 'The *Atlantic* audience . . . is the only audience that I sit down before in perfect serenity (for the simple reason that it don't require a "humorist" to paint himself stripèd and stand on his head every fifteen minutes).'[21] He is the same literary comedian who a few years before had resigned from the contributing staff of another journal with this explanation:

> I have now written for *The Galaxy* a year. For the last eight months, with hardly an interval, I have had for my fellows and comrades, night and day, doctors and watchers of the sick! During these eight months death has taken two members of my home circle and malignantly threatened two others. All this I have experienced, yet all the time been under contract to furnish 'humorous' matter once a month for this magazine. I am speaking the exact truth in the above details. Please to put yourself in my place and contemplate the grisly grotesqueness of the situation. I think that some of the 'humor' I have written during this period could have been injected into a funeral sermon without disturbing the solemnity of the occasion.
>
> (*Mark Twain's Contributions to 'The Galaxy': 1868–1871*, edited by Bruce McElderry (Gainesville: Scholars' Reprints, 1961), p. 131)

During the *Galaxy* years, the creative pressure generated by the war of the 'serious' and the 'scribbler' burst forth upon the page in the form of Mark Twain's 'Burlesque Biography'. In it, Clemens assigned the comedian to a long line of thieves, outlaws, hatchet-men, and persons of dubious progeny:

> Why it is that our long line has ever since borne the maternal name (except when one of them now and then took a playful refuge in an alias to avert foolishness) . . . is a mystery which none of us have ever felt much desire to stir.

Twains rot in Newgate; Twains work the chain-gang; the severed heads of Twains 'contemplate the people' from Temple Bar; Twains swing from the gallows; Twains walk the plank; they steal the luggage (and the very anchor) from the *Santa Maria*; and one Twain drinks himself legless, wastes seventeen rounds of ammunition taking pot-shots at George Washington from behind a tree. There are 'Richard Brinsley Twain, alias Guy Fawkes; John Wentworth Twain, alias Sixteen-String Jack; William Hogarth Twain, alias Jack Sheppard; Ananias Twain, alias Baron Munchausen; John George Twain, alias Captain Kydd'. Among the black sheep of his ancestry, a collateral line so called because 'they have got into a low way of going to jail instead of getting hanged', there are 'George Francis Train, Tom Pepper, Nebuchadnezzar, and Baalam's Ass'. Also, there is Augustus Twain—the 'born humorist'.

The same year the story was written, 1871, Clemens despaired to his brother over 'seeing my hated nom de plume (for I do loathe the very sight of it) in print *again* every month'.[22] In a matter of months he would begin *Roughing It*, in which he brought the tall tale to the American novel. The book is an exploitation by Mark Twain of Clemens's wholly futile search for gold in the West; through the use of the tall tale, Clemens converted accounts of his failures, humiliations, frustrations and rage into an exaggerated story form that could move the reader to laughter while discharging the aggression of the author.[23] In it, he binds and gags chatterbox women, deflates the braggadocio of petty stage-coach drivers and gun-slingers, dynamites the ground beneath swaggering miners, and, most importantly, turns his sword upon himself. By so enlarging his bewilderments and failures—in spite of the vitriol he sheds on his targets—there is no one who so invites the reader's sympathy as Mark Twain. As he had shown in his previous book, *The Innocents Abroad*, he could place himself in a position to effectively sabotage the stature of European Classical culture, while still remaining the 'utterly winsome sort of teddy bear'—a wide-eyed innocent in a foreign land—that Vonnegut calls him. In *Roughing It*, first-person discomfiture and innocence combine with the exaggeration of failures to render harmless the brutal evidence of Clemens's internal, and the territory's external, violence.

A man can't write successful satire except he be in a calm judicial good-humor . . . in truth I don't ever seem to be in a good enough humor with ANYthing to *satirize* it; no, I want to

> stand up before it and *curse* it, and foam at the mouth,—or take a club and pound it to rags and pulp.[24]

This admission made in 1879 must have been implicit in Clemens's search for a narrative shield after having completed *The Gilded Age*. Written in 1873, when he was first dipping his feet into the mire of business deals that would eventually bankrupt him, it reveals fully the disgust with which he watched and participated in the corruptions of the age he had so named. His growing bitterness in the 1870s, reserved for the wild speculative frenzy he saw in himself and the nation, inspired him to vent his rage on the stock market, the railroad, the Congress—even the lecture hall—and delineated the basic subject of the book, which is, in Justin Kaplan's words, 'democracy gone off the tracks'.[25] Clemens's disgust, apparent wherever his pen touched paper, proved to him that he could only treat 'the wash of today' with a satiric bitterness too caustic for his comic art and his rôle as an entertainer; he needed a medium flexible enough to accommodate his anger while still maintaining his commitment as a humorist. With *The Gilded Age*, he concluded that, in order to successfully transmit his own anger into effective comedy, he might rely on fantasy and the past.

He applied this conclusion to the writing of *Tom Sawyer*, wherein he temporarily displaced the negative barriers of his personality by inventing a juvenile character who could free him from his own participation in history as it was represented in the story. Tom Sawyer's position as a child introduced a new element of distance while almost demanding the reader's indulgence; thus because Tom Sawyer and his gang live in a world of play, they can re-enact the adult rituals of love, war, justice and death with impunity. Mark Twain, too, operates with impunity, for as Huizinga says, he 'pretends to be playing the game and, on the face of it, still acknowledges the magic circle'. Tom Sawyer's idyll is in fact surrounded by dread, yet the narrator's tolerance in maintaining the 'magic circle' of the play world charms an element of safety into the real terror and violence that exist. By instituting play—fantasy—as the reality principle in his writing, Clemens demonstrated his ability to operate within the mode of conventional fiction while maintaining a shield for his rage. He came to rely on fantasy for the full expression of his comedy; he had, after all, found his being in the tall tale.[26] His further reliance on fantasy caused him to present *Huckleberry Finn* as 'The Adventures of', and determined its format as a semi-literate boy's autobiography.

'I perhaps made a mistake in not writing it in the first person', wrote Clemens of *Tom Sawyer*, immediately after its completion. He perhaps realized that the first person allowed him to present the narrator with all sorts of immediate internal crises, thereby inviting sympathy instead of criticism, while still presenting a social comment easily as scathing as *The Gilded Age*. Thus in *Huckleberry Finn*, the humour of the book rides on the reversal of Huck's moral sentiment; his character is exemplified by his conviction that what are, to the reader, his best actions, are actually his worst. The more he chastises himself for doing the 'bad' things that will land him in hell, the more the reader is convinced that they are the same 'good' things that will send him in the opposite direction. This is one of the most important aspects of the mask which is Huck Finn's narration—the ever-present sense of denunciation with which he confronts himself. Just as Mark Twain was to refer to his creative process as that of a 'jackleg novelist' while obviously implying the opposite, Huck continually berates himself to the opposite effect, such as when he tries to prevent some thieves drowning aboard a wrecked steamboat: 'I begun to think how dreadful it was even for murderers to be in such a fix. I says to myself, there ain't no telling but I might come to be a murderer myself, yet, and then how would *I* like it?' He avers this with a straight face; and by projecting into the boy's future sense the improbable qualities of a murderer, Mark Twain reinforces the contrast between the moral worth of Huck and that of the killers over whose predicament he suffers.

Yet Huck is embarking downriver into an American inferno, and as the voyage progresses, one senses Mark Twain's precarious position in maintaining the blameless voice of the humorist without either slipping into overwhelmingly bleak satire, or negating the impact of his commentary through clownishness. As it turned out, he suffered artistic crises in both respects: in the first, he was unable to maintain Huck's generally delightful, innocent precocity in the face of the bloody feuds, and sadism of the shore folk, the anguish of Jim, and the con games of the Duke and King; in the second, the burlesque of the closing chapters threaten to make a mockery of Mark Twain's socially critical intent. As Huck travels downriver, he presents the incongruities of barbarism and gentility with a marked decrease of innocence and forgiveness—the shields of Samuel Clemens. At the first traumatic blow to his innocence, the death of Buck Grangerford, and afterwards in the Duke and King episodes, Huck's humour develops from mere precocious observation to blatant disillusionment, horror and disgust.

Upon witnessing the apocalyptic murder of Buck Grangerford, Huck utters his first unmitigated betrayal of revulsion: 'It made me so sick I most fell out of the tree.' From this point on, until the inexplicable appearance of Tom Sawyer, his humour is never as juvenile as previously; he is openly bitter when the situation demands it, as on the finaglings of the Duke and King: 'It was enough to make a body ashamed of the human race' and 'I never see anything so disgusting.' Considering his character, it is fitting that his detached innocence should be warped by the horror of the feud and the successive barbarities met with downriver. Were he to maintain an outlook emotionally unscarred in the midst of such bloody deformities, he could no longer be offered as a humane model alternative to those characters he deplores. As Huck views the increasing corruption and grows more and more critical, it becomes apparent that Mark Twain cannot deal with his subjects without revealing more of his despair than planned when *Huckleberry Finn* was begun as merely 'another boy's book'.

The book's diminishing of innocence, and the increasing blackness of humour, can be seen in the light of two successive paragraphs, wherein Buck, in *his* innocence, explains the mechanics of the feud:

> 'Well', says Buck, 'a feud is this way. A man has a quarrel with another man, and kills him; then that other man's brother kills *him*; then the other brothers, on both sides, goes for one another; then the *cousins* chip in—and by and by everybody's killed off, and there ain't no more feud.

As Huck has been up to now, Buck is unaware of the implications as he proudly describes the process of his family's extinction as though it were an arithmetic problem he has just mastered. The humour, albeit grim, depends on his naïvety; and in spite of its dark undercurrent, the dialogue is amusing because it describes the futility of the feuding process in such abstract and general terms. But when the topic is brought from the general to the particular—when Buck describes his own family's involvement—the dialogue is sickening, in spite of the fact that Buck maintains the same detached, juvenile tone:

> 'My cousin Bud, fourteen year old . . . sees old Baldy Shepherson a-linkin' after him with his gun in his hand . . . so they had it, nip and tuck, for five mile or more, the old man a-gaining all the time; so at last Bud seen it warn't any use, so he stopped and faced around so as to have the bullet-holes in front, you know, and the old man he rode up and shot him down.'

Thus in the space of a few paragraphs, with no change in the vocabulary or tone of the speaker, the quality of humour changes from bleakly absurd banter to even blacker, grimmer irony. Darkened by the shortened distance between the narrator and the subject matter, the humour exemplifies the same manner in which Huck's humour darkens as his raft floats down towards the Delta. The entire downriver experience produces a bitterness that does not dissolve until the disruptive sequence of events at the Phelps plantation. The extent to which Huck critically speaks his mind and pronounces judgement on the feud, the Duke and King, and humanity in general, shows how Mark Twain could not allow him to remain as delightfully unaware as he had been before stepping ashore. With this came an accompanying decrease in comic intensity. The final *increase* in comic intensity created in the final chapters amounts to the regression of Huck Finn to a pre-feud innocence, during which he is willing to become a shadow behind the romantic fantasies of Tom Sawyer.

Broad as the comedy is during the last ten chapters, the final sequence is in a sense the saddest part of the book. Not only does it leave the conflict between Huck's 'sound heart

95

and deformed conscience' unresolved, but it also demonstrates that Mark Twain could no longer maintain the illusion of freedom, happiness and uncorrupted nature as they are represented aboard the raft. As Bernard De Voto wrote of the 'inharmonious burlesque' of the final chapters, 'In the whole history of the English novel there is no more abrupt or more chilling descent.'[27] If the book's vernacular values were indeed abandoned by the author or undermined by his bitterness, it is worth noting, as James Cox has done, that by the time Clemens was engaged in the book's completion, he was also knee-deep in speculative ventures in 'everything from vine-yards to history games', as well as investing heavily in 'a steam generator, a steam pulley, a new method of marine telegraphy, a watch company, an insurance house, and in a new process of engraving—the kaolotype'. He was also on the verge of launching the ill-fated Webster Publishing Company, whose first publication would be *The Adventures of Huckleberry Finn*. Clemens's efforts in these ventures either never bore fruit at the outset, or were to be abandoned as financial failures. If his disillusionments with America in the Gilded Age, exacerbated by his own recurrent failures in business, caused him to lose confidence in those values of Huck Finn that were evidently beyond grasp, one can appreciate the darkening of his comedy and the frequent violent outbursts therein—not only in *Huckleberry Finn*, but in the remainder of his comic fiction.

One year after the first appearance of *Huckleberry Finn*, Clemens entered into what would be his most crippling attempt in business, organizing a company to manufacture and market the Paige Typesetter, a complicated and tempera-mental machine that was to operate only once, with only Clemens and the inventor present. That same year he began work on *A Connecticut Yankee in King Arthur's Court*; it was completed in 1889, five months after the sole operation of the typesetter. As Justin Kaplan notes, the Yankee and the Machine were inseparably twinned in the mind of Mark Twain:

> Both were tests of a perfectible world in which, contrary to all his insights and experience, friction and mechanical difficulties were equivalents of ignorance and superstition. Both expressed

a secular religion which had as an unexamined article of faith a belief not in eternal life but in perpetual motion.
(Justin Kaplan, *Mr. Clemens and Mark Twain*, pp. 280–81)

Comparisons have persistently been made between the failure of the typesetter and that of Hank Morgan's techno-logical utopia, concluding that Clemens's repeated frustra-tions in business were the sole inspiration for the reversal and holocaust in the plot that began as an innocuous burlesque entry in Mark Twain's notebook of December 1884:

> Dream of being a knight errant in armor in the middle ages. Have the notions & habits of thought of present day mixed with the necessities of that. No pockets in armor. No way to manage certain requirements of nature. Can't scratch. Cold in the head—can't blow—can't get at handkerchief, can't use iron sleeve. Iron gets red hot in the sun—leaks in the rain, gets white with frost & freezes me solid in winter. Suffer from lice and fleas. Make disagreeable clatter when I enter church. Can't dress or undress myself. Always getting struck by lightning. Fall down, can't get up.
>
> (*Mark Twain's Notebooks and Journals*, edited by R. Browning and others (Berkeley: University of California Press, 1979), III, 78)

Yet it is evident that Mark Twain was leaning towards tragedy even before getting embroiled in the problems of the Paige typesetter. A December 1885 entry in his notebook reveals this prediction for Hank Morgan:

> He mourns his lost land—has come to England & revisited it, but it is all changed & become old, so old!—& it was so fresh & new, so virgin before. . . . Has lost all interest in life—is found dead next morning—suicide.
>
> (*Mark Twain's Notebooks and Journals*, III, 216)

The timing of these entries casts doubt on the total influence of the typesetter's failure on the outcome of the book, as well as De Voto's contention that the final tragedy was a direct result of Clemens's despair over the consequent bankruptcy of 1894 and the death of his daughter Susy in 1896; for the book was completed five and seven years prior to both events respec-tively.[28] It was not that Clemens's financial and familial tragedies so overwhelmed him that he let his despair seep into the writing of the book; they must certainly have played a part, but it was deeper than this, for his despair was evident while his family was intact, and remained even after he had finally cleared his debts and regained a vast fortune. Concomitant with his personal tragedies were those of the failures, moral and concrete, of civilization in the nineteenth century. In his own country, the industrial revolution had snowballed out of hand with the accompanying corruption and moral decay that Clemens had despaired over decades before. If the typesetter represented the personal failures of Samuel Clemens, it also came to represent the failure of the technological revolution; just as *The Gilded Age* had depicted 'democracy gone off the tracks', *A Connecticut Yankee* was to depict 'technology gone off the tracks'. While as a businessman Clemens lauded Paige as one of the most original thinkers and inventors in history, as Mark Twain he was discounting all claims to human originality and the progress it might produce through technology. He says through the markedly harsh and cynical voice of Hank Morgan:

> All that is original in us, and therefore fairly creditable or discreditable to us, can be covered up and hidden by the point of a cambric needle, all the rest being atoms contributed by, and inherited from, a procession of ancestors that stretches back a billion years to the Adam-clam or grasshopper or monkey from whom our race has been so tediously and ostentatiously and unprofitably developed.

With words such as these, it is obvious that Hank Morgan suffers from a severe lack of that compassion which had given Huck Finn, for all his faults, the reader's unqualified support. This is one key to the bitterness of *A Connecticut Yankee*, and it suggests that Mark Twain, in his anxiety to write a satire vitriolic enough to contain his disgust, attempted its execution without adhering to the pleasure principle that shrouds the humorist's intent in the guise of entertainment. In its conception, the book certainly had its roots in this principle; the comic prospects of the sort mentioned in the first notebook entry are indeed ripe enough, but those burlesque elements that survive in the final product are paled to the point of becoming unwelcome intrusions when seen against the fury of

Mark Twain's satire. At sometime during the early creative process, Mark Twain decided to attack a serious subject, as he had done with *Huckleberry Finn*; the difference is that he had done so at the expense of his initial comedic intent. The result is similar to that of *The Prince and the Pauper*, in which, as James Cox notes, a book seems dedicated to the principles of comedy without adhering to them. It is granted that there are more comic elements in *A Connecticut Yankee* than in *The Prince and the Pauper*, but they depend almost without exception on the burlesque incongruity of a Yankee's presence at Camelot, a degree of comedy hardly sophisticated enough to carry and disguise the serious intent. Thus while in *Huckleberry Finn* Mark Twain fused comedy into the fabric of the moral as a powerful weapon and shield, in *A Connecticut Yankee* the comedy seems to be almost incidental and secondary to the satiric intent, and only serves to detract from it.

Hank Morgan himself declares that he is 'nearly barren of sentiment' or 'poetry'. With such an underdeveloped character as his disposal, there was no way for Mark Twain to impersonate the innocence, piety, or gravity so essential to the humour of, and sympathy for, Huck Finn. Hank Morgan is in fact a hollow shell—Clemens himself was to call him an 'ass'—resorting to mere slang and volume for verbal effect. His words depict him as with a minimum of intellect or compassion, but with an excess of ill-thought emotional bluster, spouting off his ideas with a notable lack of sensible expression. In its totality, the character of Hank Morgan could not rise above the burlesque with merely noise and slang as its defining aspects. Such narrowness could not tolerate enough analytic intelligence or humour to discharge the indignation of Mark Twain, and consequently Morgan's great democratic idealism was deflated to paltry patriotic bombast and prejudice; he became an absurd caricature of the industrial society he represented. It is not that Mark Twain's rage and despair prevented him from turning *A Connecticut Yankee* into effective comedy, for there was enough of that motivating the comic genius of *Huckleberry Finn*. The problem with *A Connecticut Yankee* was that, while in the previous book Huck's vernacular was a vehicle which by use of ironic observation and mock innocence could convert Mark Twain's indignation into humour, the underdevelopment of Hank Morgan's 'sentiment' prevented the inverted point of view upon which Huck's humour had depended. Rather than disguising it, the character of Hank Morgan clearly betrayed the indignation of his creator.[29]

Yet in his next wholly original novel, *Pudd'nhead Wilson,*[30] Mark Twain produced a work with exceedingly dire implications, but which nevertheless succeeded in its overall comedic delivery. From the depths of severe depression, Mark Twain explored in it all forms of human slavery—political, intellectual, moral, scientific, genetic, environmental, economic, and racial. He embarked in an agonizing debate over man's identity in a world regulated by both fate and coincidence— an unresolved debate, and to a great extent a manifestation of Clemens's own preoccupation with the dual identity he shared with Mark Twain. The final implications of *Pudd'nhead Wilson* are easily as bleak as those of *A Connecticut Yankee,* for while the fate of Hank Morgan's England implied an alternative, given that man might still draw in the reins of a runaway technology, the fate of Tom Driscoll and Dawson's Landing is shown as hopelessly inevitable, with no consoling justification other than that our condition is thus because it *is* thus. Yet of the two, *Pudd'nhead Wilson* is the greater comic success because in it, rather than relying on the shallow bluster of Hank Morgan, Mark Twain found an effective voice of ironic distance, that of an observer embodied in both the narrator and the final arbiter of the antagonist's fate, Pudd'nhead Wilson.

The narrative voice in the book is that of a chronicler as aloof as Pudd'nhead himself. The narrator succeds in elaborating the ironic universe represented by Dawson's Landing, not by questioning whether this universe is fact or fiction, or whether it should so exist, but by presenting his tale as a history without editorial, showing that the world itself creates its own paradoxes and burlesques. While Hank Morgan had the ambition, but not the capacity, to articulate a judgement upon the condition of his adopted world, the narrator in *Pudd'nhead Wilson* sees fit only to ironically expose those problems which Hank Morgan felt he could better. The actions in *Pudd'nhead Wilson* represent existence in a world in which the fatalities of life and coincidence combine to totally

overshadow any human claims to character or social meaning—
and the narrator, in presenting them, is very well in a position
to exclaim, 'Don't blame me.'[31] The narrator is closer to that
of *Huckleberry Finn*, who, as a child, was able to maintain a
certain degree of distance that allowed a perspective which
Hank Morgan, due to his deliberate participation in the events
he described, was denied. In choosing the perspective of an
historian, the narrator of *Pudd'nhead Wilson* is in a position to
see the events of his history as fatal, with ironic relationships
between man, society and history taking precedence over
individual desires and ambitions—something Hank Morgan
could not see. The historian can see that man is at once the
agent and victim of his own destiny—again, something that
Hank Morgan could not realize about himself, let alone those
whose existence he shared.[32]

With the aloofness of a chronicler, the narrator is able to
attack with quiet irony a preoccupation of Clemens's that can
be found in many violent outbursts in his private letters and
conversation, his literary twinship with Mark Twain. *Pudd'nhead
Wilson* began as a burlesque short story called 'Those Extraordinary Twins', as Mark Twain explained in the author's
note, which so developed through the introduction of new
characters that it became two incompatible tales, finally
separated by a 'literary Caesarean operation'. His obsession
with twinship was a permanent influence on his writings; his
most recurrent strategies were to play upon twins and pairs:
Chang and Eng, Tom and Huck, Huck and Jim, Huck and
Buck, the Prince and the Pauper, the Duke and the King,
Angelo and Luigi Capello, Thomas à Beckett Driscoll and
Valet de Chambre. The thematic emphasis placed on dual
personality and mistaken identity go back to the creative act
that invented Mark Twain, out of which came that steadily
deepening sense of internal conflict which Justin Kaplan sees
as suggested by two sets of near homonyms: Twain/twins and
Clemens/claimants.[33]

The debilitating extent to which Clemens regarded his
twinship with Mark Twain is revealed by his repeated treatment of twins as freaks, either when joined as Chang and Eng
in 'The Personal Habits of the Siamese Twins', or as the joined
and separated Luigi and Angelo in 'Those Extraordinary

Twins' and *Pudd'nhead Wilson*. At the time of his death, the last coherent words Clemens spoke before drifting into a coma were ravings about 'the laws of mentality', dual personality, and the most monstrous embodiment of literary twinship, Jekyll and Hyde. A month before his death, while noting that his birth coincided with the 1835 appearance of Halley's Comet, Clemens imagined God saying about the comet and Mark Twain, 'Here are those unacountable freaks. They came in together, they must go out together.' On the day of his death, Halley's Comet had just made its appearance of 1910.[34]

Mark Twain's treatment of twins as freaks is seen by Leslie Fiedler as the revelation of Clemens's belief that 'monsters' such as Chang and Eng—or, one might imply, the Capello brothers and their creator—are in the final analysis tragic, because their dignity and suffering incite laughter rather than tears and compassion.[35] Mark Twain himself expressed in a deleted passage from *A Tramp Abroad* that, as a performing comedian, he felt 'serious almost to sadness', with 'no impulse toward the opposite direction'.[36] In *Pudd'nhead Wilson*, he causes Angelo Capello, no longer physically joined to his brother but still psychologically as bound, to express the tragedy of a human's exploiting his freakishness out of monetary necessity with the intent of making people laugh—'slavery', he calls it, something especially pertinent in the light of *Pudd'nhead Wilson*'s having been written with the immediate intention of staving off its author's creditors. The twins' first appearance, at the home of the Widow Cooper and her daughter Rowena, culminates with all the neighbours rushing in to see the new, fine foreign birds:

> The twins drifted about from group to group, talking easily and fluently and winning approval, compelling admiration and achieving favour from all. The widow followed the conquering march with a proud eye, and every now and then Rowena said to herself with deep satisfaction, 'And to think they are ours—all ours'.

Clemens's complaints about the unmerciful grasp of public admiration are well known, though here the narrator is ironic enough to prevent the same resentment he often felt for his audiences—notably his lecture audiences—from appearing in its immediacy on the page. His fear of demeaning himself before unsympathetic audiences, which caused him some recurrent nightmares, inspired Oliver Wendell Holmes to write to him in sympathy, 'These negative faces with their vacuous eyes and stony lineaments pump and suck the warm soul. They are what kill the lecturer.'[37] In *Pudd'nhead Wilson*, the irony of the narrator presents Clemens's disgust at the possessiveness of mindless audiences in the form of sarcastic condescension, seemingly sympathizing with the widow and Rowena as they bask in the cheap thrills of hosting the celebrities:

> Eager inquiries concerning the twins were pouring into their enchanted ears all the time; each was the constant centre of a group of breathless listeners; each recognised that she knew now for the first time the real meaning of that great word Glory, and perceived the stupendous value of it, and understood why men in all ages had been willing to throw away meaner happinesses, treasure, life itself, to get a taste of its sublime and supreme joy. Napoleon and all his kind stood accounted for— and justified.

Clemens was to write through the persona of Pudd'nhead Wilson, 'The secret source of humor itself is not joy but sorrow. There is no humor in heaven.' As he wrote *Pudd'nhead Wilson* with the conscious intent of escaping bankruptcy, he faced the realization that he must exploit his sorrow in the name of an alter ego whose identity forever threatened to displace his own. Were the question of his *own* identity the sole inspiration of the book, he certainly would not have been able to extend the dilemma into social, political, economic and universally moral spheres. But this he did do, after recognizing his own internal struggle embodied in the impostures of civilization in the nineteenth century, and especially America in the Gilded Age, where imposture so seemed to *be* identity. Thus in *Pudd'nhead Wilson*, all comic and moral tension stems from the question of identity; the blurring of identity caused by Roxy's miscegenation creates an area of social and moral paradox, and the possibilities of imposture, that is Mark Twain's predominant theme.[38]

His prevailing obsessions with doubles, duplicity, changelings and dressing up play on the ambiguities of identity represented by the prevailing questions over environment and heredity. As Malcolm Bradbury writes, the world of the book is one of a paradox in which 'no one can be sure, literally or figuratively, of his own whiteness or blackness.' The absence of personal identity that could thus exist amid the confusions of the American social order, in which a man could be made or unmade by a single phrase, is first depicted in the naming of David Wilson as 'Pudd'nhead'. Wilson, a clever lawyer and 'brilliant sophist', is branded a fool for life by his neighbours because they cannot see the irony of his innocent joke about a noisy dog: 'I wish I owned half of that dog ... Because I would kill my half.' This comic view of identity embodied in the concept of two halves of a dog represents one of Mark Twain's main obsessions in the story, dualism and a confusion of identity.[39] As regards Clemens's own obsession, it is notable that Wilson is branded a 'pudd'nhead' and made an outcast *because of a joke*. When it is made, the people fall away from Wilson 'as from something uncanny'; and at the close of the book, the only way for him to gain respect from the community is to effectively 'take back his joke', that is, prove himself a master of that most humourless of professions, the law.[40]

Pudd'nhead Wilson was the last major work of fiction in which Mark Twain was able to successfully convert his rage and cynicism into comedy. His next and final novel failed in presenting this conversion; it was 'The Chronicle of Young Satan', published posthumously in an 'editorial fraud' by Clemens's literary executor, Albert Bigelow Paine, in the bowdlerized work called *The Mysterious Stranger*.[40] In order to understand Mark Twain's failure in 'playing the game' in *The Mysterious Stranger*, keeping up his art of impersonation as a comedian, one need only compare the sentiments of that work with those of *What Is Man?*, in part written concurrently. The latter gives an indication of what inspired *The Mysterious Stranger*, and contains many striking similarities which the narrator of the fiction could not disguise. While there are some sporadic attempts at burlesque in *The Mysterious Stranger*, there are few who would consider it an overall comic success; it is important as a measure of Mark Twain's failed intentions in presenting the philosophy of *What Is Man?* under the guise of fiction and humour.

Within the text is a clue to Mark Twain's final, bitter justification for the employment of laughter; no longer was it even connected with entertainment or as a means of coping with the sufferings of life. As Satan explains, laughter for Mark Twain had become purely a weapon for assault, almost a verbal version of the destructive power of Hank Morgan's arsenal.[42] Satan chides a member of the human race which he has come to despise as cowardly:

> Your race, in its poverty, has unquestionably one really effective weapon—laughter. Power, Money, Persuasion, Supplication, Persecution—these can lift at a colossal humbug,—push it a little, century by century: but only Laughter can blow it to rags and atoms at a blast. Against the assault of Laughter nothing can stand.

Had Samuel Clemens stood on the podium alongside Ulysses S. Grant and admitted this as his reason for subjecting the general to his comedic onslaught, he could have ended his career as a humorist then and there. He ended it instead with *The Mysterious Stranger*, for evident in Satan's monologues is the same open denunciation of 'the damned human race' vented in *What Is Man?*. After all, the 'colossal humbug' that Satan levels with laughter is not any given fault within the human race, but it is the human race itself. With such an admission of his intentions for the employment of laughter, Mark Twain was like the magician revealing the secret behind his tricks. An audience is always aware of being fooled by a magician, but is never content to be told just how—as Shaw said of Mark Twain, 'He has to put things in such a way as to make people who would otherwise hang him believe he is joking.'[42] The comedian's task lies in deception, and Mark Twain had surrendered his task at the writing of his last ostensible comedy.

Mark Twain: A Sumptuous Variety

NOTES

1. Justin Kaplan, *Mr. Clemens and Mark Twain* (London: Jonathan Cape, 1967), p. 227.
2. David Daiches, 'Mark Twain as Hamlet', *Encounter* 22, February 1964, pp. 70–6, (73).
3. Tony Tanner, 'Reviews and Comment', *Critical Quarterly* 4, Winter 1962, pp. 380–83, (381).
4. 'Innocence and Experience', *T.L.S.*, 12 August 1960, p. 512.
5. Kurt Vonnegut, 'Opening Remarks', in *The Unabridged Mark Twain*, ed. Lawrence Teacher (Philadelphia: Running Press, 1976), Volume I, p. xv.
6. James Cox, *Mark Twain: The Fate of Humor* (Princeton: Princeton University Press, 1966), pp. 49–50, 512.
7. Dixon Wecter (ed.), *Mark Twain to Mrs. Fairbanks* (San Marino: Huntington Library, 1949), p. 53.
8. Kaplan, p. 89.
9. Max Eastman, *Enjoyment of Laughter* (New York: Simon and Schuster, 1936; reprinted London: Johnson Reprint Co., 1970), pp. 3, 15–19.
10. Edith Kern, *The Absolute Comic* (New York: Columbia University Press, 1980), pp. 39–51.
11. Warwick Wadlington, *The Confidence Game in American Literature* (Princeton: Princeton University Press, 1975), pp. 21–2.
12. Henry Nash Smith and William Gibson (eds.), *Mark Twain-Howells Letters* (Cambridge: Harvard University Press, 1960), Volume II, p. 689.
13. Richard B. Hauck, *A Cheerful Nihilism* (Bloomington: Indiana University Press, 1971), p. 43.
14. Kenneth S. Lynn, *The Comic Tradition in America* (London: Victor Gollancz, 1958), pp. 62–4.
15. Hauck, p. 41.
16. Cox, pp. 18–19, 167–68.
17. Ibid., pp. 18–21.
18. Charles Neider (ed.), *Mark Twain: Life As I Find It* (Garden City: Hanover House, 1961), p. 44.
19. *Mark Twain to Mrs. Fairbanks*, pp. 63, 67n.
20. Albert Bigelow Paine, *Mark Twain: A Biography* (London: Harpers, 1912), Volume II, p. 786.
21. *Mark Twain-Howells Letters*, Volume I, p. 49.
22. Kaplan, *Mr. Clemens and Mark Twain*, p. 133.
23. Cox, p. 13.
24. *Mark Twain-Howells Letters*, Volume I, pp. 248–49.
25. Kaplan, p. 162.
26. Cox, pp. 128–35, 147–48.
27. Ibid., p. 172.
28. Ibid., p. 224.
29. Ibid., pp. 205–21.
30. *The American Claimant*, written previously, had revived characters from *The Gilded Age*.

31. Malcolm Bradbury, 'Introduction', in Mark Twain, *Pudd'nhead Wilson*, ed. Bradbury (Harmondsworth: Penguin, 1981), 27, 39.
32. Cox, p. 240.
33. Kaplan, p. 101; Cox, p. 21n.
34. Kaplan, pp. 386–88.
35. Leslie Fiedler, *Freaks* (Harmondsworth: Penguin, 1981), p. 213.
36. *Mark Twain-Howells Letters*, Volume I, p. 231n.
37. Kaplan, p. 88.
38. Bradbury, p. 35.
39. Ibid., pp. 18–23.
40. George E. Toles, 'Mark Twain and *Pudd'nhead Wilson*: A House Divided', *Novel* 16, Fall 1982, pp. 55–75, (74).
41. William M. Gibson, 'Introduction', in Mark Twain, *The Mysterious Stranger Manuscripts*, ed. Gibson (Berkeley: University of California Press, 1969), p. 2.
42. Cox, p. 286.
43. Kaplan, p. 382.

4

Mark Twain as Playwright

by ROBERT GOLDMAN

In an overall view of the attempts of Twain at play-writing, we are struck at once with the imposing fact that a part of more than thirty years of his literary life was spent actively writing for the stage. In interesting contrast to the lasting values of Twain's other literary achievements, not one of his plays was artistically sound, only one was financially successful, and for only three could he find a producer. Two of the full-length plays, we further note, were written in collaboration with authors as famous and successful as he, though these joint ventures were failures by almost any standard of theatrical success. But before examining these and attempting to determine why Twain could not make a happy transition from novelist-essayist-humorist to play-wright it would be beneficial to summarize the theatrical climate of Twain's times.

Just as Orion and Samuel Clemens joined the great move-ment westward over the Alleghenies, down and across the Mississippi River and across the Great Plains to the Pacific Ocean, so the theatrical scene expanded by the time gold was being mined in California. But it seems safe to believe that mark Twain's first tempting taste of the professional theatre came from times when the river-boat troupes performed at Hannibal, Missouri. Floating theatres appeared on the Mississippi as early as 1843, when Twain was 8 years old; and before the outbreak of the Civil War showboats were steaming up and down the river, bringing to small towns and small boys a repertoire of plays that ran from *Hamlet* to *The Drunkard* as well as minstrel shows.[1]

Twain's first recorded involvement with the stage came when he served on the San Francisco *Morning Call* in 1865, as reporter, drama critic and feature writer. According to Twain, he attended the local theatres every night of the week—an activity he would continue, in varying degrees, when he later settled in the East. But he was not content to remain with the dull routine of the *Call*. In quick succession he submitted 'The Celebrated Jumping Frog of Calaveras County' to the *Saturday Press*, exploited the fame brought to him by the reprintings which established him as a nationwide humorist, and made trips by steamship, first to the Sandwich Islands and then, in late 1866, to New York City. He found there a publisher for a book of short sketches; and, although he travelled extensively for the remainder of his life, he found a home in the East, and was never to return for long to the West. The theatre, then, for which he attempted to write was essentially the eastern theatre of the last half of the nineteenth century and especially the new York theatre, which from 1850 to 1900 saw the most intense activity in American theatrical history. Though the drama of this period was largely stilted and unoriginal, it gave rise to a fresh and vital approach to the American stage.

During the first quarter of the century, few cities had more than one theatre; most cities had none. Even the major centres such as New York, Boston and Charleston could not afford to keep more than one theatre open, and not more than four nights a week at that. Plays were performed by stock companies composed, for the most part, of second-rate English actors. The companies tried to attract audiences by changing the bill every night, and they attempted to boost actors within their own ranks to star status. But the companies struggled weakly, and their repertoire was essentially sterile.

In the period from 1825 to the Civil War, a developing literary nationalism, a new, more rounded sense of native American character had become manifest in the prose of Cooper, Parkman, Thoreau, Hawthorne and Melville, and in the poetry of Whitman, Longfellow, Whittier, Lowell and Holmes. Towards the end of this period, Twain's own native humour would begin to become nationally visible and attract wider audiences through less occasional pieces than those he produced for periodicals. This literary ferment naturally served to quicken interest in portraying the American character in original plays as well, especially since new theatres were being built as the population of major cities increased, and American actors were starting to challenge the predominance of their foreign counterparts on American stages.[2] By mid-century, then, the theatrical centre of America had shifted significantly toward the centres of literary activity in New York and New England.

The early years of the century had seen Philadelphia dominating theatrical life with a series of English stars who were supported by much of the cast of the 'Old Drury', a London repertory company. Such well-known stars as William Wood and William Twaitts appeared in Philadelphia at the Chestnut Street Theatre frequently enough to establish a fine company and present outstanding productions. During the second quarter of the nineteenth century, the Arch Street and Walnut Street theatres offered serious competition, and the growing pains resulted in arson and riots as the intensity of the rivalries deepened.[3] New York and Boston offered satisfactory alternative choices; so rather than go down in ruin along with the physical houses themselves, actors and companies turned to New York and Boston, thus unconsciously moving in the increasingly clear pattern which would result in the development of New York as the theatrical centre of the young nation. By 1847, the New Park Theatre was entrenched there, and the house to be known simply as The Bowery was presenting the first real competition to break the New Park Theatre's monopoly.[4] Twain's career as a dramatist, therefore, would almost inevitably be bound up with the New York stage, to which he might conceivably bring his considerable gifts as a sensitive observer of the social scene.

Although some early amateur drama was produced, the only significant native dramas written before 1800 were Royall Tyler's *The Contrast* and *The Father of an Only Child* by William Dunlap, both of which appeared in 1787 at New York's John Street Theatre. *The Contrast* introduced the now classic characteristics of the stage Yankee by showing Jonathan as ignorant, uncouth and awkward but surprisingly shrewd.

110

Dunlap was our first professional playwright, and his techniques, such as they were, dominated the drama for many years until Dion Boucicault turned his unique and fresh talents to play-writing and, with the serious treatment of the Negro character in *The Octoroon* (1859), produced a social satire of significance.[5]

Earlier there had appeared a rash of hackneyed dramas, initiated by a contest set up by Edwin Forrest for the best play dealing with an American theme. As one surveys the list of winners, a pattern of a peculiar narrowness appears, for the winning plays invariably dealt only with the theme of the native—specifically the 'noble red man'. Such pieces as James Nelson Barker's *The Indian Princess; or La Bella Sauvage* (later titled *Pocahontas*) and John H. Stone's *Metamora* were produced and played in both New York and London.

The two most important dramatists of the middle decades of the nineteenth century were probably George Henry Boker and Robert Montgomery Bird. Though a number of their plays dealt with native settings, their strength as writers lay in their treatment of foreign materials, as well as in the creation of scenes of dramatic effectiveness, and an atmosphere of inevitable tragedy. The lesser dramatists of the time still tended to treat foreign rather than native American materials almost exclusively.[6]

Two important playwrights of the later nineteenth century were Augustin Daly and Bronson Howard. Daly, of whom more will be said later in our discussion, was a drama critic before turning to play writing, and was to be influential in the development of Twain's theatrical career. Though, as Margaret Mayorga says, Daly deluged the theatre with German, French and English plays, the most significant aspect of Daly's adaptations, for our purposes, is that his English versions have no foreign flavour whatsoever.[7]

Although Daly followed his models closely, he made certain changes to ensure the native and topical quality. As an example, we find in *The Lottery of Love*, adapted from the French play *Les Surprises du Divorce* by Alexandre Bisson and Antony Mars, an interesting change in one of the characters. In the French version, one of the leading characters had been a famous ballerina. Daly, in his version, had made her a

Bloomer girl, thus referring to the feminist movement which championed women's rights about the middle of the century. Here Daly focused on a current social problem in the United States, and thereby Americanized his adaptation. (At roughly the same time, Twain was beginning to focus more sharply on similar problems and their implications, a concern which would result in such works as *Life on the Mississippi*.) Though Daly's plays reflect a more natural sense of characterization than was evidenced in most plays of the middle decades, and though he recognized the need for drama that reflected the American scene, even providing a certain impetus for the development of just such a native drama, he will be remembered in the American theatre chiefly for his producing, directing and star-making talents.

Among the dramatists whose plays Daly produced was Bronson Howard, often called the Dean of American Drama, and the first American author to succeed at earning a living as a professional playwright. Daly's production of Howard's *Saratoga* in 1870, when the boards were still crowded with French and English plays and prejudice against native American drama was still much in evidence, tended to quicken a change in attitude toward native American plays, and toward the professionalism of the American playwright. For Howard rejected conventional platitudes for realistic details of American life in his comedies of manners, and brought an engagingly original handling of plot and characterization to a true sense of form, demonstrating, as Quinn declared, that native drama need not be crude.[8] Potentially of greater significance was the fact that Daly, at about the same time as his production of *Saratoga*, was attempting to get Twain more involved in the world of the theatre, both as actor and writer.[9]

Twain has recently appeared in a leading rôle in an amateur production of James R. Planche's *Loan of the Lover* in Hartford, Connecticut, and Albert Bigelow Paine, his biographer, tells us that Henry Irving, the great English actor, observed that Twain would 'have made even a greater actor than a writer'.[10] From the first, he had felt attracted to the stage, but he had turned down Augustin Daly's offer of an acting rôle regretfully:

One of these days, somewhere in the future, I may surprise and grieve you by reminding you of that invitation, and proposing to revive it; but I mean to have the modesty to serve a decent apprenticeship before I make such a lofty venture.

I never tried the stage before; but by re-writing Peter Spyk, I managed to change the language and the character to a degree that enabled me to talk the one and represent the other after a fashion—but I am not equal to the Metropolitan boards yet.[11]

In 1873, however, though he still resisted offers either to act on or write for the stage, Twain gave Daly permission to use his travel book title, *Roughing It*, for the spectacular stage production which Daly advertised as being based on Twain's successful book, but which in reality bore little resemblance to it.[12] In August 1873, after Daly had again approached Twain, this time to write for the stage, he refused by arguing that there was more money in books than in plays. But he asked Daly to approach him again, leaving the possibility open for a later date. It was a year later that Twain actually 'intruded upon the dramatic field'.[13] After the success of *Colonel Sellers* in 1874, he continuously interrupted his work in other areas to attempt to write for the stage, either alone or in collaboration.

When Daly began coaxing Twain to invade the world of the theatre, audience taste was still, from all indications, unsophisticated, a factor that would inevitably affect the nature of Twain's work for the stage. To Mrs. Trollope, the temperament of the theatre audience at mid-century had been too often uneasy and confused.[14] There was a considerable public who had yet to accept the theatre without feeling guilty at witnessing such sinful proceedings. The strength of the theatrical businessman, later to be called the producer, and of commercial interests generally, were growing, and producers would offer lectures and art exhibits to entice customers to a theatre thus morally and culturally purged of 'degradation'. More directly, when moral lessons of a comforting nature were offered in propaganda melodramas, audiences seemed to turn out in great numbers, as witness the phenomenal success of the dramatized *Uncle Tom's Cabin* and *The Drunkard*. Along with the rather contrived situations and sticky sentiment of such works, and the seriously-intentioned dialogue which

113

seems so absurdly comic today, the audiences apparently preferred a 'show', with special emphasis on mechanical tricks and exaggerated gestures.

Actually, such factors as the dim and uneven gas-lighting of the theatres made exaggerated gestures and bombastic movement almost necessary stock-in-trade theatrical techniques if actors were to be seen by the patrons. Furthermore, danger and discomfort were a very real part of theatre-going. Aisle space was usually inadequate and auditoriums were often poorly designed for viewing and for acoustics. The gas-lights created an intense heat which was not only uncomfortable but unsafe; there is evidence of literally hundreds of theatre fires and resulting casualties to attest to that fact.[15] Thus, it seems plausible that audiences would almost inevitably demand a spectacular production, broadly conceived, rather than a subtle one, if they would come to the theatre at all. In a sense, the overwrought and extravagant, if not grotesque, designs of the theatres themselves matched those of the plays and the productions. The introduction of electric lighting, the raked auditorium and acoustical engineering, among other improvements, slowly eliminated the necessity for, at least, the posturing of the actors; but audiences seemed to expect it of them. Thus the overwrought style of the productions and the moralizing that so often characterized the dramas remained fashionable through the close of the century and Twain's career in the theatre. Therefore, men like Dion Boucicault, capable of serious artistic achievement, were writing trite plays prolifically, and designing strange and wondrous scenic effects to lure audiences.

In the last decades of the century, lesser figures, such as James A. Herne, William Gillette, Charles Hoyt, Edward Harrigan and Clyde Fitch, were contributing their own talents to the theatrical ferment. Fitch, especially, revealed considerable ability at dramatic construction and the writing of repartee, but worked often in the field of didactic melodrama. Herne popularized plays of rural life in which realistic details offset the melodramatic element,[16] while Harrigan and Hoyt, though touching on social realism (Harrigan exploited the humour in the pageant of American immigration), dealt primarily with actions commonly associated with vaudeville[17]; Gillette is best known as the originator of the spy and detective play, his *Secret Service* and *Legal Wreck* also emphasizing a certain realism of action. The work of these men was, at best, uneven, and while they contributed to the vitality of the theatre,[18] only occasionally did they reveal the qualities manifested by such as Daly and Howard that would make for a more mature American drama. A writer with the vision and ability of Mark Twain would conceivably bring considerable and welcome gifts to a theatrical scene thus artificial, and as yet, artistically undefined.

Along with and affecting these artistic developments came considerable changes in the technical and commercial aspects of the American theatre during the latter half of the nineteenth century. Following the growing unrest and riots of the '30s and '40s, innovations and changes appeared in every workaday area of the professional theatre. Certainly the westward movement, expanded by the discovery of gold in California and considerably strengthened in 1869 by the completion of the transcontinental railroad, gave an exciting and lasting impetus to increased theatrical activity. New theatres sprang up so fast throughout the country after 1850 that by 1885 there were 5,000 theatres in more than 3,500 cities and towns.[19]

With this expansion of theatrical activity and interest, commercialization inevitably took root and soon flourished. The producer of the 1860s was steadily shedding the more colourful aspects of his rôle as artist and becoming solely an entrepreneur and showman. By the 1870s a syndicate had been formed for controlling the booking, managing and housing of touring companies throughout the country. Charles Frohman, one of the all-powerful six men who controlled this theatrical syndicate, is entitled to both praise and censure for the creation of a new kind of star system which resulted in the enormous success of the syndicated theatre-chain practice. Frohman earned his label of 'Starmaker' fairly enough.[20] Through ingenious publicity and advertising methods he made Robert Edison, Julia Marlowe, Marie Doro, William Gillette, Henry Miller, John Drew, and dozens of others into personalities of nationwide fame.

The railroad circuit, or 'the road', became a lucrative source of revenue for the theatre managers while stars became national figures. The true repertory company, which had flourished during the first half of the century, was dealt the final blow by this new venture. Perhaps the crucial moment came in 1860, when Dion Boucicault, both a writer and an entrepreneur, sent out a travelling company with one play. The result, which was to contribute to the development of the 'long-run' show, was a financial success; thus the prestige of the early-century travelling star system was transferred to the travelling companies. An important further result of Boucicault's move was the shift in emphasis from the star to the play. Before the advent of the 'second-company', the audience came to see a particular star in any play from his repertory which he happened to choose. Now they came to see a 'New York hit' or a 'play by Boucicault'. Although this shift in emphasis might have been good economically for the theatre, it was not encouraging to prospective playwrights, since the long run substantially reduced the number of plays produced in a season.[21]

The times were tuned also for the steady emergence of the press agent, the publicity man, the literary agent, the road manager, the business manager; and at last, the theatrical entrepreneur, or producer, who took over the control of the production replacing the actor-manager.

The more gifted entrepreneurs possessed brilliance, power, experience, and, in some fortunate instances, talent. Augustin Daly emerged as the most powerful producer-director of the late nineteenth-century theatre. Similarly, the Wallack family was successful financially and, to the good fortune of the American theatre, artistically. Lester Wallack, son of Charles W. Wallack, who founded Wallack's Theatre in New York City, was endowed with a business sense that was equalled by an artistic sensitivity which endeared him to the artists as well as to his financially ambitious partners and family.

The conflict between artistic integrity and commercialism was perhaps nowhere better represented than in the career of Edwin Booth. It appears, despite the appeal of spectacular productions and didactic melodrama, that numbers of theatregoers still looked to the theatre for quality and substance; and, even as early as the late 1850s, Booth's subtlety and intellectualism attracted serious audiences before the dully commercial of the 1870s became popular. Shakespeare had never slipped from the affections of audiences during those lively years of change; *Lear* was enacted from Kentucky to the Bowery, and *Hamlet* was performed in canvas tents in California mining towns. By 1864 Booth was managing the brilliant New York Winter Garden Theatre and had completed his one-hundred-night run of *Hamlet*. While intellectuality and restraint best described Booth's acting style, acumen marked his business sense. Full houses and good box office receipts were not small matters to Booth, and he employed all the devices of the then popular spectaculars to please the audiences and keep them coming back for more. In many instances, realizing that the audiences were still spiritually tied to their British and European backgrounds, he imported established continental actors to co-star with him in the Winter Garden.[23] The conflict that Booth faced, and which Daly and the Wallacks resolved in varying degrees of artistic and commercial success, would confront Twain directly in his own theatrical career.

When Daly produced *Ah Sin* for Twain and Bret Harte in 1877, some years after he first approached Twain, the relationship between writer and producer was only one variety of the many in which Twain became involved. By this time, businessmen were rapidly moving into a strong position as middle-men with the vague title of 'agent'.[24] Twain remained troubled during all of his transactions in the theatre, and it is not too presumptuous to lay part of the responsibility on his own wilful determination to arrange matters, financial and otherwise, to his own liking. One cannot help wondering how he might have fared later had he been able to work as he did with *Colonel Sellers* and while the theatrical scene was still dominated by the actor-manager, whose main concern was to offer himself as the star attraction by securing a play ready-made for his particular talents and by dealing directly with the writer who could produce such a vehicle. It might have been less disastrous for Twain had he come in contact with fewer hard-handed businessmen. But the establishment of the theatre as big business was beginning by the time Daly first approached Twain.

Twain's artistic concerns are revealed in his theatre criticism, largely satirical or otherwise humorous, and in other, less public sources. During his tenure with the San Francisco *Morning Call*, his reviews were naturally journalistic in style and tone, but later there were significant exceptions that reveal his love for the drama and his concern for the state of the American theatre; among them were 'The Indignity Put Upon the Remains of George Holland by the Rev. Mr. Sabine'[25] and 'About Play-Acting'.[26] The former article, published by *Galaxy* magazine in February 1871, defended the theatre as a respectable arena for a profession; the latter, published by the *Forum* in October 1889, made a constructive suggestion concerning what the author felt was lacking in the New York theatre—a sense of the tragic. In a letter to his sister in October 1853, he was obviously impressed by the acting skill of Edwin Forrest and in ways that suggest his concern for appropriateness in acting rather than mere histrionics:

> Edwin Forrest has been playing for the last sixteen days at the Broadway Theatre, but I never went to see him until last night. The play was the 'Gladiator'. I did not like parts of it much, but other portions were really splendid. In the latter part of the last act, where this 'Gladiator' (Forrest) dies at his brother's feet, (in all the fierce pleasure of gratified revenge), the man's whole soul seems absorbed in the part he is playing; and it is really startling to see him play 'Damon and Pythias'—the former character being his greatest.[27]

That Twain was aware of the dramatic effects of costuming, lighting and staging is implicit in many of his articles. This knowledge of the technical aspects of theatre is evident even when his primary purpose is satire or humour, as in the following review that appeared in the Virginia City *Territorial Enterprise* on 13 September 1863:

> When I arrived in San Francisco, I found there was no-one in town—at least there was nobody in town but 'the Menken'—or rather, that no one was being talked about except that manly young female. I went to see her play 'Mazeppa', of course. They said she was dressed from head to foot in flesh-colored 'tights', but I had no opera glass, and I couldn't see it, to use the language of the inelegant rabble. She appeared to me to have but one garment on—a thin tight linen one, of unimportant dimensions; I forget the name of the article, but it is in-dispensable to infants of tender age—I suppose any young

mother can tell you what it is, if you have the courage to ask the question. With the exception of this superfluous rag, the Menken dresses like the Greek Slave; but some of her postures are not so modest as the suggestive attitude of the latter. She is a finely formed woman down to her knees; if she could be herself that far, and Mrs. H. A. Perry the rest of the way, she would pass for an unexceptionable Venus. Here every tongue sings the praises of her matchless grace, her supple gestures, her charming attitudes. Well, possibly, these tongues are right. In the first act, she rushes on the stage, and goes cavorting around after 'Oliska'; she bends herself back like a bow; she pitches head-foremost at the atmosphere like a battering-ram; she works her arms, and her legs, and her whole body like a dancing-jack: her every move is as quick as thought; in a word, without any apparent reason for it, she carries on like a lunatic from the beginning of the act to the end of it. At other times she 'whallops' herself down on the stage, and rolls over as does the sportive pack-mule after his burden is removed. If this be grace, then the Menken is eminently graceful.[28]

Thus Twain appeared to have valid critical standards regarding acting styles, costuming, staging and character motivation.

Twain's awareness of dramatic weaknesses extended itself even to self-criticism. In 1907 he confessed to Albert Bigelow Paine that 'there was never any question with the managers about my plays. They always said they wouldn't act. . . .'[29] The fact that Twain recognized the technical weaknesses in his plays only adds confusion to an already disturbing paradox in his play-writing career. He showed by his dramatic criticism that he was aware of the technical problems of acting and production; yet he was unable or unwilling to analyse objectively the technical weaknesses in his own plays—an analysis that could have possibly salvaged a promising script, as in the case of *Simon Wheeler, Amateur Detective.*

Twain's notebooks and letters indicate that he regularly attended the theatre after he settled in the East, and that he initiated and was active in amateur dramatic endeavours around his home. Then, his magnificent lecturing talents were hardly those of a person without a sense of the dramatic.[30] The major question thus poses itself: how is it that a writer with this concern, awareness, and vision, would come to write and

119

produce plays which so frequently lacked character motivation and represented, all in all, little more than the flimsiest and weakest dramatic writing?

A possible answer is implicit in his oft-stated opinion that he wanted to and could produce a money-making script in a short time with a minimum effort. Not to be overlooked, likewise, is his basic attitude towards the art of writing for the stage; he never indicated that he hoped for anything but financial success, a factor which need not have eliminated artistic quality as well, but did in Twain's case. Manuscript sources and letters, then, give evidence of his impatience and stubbornness when dealing with theatrical people, themselves never renowned for even temperaments. Strangely enough, his innate genius would never demonstrate a penchant for writing comedy for the nineteenth-century American stage. His own faults aside, the native American drama which might have provided him with a style—extravagant or realistic—which he could successfully employ was never to be realized in his productive years as a playwright.

One special purpose, then, of the following pages is to consider Twain's preoccupation with the business aspects of the production of his plays, which led him to neglect, thereby, the 'polishing of the diamonds' that Brander Matthews said his plays needed.[31] This chronic preoccupation will be evident as we summarize the history of the production or attempted production of each play. When his plays failed, Twain's annoyance seemed to be limited to the inconveniences of troublesome agents, stubborn managers, inept collaborators, and unpredictable stars. He may have been aware of the weakness of his scripts, but he habitually attributed their failures to the legal entanglements and confused business dealings which he seemed to fall into during all of his life.

Of Twain's produced plays, the single financial success was *Colonel Sellers* (1874), adapted from *The Gilded Age*. It turned a profit of $70,000 for Twain, a sizeable fortune in those days, and made an 'overnight' success of an obscure actor, John T. Raymond, who portrayed the title rôle. After reading the script, we must nevertheless conclude that Raymond did more for the play than the play did for Raymond, Twain's remarks to the contrary notwithstanding. The critics were unanimous

in praising the comic abilities and originality of the chief actor,
while criticizing the play as 'slender' and as a 'grotesque
sketch'. Though 'grotesque' is a rather harsh judgement,
'slender' is a kind evaluation of the script. With the exception
of Sellers, no character has any depth or definition. The
occasional moralizing is out of key with the tenor of the piece,
and the dialogue is neither consistent nor controlled. Throughout his life, Twain berated Raymond for not giving more
dimension to the part of Sellers, whereas he should have
recognized that the author, not the actor, should give
'dimension' to his characters.

This brings us to a major reason for Twain's failure as a
dramatist. He was able in *Huck Finn*, for example, to make his
characters connotative and suggestive which is exactly what a
dramatist should do, only more so. Twain, however, made his
characters denotative, thereby failing to consider that the
actor must bring the character to life through the imagination
of the audience. In a novel, the characters come to life through
the words of the author. In not one of Twain's plays, with the
possible exception of *Is He Dead?*,[32] was there a character with
more than one dimension. Most characters in Twain's novels
are 'types'; that is, they are to some degree universal and
recognizable to many people. In addition they also have some
unique quality which prevents them from being stereotypes.
In Twain's plays, however, the characters are either known or
recognizable types or lack any individuality to make them
other than boring stereotypes. Without 'real' characters, it is
impossible to have 'real' drama.

It was probably the financial success of *Colonel Sellers* which
precipitated Twain's collaborative effort with Bret Harte.
Even though they had had a previous misunderstanding,
Twain acquiesced when Harte invited him in 1877 to
collaborate on a play. The result of this effort was *Ah Sin*, a
poorly constructed farce crammed with caricatures rather
than characterizations. But the story of the production of the
play is incomplete without a mention of the personal animosity
which grew between the two authors. Twain, for many
personal and business reasons including what he said was an
insulting remark directed by Harte toward Olivia Clemens,
dismissed Harte in spoken and written word, not only as a

friend, but as a writer, critic and human being. His contempt was poured forth in such torrents that Harte, after writing one stinging letter, withdrew from the collaboration before opening night and withdrew from the verbal battle with Twain as well. But Twain continued to pour invective upon Harte even until he undertook his autobiographical dictation in the latter years of his life.

Their play should have been successful. Though poor, it was as good as *Colonel Sellers*, and much better than many nineteenth-century plays which found favour with audiences. Twain spent more time revising, before and after the Washington tryout, than with any other of his dramatic attempts. His public relations were good for a change and the production was well publicized. Furthermore, it was staged by Daly and had as its star Charles Parsloe, who had been critically well-received for a similar part in Harte's other dramatic attempt, *Two Men of Sandy Bar*. In addition, the critics, though finding weaknesses, received the play kindly for the most part and were unanimous in their praise for Parsloe's performance of the 'Heathen Chinee'. Unfortunately, however, the play opened 31 July to run through August, a month even now avoided by producers for opening a play, despite air-conditioned theatres. Although the first week of the run showed promise, with well-filled houses, the audiences soon diminished and the play went on the road with no better luck. Since there was no 'Broadway success' to advertise, the provinces proved fruitless. The main weakness of the play is in its incoherence: its apparently haphazard sequence of events. Twain elsewhere made the distinction between 'farce' and 'comedy'; this plot calls for comedy, not farce, but farce is what we get. One of the main elements in comedy is its presenting the normal and sane as right, thereby exposing the abnormal or insane. The contrast between normal and eccentric behaviour is an important, even essential, ingredient in comedy. What we get in *Ah Sin* and in *Colonel Sellers as a Scientist* is abnormal and eccentric behaviour alone.

Most reviews took note of the obvious delight of the audience, while commenting on the dramaturgical weaknesses of the play itself. Still the play could very well have reaped the financial rewards Twain was seeking had a more propitious date for opening been selected. Another helpful move would have been for Harte to accept Twain's proposal to launch the play in San Francisco, where the climate is mild even in summer. Also the topical references to the Chinese coolie would have had more impact there. The news of any success on the West Coat would have filtered back to New York, for added publicity, thereby enhancing the chances for a long run. But weather conditions, clash of personalities, poor writing, lukewarm reviews—all combined to doom *Ah Sin* to indeed 'a most abject and incurable failure'.

The last play to be produced, *Colonel Sellers as a Scientist* (1884), was also a collaborative effort, this time with William Dean Howells. It is perhaps stretching a point to call this a 'produced' play since it had a 'run' of only one New York performance. Although there were stormy moments during this collaboration too, the friendship was too deep, too real, to be wrecked by Twain's irascibility or Howell's near-psychotic fear of personal criticism. It was Twain's idea to capitalize on the popularity of the character of Colonel Sellers by having him reappear ten years later as an eccentric do-gooder and pseudo-scientist. However, the rôle was so closely identified with Raymond that no other actor would touch it, and Raymond felt that the play was weak and the eccentricities of Sellers were exaggerated to such an extent that he seemed a 'lunatic' rather than the lovable speculator. This judgement, along with the unreasonable financial demands made by Twain and the dislike that each felt for the other, caused Raymond to turn down the part. After many fruitless hours of searching for producers and an actor acceptable to both authors, Howells assigned his rights to the drama to Twain, who leased them in turn to Burbank, an elocutionist and impersonator, who was unable to give the part the quality needed to capture the fancy of the audience. So after a tryout in New Brunswick, New Jersey, the play opened and closed in New York City on the same day in September in 1884.

Again the problems which beset this attempt hint at yet another reason why Twain consistently failed as a playwright. He did not understand the proper and necessary relationships between dramatists and actors. The novelist creates in a vacuum, but the dramatist must deal with and consider that other creative artists are needed to make his work come alive. The actors' work extends the playwright's basic conception and the playwright must depend on the actors. Twain's attitude towards Raymond in particular, and the casting of his plays in general, indicates his lack of understanding of this dependency.

If one considers and accepts the dictum that drama can be literature, but literature is never drama, we can conclude that Twain's success as a novelist and general prose writer and failure as a playwright stem partially from the fact that he understood the making of literature but not drama. Twain the novelist had literary skill and philosophic penetration, but Twain the playwright was unable to synthesize verbal, physical, auditory and visual elements to create a live image of the human condition.

A script for which Twain had high hopes but which never saw production was *Simon Wheeler, Amateur Detective* (1887). Although the idea of the play was applauded by Twichell, Daly and Boucicault, the finished product was judged unplayable by producers. With a little restraint on the part of Twain in delineating the comic characters, and a willingness to do judicious and extensive cutting, this perhaps could have been a very funny vehicle for a clever actor. *Is He Dead?* is another play which could not find a producer but which, in my opinion, is the best of all Twain's efforts. It is closer to high comedy than any of the others, and has a coherent structure so noticeably lacking in the other attempts. The dialogue does not ring as true as in many of his novels and stories, but it is not so glaringly artificial as in the other plays. The extant evidence shows that Twain was not so persistent in his attempts to get this play produced as he had been in the past. Had he persisted, *Is He Dead?* might have provided him with the theatrical success he sought but failed to receive after *Colonel Sellers*. There is no evidence that any effort was made to get 'The Death Wafer', a one-act melodrama, produced. If there had been, it is inconceivable that a producer would have read beyond the first page, so contrived is the language, so stilted is the dialogue, so shallow are the characters.[33] Twain's adaptation of *Tom Sawyer*, the pantomime titled 'Love on the Rail', and the clever *Meisterschaft* likewise failed to impress any producers.

In addition to the plays previously mentioned, Twain wrote several pieces in apparent dramatic form which have been called variously 'plays', 'dialogues', 'pantomimes', 'burlesques', 'charades', or 'sketches' by Twain bibliographers and scholars but are not considered serious attempts at play-writing by this writer as they were not written for stage presentation. A few of these are the unfinished fragment, *The Quaker City Holy Land Excursion*; 'What is Man?'; the two acting charades, *A Champagne Cocktail* and *A Catastrophe*; 'The Dervish' and the 'Offensive Stranger'; the 'Burlesque Il Trovatore'; and the burlesque review of *Ingomar the Barbarian*. They were all written for Twain's own amusement or that of his friends and family, for dramatic effect though not for drama, or for when he felt the dialogue form was the best mould in which his satirical die could be cast.

Although an account of Twain's play-writing would seem to indicate, for the most part, a wste of his time and effort, a more positive point of view may be suggested. With the exception of *Colonel Sellers*, *Tom Sawyer* and *Is He Dead?* which were adapted from prose works already published, the plays eventually found their places completely, partially, or tangentially in later works of different genres.

A play fragment, 'Brummel and Arabella', was incorporated into *Simon Wheeler, Amateur Detective*, and this play found itself used several times thereafter. The idea of burlesquing the private and police detective was employed in 'The Stolen White Elephant' and 'A Double Barrelled Detective Story'. Eventually Twain started to turn the play itself into a novel. Though he never completed it, he left ten chapters, as well as outlines and working notes for the remainder, which have been edited and published. The burlesque *Hamlet* made use of anachronisms which foreshadowed some of the effects in *A Connecticut Yankee*; *Meisterschaft* was published first as a magazine piece and was included in Paine's Definitive Edition. 'The Death Wafer' was rewritten as a short story which was included in *Harper's Monthly* in December 1901, while *Colonel Sellers as a Scientist* was transformed into *The American Claimant*. Furthermore, his notations for plots for dramas, in many instances, became successful short stories. We may conclude, then, that Twain's play-writing, though not successful in itself, was valuable as an apprenticeship for future and more successful efforts.

But we should now try to come to grips with a rational explanation as to *why* Twain failed as a playwright, especially in the light of evidence that Twain thought dramatically in his novels and stories. It is not unusual for an author to succeed in one *genre* but fail in another. Indeed, Howells and James also found little success in writing for the stage and Chekhov had no success with the novel.

One probable reason for Twain's failure as a dramatist was his preoccupation with theatrical business details and his concern about the financial potentialities of the play rather than the literary potentialities. The time he spent haggling with producers, and arguing with actors, could more profitably have been devoted to revising and polishing his work. It is true that Twain thought of the financial potentialities of his other works and lectures, but business considerations were never the sole *raison d'être* for writing or performing. There was never a conflict between 'artist-playwright' and 'business-playwright' as there sometimes was between the 'artist and businessman-novelist', but solely a get-rich-quick attitude towards play-writing which prevented any polishing of the plays for artistic reasons. Brander Matthews' statement that Twain had dramatic genius but 'could not polish it for the stage'[34] sums up one critic's evaluation of Twain as a playwright, but I feel that Twain '*would* not polish it' is nearer the truth.

Added to this was his inability to adapt his own style to playwriting. Again, using *Huckleberry Finn* as an example, we note that in his best fiction Twain carefully set the scene with minute description of the physical surroundings, and projected into this setting fully drawn characters who used dialogue and performed actions fully consistent with their personalities. One could transpose, for example, the Boggs-Sherburn episode to the stage without changing setting, dialogue or action and retain the effectiveness of the scene. But when Twain turned to play-writing, he persisted in imitating the artificial and contrived style of many of the playwrights of his day.

O'Dell's simplistic explanation of Twain's failure as a playwright that he 'simply could not write plays', fails to deal with the problem of 'why'. Twain's humour in his novels and short stories evolves mainly from the 'narrator's' comments on an action or incident itself. A playwright must be able to render amusing or interesting a situation (the occasional 'aside' notwithstanding) without comment. Twain failed to recognize this as evidenced in his notebook entry where he discusses an invention to be used in *Colonel Sellars as a Scientist*. The invention is a phonograph machine to play 'sailors' cursing' at sea. Twain comments on this by saying it is to be used during a storm when 'they are too busy to curse for themselves.' The humour evolves from the comment rather than the incident, but when writing the scene for the play Twain failed to recognize this. Twain, in other words, did not know or refused to accept that a novel narrates while a play enacts.

Twain employed social satire and topical humour in most of his dramatic works, though much less centrally than he did in his other writings. In *Colonel Sellars*, the major targets for his satire are political corruption and the jury system, which he found ineffective; in *Simon Wheeler*, private detectives in general and the Pinkerton Agency in particular are burlesqued, while unfair police tactics are also examined. *Colonel Sellars as a Scientist* takes aim at spiritualism, temperance societies, American reverence for useless European titles, and the sudden avalanche of outlandish scientific and technical products being offered for patents.

Social satire and topical humour can enhance drama; certainly social criticism can be effective, and social reform has been achieved by facile or capable dramatists who have used satire aptly. Twain, however, could not take the local problem or point of satire and create the universality required to expand its very limited scope and make it poignantly effective as drama. He accomplished this in *Huckleberry Finn*, *A Connecticut Yankee* and *The Prince and the Pauper*, and to a lesser extent in *Tom Sawyer* and other stories and novels, but his dramas failed to arouse more than a superficial, knowing smile at a topical situation. Huck Finn's indignation or sense of moral injustice concerning Jim's predicament becomes the reader's indignation toward all institutions which suppress man's freedom. But, while we might laugh at Colonel Sellars' speaking to a temperance society when in his cups, we do not go beyond that to wonder at the hypocrisy of many 'do-gooder' reform movements. Twain's plays failed to probe in depth the human condition within the social environment, a major requisite for lasting drama.

When Rodman Gilder gave his article for *Theatre Arts* the title of 'Mark Twain Detested the Theater', he was quoting an opinion by Howells unfairly and out of context.[35] It is true that Twain as a theatre critic viewed many plays with a jaundiced eye, or used his critical licence to expound his satire and humour, but the letters and notebooks attest to his having enjoyed evenings at the theatre regularly throughout his life while counting among his friends many actors, producers and playwrights. Two major essays, furthermore, expressed a respectful philosophy toward the theatre as an institution. 'The Indignity Put Upon the Remains of George Holland by the Rev. Mr. Sabine', published in *Galaxy* magazine in 1871, defended the acting profession and held that the theatre was a noble and worthy institution. 'About Play-Acting', published in October 1898, in the monthly *Forum*, cited the need for a national tragic theatre. It noted the over-abundance of comedies in this country and in England and admitted that while 'comedy keeps the heart sweet', a return to the classical tragedies on occasion would enable one to 'enjoy the comedies all the better'. This was hardly the attitude of a man who 'detested the theater'.

The Twain biographers, scholars and critics have treated him as a novelist, essayist, social critic, inventor, businessman, journalist, humorist, lecturer, short story writer, historian, traveller, riverboat pilot, and husband and father. But they have failed to recognize adequately the fact that from 1865, when he was a reporter for the San Franscisco *Morning Call*, to 1900, when he wrote his last play, Twain was often occupied with the professional theatre as reviewer, playwright, or collaborator.

Mark Twain as Playwright
TWAIN'S DRAMATIC WRITINGS

A. Published

Ah Sin. Written in collaboration with Bret Harte, edited by Frederick Anderson (San Francisco, California, 1961).

'Brummel and Arabella' (*circa* 1871). This is a fragment of approximately 28,000 words. It was incorporated fully into *Cap'n Simon Wheeler, Amateur Detective*. Published in *Mark Twain's Satires and Burlesques*, edited with an introduction by Franklin R. Rogers (Berkeley and Los Angeles, 1967), pp. 207–15.

'Burlesque *Hamlet*' (1881). A subtitle to this piece is 'Hamlett's Brother', pencilled in Twain's hand on the first page of the manuscript. It is incomplete, with the action going only through Act II, Scene 2 of Shakespeare's play. Extracts from a printed version of *Hamlet* with Twain's additions of about 25,000 words make up the manuscript. Published in *Mark Twain's Satires and Burlesques*, edited with an introduction by Franklin R. Rogers (Berkeley and Los Angeles, 1967), pp. 49–87.

Cap'n Simon Wheeler, the Amateur Detective (1877). Published in *Mark Twain's Satires and Burlesques*, edited with an introduction by Franklin R. Rogers (Berkeley and Los Angeles, 1967), pp. 216–306.

Colonel Sellers as a Scientist. Written in collaboration with William Dean Howells, edited with an introduction by Walter J. Meserve (New York, 1960).

Meisterschaft. Published in *Merry Tales* (New York, 1892). Reprinted in the Definitive Edition, Volume XV (New York, 1923).

The Quaker City Holy Land Excursion: An Unfinished Play. Privately printed, 1927.

B. Unpublished

Bartel Turaser (*circa* 1899). This manuscript is not extant but is mentioned in an unpublished letter in C. Waller Barrett Collection, University of Virginia Library. The correspondence is addressed to Dr. C. C. Rice, a personal friend of

Twain, to whom the author must have sent the manuscripts. The letter is dated 27 February 1899. Included is the mention of *In Purgatory*.

Colonel Sellers (1874). This is extant as a prompt copy with some notes in Twain's hand. Also housed with this is a full-length revision which differs from the prompt copy only in the respect that the first scene of the latter has been integrated with the first act of the revision, and the steamship intrigue involving Laura and Clay has been eliminated.

'The Death Wafer' (1900). This one-act script contains 58 pages and about 6,000 words. Also, there is a typescript copy of 26 pages.

In Purgatory (*circa* 1899). This manuscript is not extant. See annotation under *Bartel Turaser*.

Is He Dead? (1897). This manuscript is an amanuensis copy of 136 pages and approximately 13,500 words.

'Love on the Rail' (*circa* 1887). The manuscript of this pantomime is in Twain's handwriting, and consists of 7 pages of about 700 words.

The Prince and the Pauper (1889). This manuscript is by Abby Sage Richardson, but includes 45 pages of about 4,500 words of revisions in Twain's own handwriting. The 70 pages of the Richardson manuscript have been edited throughout by Twain.

Tom Sawyer (1884). Included here are a handwritten, complete script of the play, notes for a 'Tom and Huck' play, a pencilled synopsis on lined notepaper in Twain's handwriting, a typescript with pencilled corrections which is a copy of the handwritten script, and additional complete scenes and notes in his handwriting.

NOTES

1. Minnie M. Brashear. *Mark Twain: Son of Missouri* (Chapel Hill, 1934), p. 142.
2. Laurence Hutton, *Curiosities of the American Stage* (New York, 1891), pp. 7–8.
3. John Coleman, *Players and Playwrights I Have Known* (Philadelphia, 1890), pp. 31–3.
4. Joseph N. Ireland, *Records of the New York Stage from 1750 to 1860* (New York, 1866), I, 172–73.
5. Barnard Hewitt, *Theatre U.S.A.: 1668 to 1957* (New York, 1959), pp. 183–87.
6. Arthur Hobson Quinn, *A History of the American Drama from the Beginning to the Civil War* (New York, 1923), pp. 337–67.

Mark Twain as Playwright

7. *A Short History of the American Drama* (New York, 1932), p. 3.
8. Quinn, 'Bronson Howard and the Establishment of Professional Playwriting', *A History of the American Drama from the Civil War to the Present Day* (New York, 1927), pp. 39–65.
9. Joseph F. Daly, *The Life of Augustin Daly* (New York, 1912), pp. 146–47.
10. Albert Bigelow Paine, *Mark Twain, A Biography* (New York, 1912), II, 571.
11. Daly, p. 146.
12. Frank Morgan Flack, 'About the Play "Roughing It" as Produced by Augustin Daly', *Twainian*, V (July–August, 1946), 1–3. See also Paine, *Biography*, II, 1000.
13. Daly, p. 147.
14. Frances M. Trollope, *Domestic Manners of the Americans* (London, 1842), pp. 129–35.
15. Ben G. Henneke, 'The Playgoer in America' (unpublished Ph.D. dissertation, University of Illinois, 1956), pp. 14–20.
16. Quinn, *History of American Drama from Civil War to Present Day*, pp. 125–26.
17. Ibid., pp. 96–103.
18. Ibid., pp. 96, 162, 218–38.
19. Hewitt, p. 217.
20. O. S. Coad and Edwin Mims, Jr., *The American Stage* (New Haven, 1929), p. 279.
21. Hewitt, 'Resident Company versus Travelling Star', *Theatre U.S.A.*, pp. 161–217.
22. Quinn, *A History of the American Drama from the Beginning to the Civil War*, p. 387.
23. William Winter, *Life and Art of Edwin Booth* (New York, 1893), pp. 151–53.
24. Hewitt, pp. 256–57.
25. Also reprinted in Paine, II, 1624–627.
26. Reprinted in *The Man That Corrupted Hadleyburg and Other Stories and Essays* (New York and London, 1900), pp. 278–87.
27. Letter in the Mark Twain Papers, University of California at Berkeley. Hereafter cited as MTP.
28. Published in *Mark Twain of the Enterprise: Newspaper Articles & Other Documents 1862–1864*. Edited by Henry Nash Smith with the assistance of Frederick Anderson (Berkeley and Los Angeles, 1957), pp. 78–80.
29. Paine, *Biography*, II, 1414.
30. Robert A. Wiggins, 'Mark Twain and the Drama', *American Literature*, XXV (November, 1953), 279–86.
31. Brander Matthews, 'Mark Twain and the Theater', *Playwrights on Playmaking and Other Studies of the Stage* (New York, 1923), p. 183.
32. See Annotated Bibliography.
33. Ibid.
34. Matthews, p. 183.
35. XXXVIII (February, 1944), 109–16. The precise statement by Howells was, 'As for plays, he detested the theater, and said he would as lief do a sum as to follow a plot on the stage.' See *My Mark Twain*, p. 16.

5

Huckleberry Finn, 'Sivilization', and the Civilization of the Heart

by A. ROBERT LEE

1

Hemingway's celebrated *dictum* in *Green Hills of Africa* (1935)
that 'all modern American literature comes from one book by
Mark Twain called *Huckleberry Finn*'[1] might not tell the whole
truth, but it does tell a sufficient truth and one which honours
both its recipient and its maker. Hemingway's generosity—a
rising literary Modern paying homage to a major forerunner
oftener than not at the time judged only a tall-story
'humourist' and American children's writer[2]—recalls the
tribute Herman Melville paid to Hawthorne in his two-part
'Hawthorne and his Mosses' in the *Literary World* for August
1850, a similarly handsome, discerning affirmation of writerly
fellowship.[3] For as closely as Melville felt himself 'fixed' and
nourished by his New England contemporary, so Hemingway
recognized a debt in kind to a writer whose sheer distinctive-
ness of idiom confirmed his own.

Hemingway no doubt had first in mind the palpable
humanity of Twain's novel, its decisive, unsermonly moral
sureness of touch. He must, too, have discerned in the book's
voice, so apparently artless, unliterary and shot through with
spectacular ungrammaticality, precedent for his own emerging

declarative style. Twain's irony, cutting several ways at one and the same time and always shrewdly understated, clearly also made its impact. Certainly, the author of *The Sun Also Rises* (1926), the other major novels, and the Nick Adams and war and travel stories, had good creative reason to think *Huckleberry Finn* a masterpiece. The indebtedness shows everywhere and to advantage. But the judgement offered by Hemingway deserves to stand at a more general level. For the novel indeed does amount to a cornerstone of American literature, a classic (despite flaws which would have sunk a lesser work) amply rich enough on its own terms and at the same time the crucial, transforming link between the great American Renaissance writings of the nineteenth century— pre-eminently Emerson's addresses and poems, *The Scarlet Letter* (1850), *Moby-Dick* (1851), *Walden* (1854), 'Song of Myself' (1855) and the poetry of Emily Dickinson—and the fictional line which leads on through the American Naturalists to Faulkner, Fitzgerald, Hemingway himself, and well beyond.

As a 'voice', *Huckleberry Finn* works to irresistible effect, its idiomatic good ease and grain made to mask the most trenchant indictment of human cruelty and an array of error from false piety to slavery. It reflects Twain's mastery of a kind of 'alternative' or adolescent and regional frontier counter-language against which to site, and for ever pillory, the official values of a slave-holding, meanly provincial and puritanized 'St. Petersburg', not to say the larger historic 1840s American South of which for Twain it was symptomatic. Where better, or more memorably, has a colloquial American idiom been realized on the page? Twain's command of Huck's own speaking voice, and of those which surround it, bespeaks a genius both of ear and tongue, the ability to make vernacular speech say infinitely more than the speaker realizes and wholly to implicate the reader in the irony of that discrepancy.

And in taking us down the central, arterial waterway of America, the Mississippi as the Abraham of rivers as Herman Melville calls it in his own ensnaring river masquerade, *The Confidence-Man* (1857), Twain unmistakably refers to the larger paradigm of the human journey, the river as at once vividly literal (and rendered so memorably in *Life on the Mississippi*, 1883) and equally the implicit current of life itself, a trajectory of defeats and gains, errors and awakenings. In this, it invites comparison with, among others, George Eliot's 'rush of water' as she calls the floss in *The Mill on the Floss* (1860), Dickens's Thames in almost any of his London novels, Conrad's serpentine Congo in 'Heart of Darkness' (1902), or behind them, the central peregrinatory journey of *Don Quixote*. None of these 'rivers', distinctively imagined as they are, however, has also had to linger in a phrase akin to 'sold down the river', the Mississippi as sumptuous Nature but as Twain further demonstrated in *Pudd'nhead Wilson* (1894), an indicting reference back to its place in the historic, unconscionable rot of cotton slavery.

Huckleberry Finn himself, furthermore, has now become part of the stock of legendary Western archetype. Yet he belongs, too, in a long tradition of American fictional journeyers, youthful and usually male tyros who secure their rights to selfhood only after the most arduous *rite-de-passage*. Usually, too, they journey with a companion-mentor, often older, non-white and, at least on Leslie Fiedler's argument in *Love and Death in the American Novel* (1960), implicitly tied into some unstatedly and darkly sexual *Brüderschaft*. The list, besides Huck and Jim, is considerable: Cooper's Natty Bumppo and Chingachgook, Melville's Redburn and the Ishmael-Queequeg pairing of *Moby-Dick*, Hawthorne's Blue-stocking ingénus in 'My Kinsman, Major Molineux' and 'Young Goodman Brown', Crane's Henry Fleming in *The Red Badge of Courage*, and in our own century, loners from Hemingway's Nick Adams and Jake Barnes through to Ellison's Invisible Man and Mailer's D. J. and Tex in *Why Are We In Vietnam?* and who especially count among their number that 1950s adept in the countervailing uses of the vernacular, J. D. Salinger's Holden Caulfield.[4] For all of them, paired or in Melville's phrase from *Moby-Dick* 'isolato', journeying involves a major act of self-parenting.

Above all, however, and behind all of these elements—the book's marvellous voicing, its river-iconography, its 'history' (derived in large part from Twain's own Missouri boyhood and his Mississippi river-pilot experiences and observations), Huck as an archetype of all boyhood—there lies the most rooted moral conviction, not in the sense of some petty, sermonistic 'motive' of the kind Twain rightly orders 'banished' in his Notice, but conviction infinitely deeper and more capacious. For within the river journey of Huck and Jim and their raft republic of two, Twain depicts where and how a truly human value is to be learned and against every threat nourished and protected.

In redirecting attention back to the moral resonance of *Huckleberry Finn*, a no doubt antiquated and incorrigibly Anglo-Saxon focus in an age of French and Yale deconstructionism, one perhaps risks sounding obsolescent, or at least in retreat from the newer semiotic orthodoxies. Which, however, is not to avoid recognizing the integral relationship of the novel's language with its moral vision. A concern with Twain's moral intelligence, too, can risk making the novel sound solemn, less than its great buoyancy as narration. Nevertheless, its moral claims are finally what make *Huckleberry Finn* quite so momentous, the serious, unremitting humanity of Twain's comic vision and art. His achievement is to have captured with unique authority an abiding measure of human worth.

In this respect the note which needs to be underlined Twain establishes at the very outset of *Huckleberry Finn*, and returns to, almost exactly, in the novel's literal closing paragraph. With the memory, perhaps, of *The Adventures of Tom Sawyer* (1876) in mind, Twain makes his transition into the altogether more consequential world of *Huckleberry Finn* in the following terms. The voice is Huck's, live-sounding from the start and unselfconsciously wry:

> The Widow Douglas, she took me for her son, and allowed she would sivilize me; but it was rough living in the house all the time, considering how dismal regular and decent the widow was in all her ways; and so when I couldn't stand it no longer, I lit out. I got into my old rags, and my sugar-hogshead again, and was free and satisfied.[5]

Put alongside the celebrated leave-taking which concludes the novel (after the problematic Phelps Farm chapters), we can hardly fail to note the continuity of motif. Huck hasn't necessarily changed, but we have. Our whole reading experience—of the shoreline feuds, the treatment of Jim, the

sham-chivalry and gangsterdom—works to gloss Huck's
ingenuousness of voice:

> Tom's most well, now, and got his bullet around his neck on
> a watch-guard for a watch, and is always seeing what time it is,
> and so there ain't nothing more to write about, and I am rotten
> glad of it, because if I'd a knowed what a trouble it was to make
> a book I wouldn't a tackled it and ain't agoing to no more. But I
> reckon I got to light out for the Territory ahead of the rest,
> because Aunt Sally she's going to adopt me and sivilize me and
> I can't stand it. I been there before.
> THE END. YOURS TRULY, HUCK FINN (245)

Not only does Twain here confirm the fine tuning of Huck's
vernacular, he reaffirms the novel's organizing antimonies:
being 'free and satisfied' as against 'sivilization' in the form of
St. Petersburg and the co-threats of the Widow Douglas and
Aunt Sally and the dire scale of custodial good intention
represented by their 'mothering'; the urge to 'light out' for free
territory as against house-bounded St. Petersburg gentility;
and also, if only as an implicit call to memory in the reader,
the dialectic of 'sound heart' and 'deformed conscience' which
the novel at large acts on at every turn. For Huck's true
civilization, never intrudingly moralized by him or Twain, lies
in the triumphant unadoptability of his Mississippi adventures, whether faced alone, or with Jim, and whether aboard
the raft or on shore. His civilization, and ours by proxy,
belongs to the heart and transcends utterly all the communal
bad faith about him—all the 'sivilization'—be that expressed
as Pap Finn, the Duke and the Dauphin, slavery, St. Petersburg and the other river towns, or America itself.

2

The account which follows analyses a half-dozen or so key
sequences in *Huckleberry Finn*, each linked into and building
upon and confirming the other and indicative of the novel's
overall moral design. First, St. Petersburg itself as fictional
and moral terrain: the world *Huckleberry Finn* ushers us into
only ostensibly carries over from *The Adventures of Tom Sawyer*,
the border-state Southern river town, primly respectable,
outwardly cosy, and still presided over by its Judge Thatchers,

Aunt Pollies and Widow Douglases. For though abrim with a kind of Sunday School rectitude, its surface social good-orderliness barely conceals the great pockets of violence within. It harbours among other things feuding, drunken rage, threats to women, lynch-law, and above all, slaveholding. This St. Petersburg, in other words, exists at barely a generation's remove from an anything-goes frontier lawlessness. Far from simply extending the *Tom Sawyer* backdrop, it might be thought more closely twinned with the Dawson's Landing of *Pudd'nhead Wilson*, a town also almost intolerably bored with itself and whose emblem Twain makes the pampered, sun-contented cat, 'asleep and peaceful'. Excitement, of any kind, violent or not, clearly will prove welcome, and excitement it gets: a 'murder'; an escaped slave; and justice to be meted out on the ancestral equation of white domination over black.

All of this Twain wonderfully foreshadows in Tom Sawyer's gang and derring-do rituals. For Tom, and his fellow fantasists, by their games of chivalry-in-small and Southern Romance, point us two ways at once: indeed backwards into the novel *Tom Sawyer* and the nostalgic, releasing power of childhood play; but also, and altogether more soberly, forwards, by anticipating (and aping) the codes of the St. Petersburg adult community. Tom's acting-out, his 'oaths' and requirements about 'the correct thing to do' (10) could hardly work to better purpose. For what in Tom's terms amounts to 'excitement'— the graveyard caper, the casual imagining of robberies, murder and rescues, the tricking of the grown 'boy' in the form of Nigger Jim—will all have their counterparts in the journey Huck and Jim undergo down-river from Jackson's Island. Where Twain especially triumphs is in making sure we sense not so much a changed St. Petersburg, but a changed Huck Finn, that is, a Huck who has his doubts about the charades and is dubbed as a consequence a 'perfect sap-head' (14), who is conspicuously less Tom's acquiescent first lieutenant than the son of Pap Finn (himself previously thought no more than the town's joke drunk rather than a thoroughly dangerous redneck and racist thug suffering the DTs), and the Huck who shows his unSawyerish savvy in later recognizing that a female drowned body floats face downwards.

Huck, thus, is made to point to his own impending passage-out, first from the 'smothery' gentility of the Douglas/Watson menagerie, then from the Tom Sawyer domain (to which he returns in pointed contrast in the Phelps Farm sequence) and finally from his own father's brute unfatherliness in locking him up and threatening injury in hopes of getting his hands on the treasure from the Cave. Huck's escape, thereby, blends crucially into Jim's. The pair, boy and man (terms in this context ironically interchangeable), 'free' outcast and freedom-seeking slave, personify two classic American refugees from the prevailing order. Nor, at any point, does Twain allow Huck to be thought some conscious avenging angel. Quite the reverse: Huck throughout goes on speaking the language he has been taught, about uppety niggers, 'Ablition', Conscience and the like. He also assumes that all slaves are the 'children' of required stereotype, trickable and ever prey to superstition and therefore objects of fun. The more Huck's river experience contradicts the language he speaks, however, and the assumptions which have shaped it, the more formidable becomes the moral power of Twain's irony.

The first live intrusion into this St. Petersburg undisturbed moral cosiness with its important Aunt Polly–Tom Sawyer axis occurs with the arrival of Pap Finn. Both in talk and demeanour he incarnates poor-white Southernness, an object of embarrassment to his social betters yet of potential salvation. The behaviour is all authentic viciousness and his talk shows its paces not only in the homespun witty snarl (his derision of Huck's ability to read and new clothes, for instance), but in the set-part he plays of Reformed Drunkard before the new judge's Temperance. Huck may chafe against Sunday School piety and the like. Twain makes Pap use it graphically against itself. For where his hypocrisy is painfully explicit, not to say funny, St. Petersburg's is modulated and masked in provincial high manners.

Pap amounts to a virtuoso portrait, with just enough of Huck himself in his make-up to prevent him from becoming the gargoyle. His contempt for the St. Petersburg 'quality' is palpable. He talks a ready violence and racism; indeed his whole existence hovers dangerously on a brink between life and death, his own and also Huck's. Each beating and threat and drunken outbreak could easily turn him into the murderer of his own son. In fact and as local myth he truly vacillates between a figure of life and one of death. The town at first has reason to think him drowned but he reappears on the news of Huck's gold; when Huck first sees him in 'his own self' (17), he might be an apparition become human flesh; in his temporary new-found temperance he professes all the signs of the 'born-again' Prodigal Son; at a later stage, Huck by faking his own death throws suspicion on both Pap and Jim as his killer; and Pap in his turn imagines Huck as his killer or Angel of Death. Finally, when Pap does drown, it is Jim who prevents Huck from seeing the water-logged corpse, a true act of fathering. The whole intricate father-son, son-father paradigm Twain works through with consummate tact.

As, too, the rogue Southerner—hobo, redneck, and barely controlled alcoholic—in almost everything he says Pap also makes explicit the communal lie which passes as a rationale for slavery. Slaves are property, sub-human and necessary commodities. Therefore, backed by selective quotations from the Bible and a most careful sexual ranking-system, slave-ownership can be discussed in the defensive terms of invest-ment, studding, disposal and the general good management of resources. Those, like Jim, who have been allowed out of the field and into the house, have suitably been de-individuated into Aunts and Uncles, amiable domestics. Typically, how-ever, Jim himself has his own family and children, all tenanted out and likely at any time to sale down the river. Thus, when in a characteristic outburst Pap drunkenly reports having seen a light-skinned Ohio freedman, he splutters into a diatribe whose comedy of outrage makes sobering parody. The language has all to do with rights, especially rights of property and the vote which to Pap's untutored eyes are being violated in full view, and which, though expressed more decorously, are also those of St. Petersburg:

> Oh, yes, this is a wonderful govment, wonderful. Why, looky here. There was a free nigger there, from Ohio; a mulatter, most as white as a white man. He had the whitest shirt on you ever see, too, and the shiniest hat; and there ain't a man in that town that's got as fine clothes as what he had; and he had a gold watch and chain, and a silver-headed cane—the awfulest old gray-headed nabob in the State. And what do you think? they

said he was a p'fessor in a college, and could talk all kinds of languages, and knowed everything. And that ain't the wust. They said he could *vote*, when he was at home. Well, that let me out. Thinks I, what is the country a-coming to? It was 'lection day, and I was just about to go and vote, myself, if I warn't too drunk to get there; but when they told me there was a State in this country where they'd let that nigger vote, I drawed out. I says I'll never vote agin. Them's the very words I said; they all heard me; and the country may rot for all me—I'll never vote agin as long as I live. And to see the cool way of that nigger—why, he wouldn't a give me the road if I hadn't shoved him out o' the way. I says to the people, why ain't this nigger put up at auction and sold?—that's what I want to know. And what do you reckon they said? Why, they said he couldn't be sold till he'd been in the State six months, and he hadn't been there that long yet. There now—that's a specimen. They call that a govment that can't sell a free nigger till he's been in the State six months. Here's a govment that calls itself a govment, and lets on to be a govment, and thinks it is a govment, and yet's got to set stock-still for six whole months before it can take ahold of a prowling, thieving, infernal, white-shirted free nigger, and—. (24–5)

The inspired confusion and double-think barely need comment, except to say that Twain knew convention did not permit the full verbal obscenity of a Pap Finn to get into print. The revolving cluster of 'free', 'sold', 'white' and 'nigger' will echo throughout the novel: whether in Huck's mouth ('*I* warn't to blame, because *I* didn't run Jim off from his rightful owner' (75)); Jim's own ('I owns myself, en I's wuth eight hun'd dollars. I wish I had de money, I wouldn't want no mo' (41)); or even in the version of things which allows that 'Tom Sawyer had gone and took all that trouble and both to set a nigger free!' (242). It cannot escape notice, furthermore, that if Pap's and these other expressions of confused property language work half-comically, St. Petersburg in the form of the Widow proposes nothing less than literally to sell Jim for 800 dollars, and that the sorry drama of slave-ownership goes on even into death as Jim is 'freed' in accordance with the Widow's will. For all their fugitive status, both Huck and Jim, and Pap behind them, are embroiled in a murderous property war, white over black, parent over child. The genius of creating a speech like Pap's lies in important part in throwing the moral response upon the reader, each turn of phrase to be deciphered as referring back into a St. Petersburg South willing to trade in human stock on the same untroubled standard it preaches its Sunday School pieties.

3

So thrown together, Huck in escape from his father and Jim 'run off' (38) to avoid being sold down the river by the 'Old Missus', the pair begin the journey which will take them down the Mississippi and even more towards each other. Both will be revealed as implicated in 'murder': Huck in attempting to fake his own death (unsqueamishly having stuck the pig and used its blood as evidence) and Jim ironically as Huck's suspected assassin. From death, thus, they find in each other resources for life. But theirs is a kinship free of coyness or sentimentality. Huck willingly goes on playing upon Jim as a superstitious darkie while Jim sees in Huck a 'hanting', a white ghost back from the shades. Further, Huck's idiom continues to reveal him using St. Petersburg language against itself:

> People would call me a low down Ablitionist and despise me for keeping mum—but that don't make no difference. I ain't agoing to tell, and I aint agoing back there anyways. (38)

This is given as an instinctual assurance to Jim, who cites 'a nigger trader' out to buy him and his own confused efforts to get rich by investing in 'stock', which he thinks means cattle rather than human and capital shares. His comic degradation of the language again richly underscores the degradation which passes as the normal language of value in St. Petersburg and its neighbouring slave territory. Perhaps the dead man they find (44), stripped of his clothes and shot in the back ('too gashly' says Jim), offers a form of epitaph to their own former selves, their mutual 'deaths' in St. Petersburg.

For at Jackson's Island, they inaugurate the bond which will carry them down the Mississippi—into both its life-enhancing powers and also its mists, eddies and array of shoreline threats. But it is a bond which though it must be

141

earned and contend against odds like the fact that Huck causes Jim to get stung by a rattler and later tricks him into thinking him dead in the fog and returned as a ghost, will at least be of their own uncoerced making. And having killed one identity in St. Petersburg, Huck launches (as does Jim in fact) upon a series of others, the first of which has him playing a girl, one who can neither thread a needle or catch in female fashion and whose name under the shrewd but benign questioning of Mrs. Loftus finally conflates into 'Sarah Mary Williams George Elexander Peters' (53). The 'acting out', great fun in itself, again moves on from Tom Sawyerism, however. It reveals the unfantasized threat at hand—that Jim is suspected of Pap's murder (as loaded a paradox as any in the book) and that they have not in truth floated out of St. Petersburg's reach at all. Fleeing back to Jim, Huck breaks through historic racial ban, colour and age, and offers a moment of crucial mutuality: 'Git up and hump yourself, Jim! There ain't a minute to lose. They're after us!' (54). The force of 'us' in this context cannot be underplayed. Huck and Jim by what they are and what they now propose strike at the deepest prohibitions of their culture.

It therefore comes as perfectly appropriate that throughout Chapter XII (and again Chapter XIX) Twain offers the most flawless of pastoral idylls, two beings set against a momentarily benign Mississippi river and for an interval freed of all false 'sivilization' and 'smotheriness'. The poise of Twain's writing is manifest:

> It was kind of solemn, drifting down the big still river, laying on our backs and looking up at the stars, and we didn't ever feel like talking loud, and it warn't often that we laughed only a little kind of a low chuckle. We had mighty good weather, as a general thing, and nothing ever happened to us at all, that night, nor the next, nor the next.
>
> Every night we passed towns, some of them away up on black hillsides, nothing but just a shiny bed of lights, not a house you could see. The fifth night we passed St. Louis, and it was like the whole world lit up. In St. Petersburg they used to say there was twenty or thirty thousand people in St. Louis, but I never believed it till I see that wonderful spread of lights at two o'clock that still night. There warn't a sound there; everybody was asleep. (55–6)

The spiritual ease represented by the nightime drift of the Mississippi is again met with after Huck's encounters in the Shepherdson/Grangerford feud, raft and river as sanctuaries against the murderous deadlock of Southern code behaviour:

> I never felt easy till the raft was below there and out in the middle of the Mississippi. Then we hung up our signal lantern, and judged that we was free and safe once more. I hadn't had a bite to eat since yesterday; so Jim he got out some corn-dodgers and buttermilk, and pork and cabbage, and greens—there ain't nothing in the world so good, when it's cooked right—and whilst I eat my supper we talked, and had a good time. I was powerful glad to get away from the feuds, and so was Jim to get away from the swamp. We said there warn't no home like a raft, after all. Other places do seem so cramped up and smothery, but a raft don't. You feel mighty free and easy and comfortable on a raft. . . .
>
> Sometimes we'd have that whole river all to ourselves for the longest time. Yonder was the banks and the islands, across the water; and maybe a spark—which was a candle in a cabin window—and sometimes on the water you could see a spark or two—on a raft or a scow, you know; and maybe you could hear a fiddle or a song coming over from one of them crafts. It's lovely to live on a raft. (98–101)

The 'down-home' food—corn-dodgers, pork, cabbage and greens and the like eaten against the ebb of the river—again offers an outward sign of inward grace. The 'other places' which seem so 'cramped up and smothery' belong on shore and with 'sivilization'. Between Huck and Jim, free and safe and with the whole river to themselves, there exists by contrast undeniable civilization.

Not that the Mississippi itself is projected as an unchanging, benign deific spirit. Far from it. Apart from its potential natural dangers, it has no means of resisting the intruding corruptions of the shore. The Duke and Dauphin will get aboard the raft. A river steamer will run the raft down. The river will carry fever and several corpses as well as slave and other different illicit freight. Around it, too, besides Pap, the Duke and Dauphin, the Shepherdsons and Grangerfords, and Colonel Sherburn, assemble a whole riff-raff of *canailles*, robbers, murderers, sneak-thieves and would-be lynchers.

And as if to confirm that the Mississippi can also be a Melvilleian theatre of false 'confidence', after Chapter XII has given the account of drifting down-river, Huck and Jim come upon the aftermath of a robbery and the murder of one of the gang-members (59–60). In the escape, Huck once more takes the defensive manoeuvre of pretending to be what he is not (in this case the distressed son of 'pap, and man, and sis' (63)). That the wreck at the centre of all this action should be the *Walter Scott*, the admired literary voice of Romance and to whom Twain once acerbically ascribed responsibility for the ruin of the South, adds further ironic point.

The river again contributes to Huck's education when (in Chapter XV) he gets separated from Jim in the fog. Playing on received stereotype, he tricks Jim into thinking the whole episode a dream. The assumption rests upon the idea of Jim as enshrouded by voodoo, 'conjure', still not free of the Tom Sawyer bric-à-brac. In seeing through the hoax, Jim chastises Huck, and his words—suitably cast in dialect—assume quite devastating moral authority. Pointing to the debris which has attached itself to the raft, he says:

> 'When I got all wore out wid work, en wid de callin' for you, en went to sleep, my heart wuz mos' broke bekase you wuz los', en I didn't k'yer no mo' what become er me en de raf'. En when I wake up en fine you back agin', all safe en soun', de tears come en I could a got down on my knees an kiss' yo' foot I's so thankful. En all you wuz thinkin 'bout wuz how you could make a fool uv ole Jim wid a lie. Dat truck dah is *trash*; en trash is what people is dat puts dirt on de head er dey fren's en makes 'en ashamed.'
>
> Then he got up slow, and walked to the wigwam, and went in there, without saying anything but that. But that was enough. It made me feel so mean I could almost kissed *his* foot to get him to take it back.
>
> It was fifteen minutes before I could work myself up to go and humble myself to a nigger—but I done it, and I warn't ever sorry for it afterwards, neither. I didn't do him no more mean tricks, and I wouldn't done that one if I'd a knowed it would make him feel that way. (73–4)

Learning that Jim 'would feel that way', like kissing his foot, marks feeling that cuts into, and through, 'sivilization' like a knife. Huck secures his dignity in the account he gives, but only as it is released to him morally by Jim's better, tested dignity in the face of all conceivable odds.

4

From this Twain directs us even more certainly to the moral centre of *Huckleberry Finn*, and inevitably the focus has to do with slavery, both as historic nineteenth-century American fact, and as the expression of other forms of 'enslavement'— notably the ruling illusions of white racial ascendancy and Southern chivalry. Whatever Huck has come to 'know' through Jim, he still has to contend against the internalized voice of Conscience, the language of St. Petersburg with its base in slaveholding and which he has been taught to speak by hallowed white-supremacist tradition. Given Huck's increasing divisions, between heart and head, instinct and culture, his monologue as to the implications of aiding Jim to Free Territory underscores how deeply 'sivilization' contradicts his natural civilization of the heart. His language, despite itself, works to the contrary of his regional and Sunday School training with its fundamentalist theology and rhetoric:

> Jim said it made him all over trembly and feverish to be so close to freedom. Well, I can tell you it made me all over trembly and feverish, too, to hear him, because I begun to get it through my head that he *was* most free—and who was to blame for it? Why me. I couldn't get that out of my conscience, no how nor no way. It got to troubling me so I couldn't rest; I couldn't sat still in one place. It hadn't ever come home to me before, what this thing was that I was doing. But now it did; and it staid with me, and scorched me more and more. I tried to make out to myself that *I* warn't to blame, because *I* didn't run Jim off from his rightful owner; but it warn't no use, conscience up and says, every time, 'But you knowed he was running for his freedom, and you could a paddled ashore and told somebody.' That was so—I couldn't get round that, noway. That was where it pinched. Conscience says to me, 'What had poor Miss Watson done to you, that you could see her nigger go off right under your eyes and never say one single word? What did that poor old woman do to you, that you could treat her so mean? Why, she tried to learn you your book, she tried to learn you

145

your manners, she tried to be good to you in every way she knowed how. *That's* what she done.' (74–5)

Conscience operates inside Huck as the expression of a Bible-sanctioned Protestant ethic of property. In allying himself with Jim, he dangerously allies himself against 'siviliza-tion' as taught by Miss Watson through the Bible ('your book') and 'manners', not that either Bible or manners inhibits her from proposing to sell Jim any more than they do the Duke and the Dauphin who later traffick in him for 'forty dirty dollars'. The inversion of Huck's moral language gains still greater point when Jim vows to 'buy his wife' (75) out of slavery and with her then to buy their children back. He also adds, his language at one with Huck's, that 'if their master wouldn't sell them, they'd get an Ab'litionist to go and steal them' (75). What remains for Huck is in effect to make his moral instincts over into his own 'property'.

Twain continues this language of false conscience supremely. It is language which blends Divine Sanction into slave-holding and recalls the earnest moralizing of pulpit and Sunday School. Providence speaks to Huck on the side of slavery and against 'Ab'lition':

> And to think of *me*! It would get all around, that Huck Finn helped a nigger to get his freedom; and if ever I was to see anybody from that town again, I'd be ready to get down and lick his boots for shame. That's just the way: a person does a low-down thing, and then he don't want to take no conse-quences of it. Thinks as long as he can hide it, it ain't no disgrace. That was my fix exactly. The more I studied about this, the more my conscience went to grinding me, and the more wicked and low-down and ornery I got to feeling. And at last, when it hit me all of a sudden that here was the plain hand of Providence slapping me in the face and letting me know my wickedness was being watched all the time from up there in heaven, whilst I was stealing a poor old woman's nigger that hadn't ever done me no harm, and now was showing me there's One that's always on the lookout, and ain't agoing to allow no such miserable doings to go only so fur and no further, I most dropped in my tracks I was so scared. Well, I tried the best I could to kinder soften it up somehow for myself, by saying that I was brung up wicked, and so I warn't so much to blame; but something inside of me kept saying, 'There was the Sunday

school, you could a gone to it; and if you'd a done it they'd a
learnt you, there, that people that acts as I'd been acting about
that nigger goes to everlasting fire.' (178)

The inversions and upside-down morality come over dramatically: Bible-belt Christianity in the service of slaveholding
and its agency the Sunday School and adoptive Miss Watsons.
To challenge this equation is for Huck to be 'brung up
wicked', to be made to signal the gap between heart and
conscience.

Nonetheless, he writes a letter to Miss Watson about Jim,
feeling 'good and washed free of sin for the first time I had ever
felt so in my life' (179), his language ironically that of the
born-again, saved Sinner. But Twain has him set against such
salvation the counter-image of Jim whom he proposes returning to his rightful owner. The passage which then follows
locates the absolute moral lodestone of the novel:

> somehow I couldn't seem to strike no places to harden me
> against him but only the other kind. I'd see him standing my
> watch on top of his'n, stead of calling me, so I could go on
> sleeping; and see him how glad he was when I came back out of
> the fog; and when I come to him again in the swamp up there
> where the feud was; and such-like times; and would always call
> me honey, and pet me, and do everything he could think of for
> me, and how good he always was; and at last I struck the time I
> saved him by telling the men we had small-pox aboard, and he
> was ever so grateful, and said I was the best friend old Jim ever
> had in the world, and the *only* one he's got now; and then I
> happened to look around, and see that paper.
>   It was a close place. I took it up, and held it in my hand. I
> was a trembling because I'd got to decide, forever, betwixt two
> things, and I knowed it. I studied a minute, sort of holding my
> breath, and then says to myself:
>   'All right, then, I'll *go* to hell'—and tore it up. (179–80)

The 'hell' to which Huck consigns himself, and which has
taught him to speak as he does, draws self-incriminatingly upon
slavery, St. Petersburg and its institutions, and the elaborate
hypocrisy by which slave-holding historically attempted justification. Huck's choice, 'betwixt two things', at one obvious
level is whether to save or damn Jim. In fact it is as much and
possibly more whether to save or damn himself. It amounts to

the choice for heart over head, civilization over 'sivilization'. And in opting for Jim, wittingly or not, he opts to repudiate the massive double-standard of a South founded on slavery and using its Bible Belt Christianity and 'manners' to aid and abet. To go to a 'hell' appointed by this historic order is to parody, and outflank, just such a South, as in like manner the kinship Huck learns with Jim transcends all the Southern-folks false kin and gentility on which he has been raised. And if the moral point still has not been grasped, a moment later and once more in a language which doubles back on itself Twain has Huck resolve 'to go to work to steal Jim out of slavery again' (180).

5

In linking the Jackson's Island episodes to that in which Huck writes his letter to Miss Watson, I have, of course, been contracting a fair amount of the novel; thus if 'hell' is Huck's destination we need to consider in some particularity how he journeys there. One of the earliest testing grounds in this raft odyssey has to do with the Shepherdson-Grangerford feud, Southern chivalry unpacked for its licence to kill with no ironic holds barred.

'Col. Grangerford was a gentleman, you see. He was a gentleman all over; and so was his family' (89): so Huck defers to the assumed high gentry of the shoreline Mississippi world. But beneath the Grangerford pose, and its nemesis in the Shepherdson clan, lies jungle law, stylized and costumed to be sure, but jungle law all the same. Huck enters this terrain under yet another name, that of George Jackson. He quickly begins to spot the clues to the spuriousness of Grangerford aristocracy: the mock-baronialism of the estate; the ill-assorted 'parlors' and the grotesque clock on the mantle-piece; the 'big outlandish parrot' (85) made of chalk and the Dickensian crockery; the oil-cloth table cover with its 'red and blue spread-eagle' (85); the library (the Bible and *Pilgrim's Progress* pre-eminent) 'full of beautiful stuff and poetry' (86); and the ceremonial portraiture, a mixture of the pretentious and the maudlin. The whole could easily be the detail from an Ambrose Bierce parody. The culmination of this funny-grotesque décor is Emmeline Grangerford and her scrap-book poems, especially

148

the Ode to Stephen Dowling 'that fell down a well and was drownded' (87).

The impact of all this reads comically enough on its own terms. But matters turn sharply grimmer with each ritual killing and revenge, especially that of Huck's new friend Buck. Light comedy especially darkens when Huck hears the chant, 'Kill them, Kill them!' (97), and when, as increasingly happens when he leaves the raft for the shore, he feels 'sick' (97). This amounts to Tom Sawyer's play world transformed into reality: one of Chivalry which actually causes death; picture-book romance which becomes tawdrily lifelike; and Honour to be revealed as coded, mindless violence. Little wonder the observation has occasionally been made that the Code of the West was born in the South, something to which Owen Whister's *The Virginian* (1902) and Walter Van Tilburg Clark's *The Ox-bow Incident* (1940) both importantly attest. Huck finally, once more, has to take the evidence of his senses over Southern myth when he sees the gang killing. Reality now becomes the nightmare, the threatening dream:

> I wished I hadn't ever come ashore that night, to see such things. I ain't ever going to get shut of them—lots of times I dream about them. (97–8)

No sooner have Huck and Jim broken free of the feud, and with but a moment's respite aboard the raft (Chapter XIX), than they find themselves up against the Duke and the Dauphin, confidence-men *par excellence*. In them, as in Pap Finn earlier, Twain blends a mean, darker vein into all the fun and verbal knock-about: the pair will lie, cheat, steal, put Jim out for sale, mock the impaired, and take every advantage of backwoods Arkansas credulity. If they raise a laugh, it cannot be other than an uneasy one, humour adroitly angled to cause radical discomfort.

The Duke and Dauphin first appear in the guise of 'aristos', fake European royalty out to con and win the deference of a supposedly levelling frontier society. They also serve as joke-forms of the Judge Thatcher-Miss Watson-Aunt Polly world: one purports to have been a teacher, a lecturer and 'medical' mesmerist, the other a preacher and missionary. Both can work a crowd, talk in the style of the professional, and flatter and deceive, whether as men of medicine, the law, temperance, quality theatre people or simply visiting 'kin'. Their mastery of the spoken word situates them always 'on stage', both in reality as in the Wilks Farm caper or in the tented shows and greasepaint of the mock-Shakespeare, David Garrick and Edmund Kean the Elder (126) reincarnated in the form of actors playing other actors. Huck, as always, offers the monitoring response:

> It didn't take me long to make up my mind that these two liars warn't no kings nor dukes, at all, but just low-down humbugs and frauds. But I never said nothing, never let on; kept it to myself; it's the best way; then you don't have no quarrels, and don't get into no trouble. If they wanted us to call them kings and dukes, I hadn't no objections, 'long as it would keep peace in the family; and it warn't no use to tell Jim, so I didn't tell him. If I never learnt nothing else out of pap, I learnt that the best way to get along with his kind of people is to let them have their own way. (106)

Pap's 'kind of people' locates them perfectly, parodic incarnations of the Franklinesque self-made man. Huck, in fact, in a yet further defensive gesture, almost matches their manipulative powers when he tells them the weepy tall-tale of his drowned family from Pike County Missouri, one confidence feat for another. These interwoven masquerades culminate in the mock-Shakespeare, a Twainian slap against bardology but also at small-town credulity which amazes (as Oscar Wilde found on his American tours) at theatre lights and sound over all possible sense. In the midst of the rehearsals and shenanegans, there takes place the Boggs-Sherburn episode (Boggs needs further comment), again actual and murderously 'live' theatre to contrast with the riverside shows. In the comic garbled Shakespeare Twain in part takes revenge on behalf of every schoolchild obliged to learn the bard as scripture. But he also turns the occasion to moral advantage when he has the Duke and Dauphin dress Jim up as King Lear:

> [The Duke] dressed Jim up in King Lear's outfit—it was a long curtain-calico gown, and a white horse-hair wig and whiskers; and then he took his theatre-paint and painted Jim's face and hands and ears and neck all over a dead dull solid blue, like a man that's been drownded nine days. Blamed if he

warn't the horriblest looking outrage I ever see. Then the duke
took and wrote out a sign on a shingle so—
Sick Arab—but harmless when not out of his head. (132)

The comedy once more cuts two ways. Jim has indeed reason
to be 'out of his head', and though meant to be got up as
spectacle, who better to be thought a Mississippi king, 'blue-
blood' royal, or Muslim notable?

The Wilks episode thus acts as a transfer from stage to life.
In having them impersonate the two heirs, Twain rings the
moral changes on property, inheritance, false and true owner-
ship, so that life becomes art but this kind of art a kind of
anti-life. It is also art which carefully negotiates between the
comic and the black-farcical: the funereal pieties which hover
around death and burial; the jokes about the hair-lipped girls;
the Feydeau theatricality of the buried inheritance. Huck's
response strikes the moral note: 'It was enough to make a body
ashamed of the human race' (137). But right as that is, Twain
again reverses the process as the two 'Royal Nonesuch
rapscallions' (193) are tarred and feathered. Huck finds himself obliged to change sympathies:

> Well, it made me sick to see it; and I was sorry for them poor
> pitiful rascals, it seemed like I couldn't ever feel any hardness
> against them any more in the world. It was a dreadful thing to
> see. Human beings *can* be awful cruel to one another. (194)

This supreme understatement looks once more to the reader to
complete the full moral import of the entire escapade.

The Sherburn matter (Chapters XXI and XXII) also plays
one moral end of the spectrum against the other. First, and
with Huck as our vantage-point, Boggs, the town-drunk,
watched fearfully by his daughter, lets drink get the better of
him and having challenged the Colonel is duly gunned down,
all in accordance with the code of the duel. The pendulum
then swings the other way. The crowd rises, mob-like, resolved
to lynch the Colonel. His speech outfaces them, a voice, as
Henry Nash Smith and others have rightly noted, which
anticipates the sardonicism of the Twain who later wrote *What
Is Man?* (1906) and the even grimmer *The Mysterious Stranger*
(post., 1916).[6] Huck's observing of both the speaker and those
spoken to amounts to still another implicit moral call to arms:

The idea of *you* lynching anybody! It's amusing. The idea of
you thinking you had pluck enough to lynch a *man*! Because
you're brave enough to tar and feather poor friendless cast-out
women that come along here, did that make you think you had
grit enough to lay your hands on a *man*? Why, a man's safe in
the hands of ten thousand of your kind—as long as it's day-time
and you're not behind him. (123)

Boggs, the mob, and Sherburn, play mutual supporting rôles
in the drama. Only Huck moves on and out of this moral and
historical stasis.

6

Having so 'journeyed' through the Mississippi's fogs and eddies
and through their counterparts in shoreline society, Huck
arrives at Phelps Farm. Immediately, he is forced into a last
metamorphosis, not this time as 'Sarah Mary Williams George
Elexander Peters', or 'George Jackson', or the orphan survivor
of a drowned family, or the stage-hand, or the 'low-down
Ab'litionist', but of all people as Tom Sawyer, a prior self left
well behind and at odds with the river-journey undertaken in
Jim's company. These last ten chapters understandably have
long been a source of unease, and Twain's difficulties in finding
a right ending to *Huckleberry Finn* are well documented.[7] For
some they usefully support the contrast of Tom's play world
with Huck's real world. For others, they reveal an imaginative
failure of nerve, Twain's inability to deliver on the moral logic
of the novel—for instance, by avoiding the patent sentimentality of a Miss Watson deathbed repentance and by *now*
selling Jim down the river, in the historically likelier manner of
Pudd'nhead Wilson's ending.

Parts, to be sure, are perfectly on line as in the following
exchange about a boat which has blown up on the river:

'Good gracious! Anybody hurt?'
'No'm. Killed a nigger.'
'Well, it's lucky; because sometimes people do get hurt.' (185)

But what are we to make of Huck's subsequent comment that
Jim was acceptable because he was 'white inside' (250)?
Further, the fantasy games which the real Tom introduces—

the false imprisonment and escape and the Count of Monte Cristo costume adventure—one suspects for most readers becomes wearing, though Tom's conversion of the bullet into a kind of charm nicely modulates between his own world and reality.

For Huck, finally, there can be only 'the Territory ahead', American time and space as yet for him unfilled by 'siviliza-tion'. Like his many American fictional compeers, he returns to Ishmaelism, unadoptable and 'lighting out'. When Jim, in the last thing he says, reveals that Pap Finn did truly die and not just disappear, it confirms Huck as both orphan and his own father and thus still further unadoptable by any new Aunt, Widow or St. Petersburg. Even through the imperfec-tions of the last chapters, Twain never lessens the projection of Huck as the live human embodiment of the civilized heart. His, after all, represents a morality beyond 'sivilization' and which draws upon the tested bond with Jim and the pro-foundly civilized memory of 'there warn't no home like a raft' (99).

NOTES

1. Ernest Hemingway, *Green Hills of Africa* (New York: Scribners, 1935).
2. Twain, that is, as a humorist in the vein of pseudonymous comic writers like Petroleum V. Nasby (David Ross Locke) or South-West tall-story makers like Augustus Baldwin Longstreet, George Washington Harris, Thomas Bangs Thorpe or Henry Clay Lewis. See, for instance, an anthology like *Humor of the Old Southwest*, ed. Hennig Cohen and William B. Dillingham (Boston: Riverside Press, Houghton Mifflin, 1964), and the still classic study, *American Humor: A Study in the National Character* by Constance Rourke (New York: Harcourt, Brace and Co., 1931).
3. Herman Melville, 'Hawthorne and his Mosses', *Literary World*, 17 and 24 August 1850.
4. For useful comparisons between *Huckleberry Finn* and *The Catcher in the Rye*, see Charles Kaplan, 'Holden and Huck: Odysseys of Youth', *College English*, XVIII (November 1956), pp. 76–80; Edgar Branch, 'Mark Twain and J. D. Salinger: A Study in Literary Continuity', *American Quarterly*, IX (Summer 1957); and Arvin R. Wells, 'Huck Finn and Holden Caulfield: The Situation of the Hero', *Ohio University Review*, II (1960), pp. 31–42.

5. Page references throughout are to *Adventures of Huckleberry Finn*, ed. Henry Nash Smith (Boston: Riverside Press, Houghton Mifflin, 1958), p. 3.
6. See, especially, Henry Nash Smith, *Mark Twain, The Development of a Writer* (Cambridge; Harvard University Press, 1962); also Walter Blair, *Mark Twain and Huck Finn* (Berkeley: University of California Press, 1960); Van Wyck Brooks, *The Ordeal of Mark Twain*, rev. ed. (New York: Dutton, 1923), and Bernard de Voto, *Mark Twain's America* (Boston: Little, Brown, 1932).
7. See Henry Nash Smith (op. cit.), and for a reconstructed version of the novel, John Seelye: *The True Adventures of Huckleberry Finn* (Evanston: Northwestern University Press, 1970).

I would again like to acknowledge the award of an American Council of Learned Societies Fellowship during 1981–82 when much of this essay was first drafted.

6

Mark Twain and the Future of Picaresque

by LYALL POWERS

Associating Mark Twain with the term 'picaresque' will strike
no reader as an original idea. Twain on several occasions
conspicuously encouraged that association—or so it has
seemed. But it has usually been a loose and perhaps
irresponsible association, as it usually connects Twain and
Cervantes. That in itself is acceptable enough: Cervantes'
'Exemplary Novel' *Rinconete and Cortadillo* (1613) is truly a
picaresque tale of the adventures of two boys who are more
than faintly anticipatory of Twain's famous pair, Tom and
Huck.[1] It is not with this tale in mind, however, that the
association is usually made, but with *Don Quixote*—and as a
paradigm of 'picaresque'. A footnote in a popular 'critical
edition' of *Adventures of Huckleberry Finn* is typical: it identifies
Don Quixote as 'the "hero" of Cervantes' picaresque narrative
(1605)'.[2] But perhaps that association and definition are not
altogether red herrings, for they may encourage us to attempt
to make distinctions that could prove useful: (1) to distinguish
between *Don Quixote* and the true picaresque novel: (2) to see
how that distinction might enable us to locate Twain's novels
in a particular literary tradition; and (3) to discover how such
a distinction can help clarify some problems in three of
Twain's major works—*The Adventures of Tom Sawyer, Adventures
of Huckleberry Finn*, and *A Connecticut Yankee in King Arthur's
Court.*

The picaresque novel begins properly with the Spanish works *Lazarillo de Tormes* (1554) and *Guzman de Alfarache* (1599, 1604), and continues in such non-Spanish works as *Moll Flanders* (1722), *Gil Blas* (1715, 1724, 1735), and *Roderick Random* (1748). The true picaresque novel is characterized by certain unmistakable features. It is the story of the peregrinations of a low-born hero, an alien obliged to live by his wits in order to survive in a hostile and hypocritical society. It is cast in the mould of autobiography, and thus involves a double time sequence—the time of the adventures recounted and the time of recounting them. That duality makes possible the moralizing implications of the autobiographer, particularly visible in *Guzman* and in the eighteenth-century, non-Spanish works. The dilemma of the picaro is that he must choose between conforming to the mores of the society in which he finds himself in order to survive, and adhering to what innate moral principles he may possess. Richard Bjornson aptly calls this dilemma the picaresque 'double-bind'.[3] The Spanish picaresque novel typically ends unhappily with the loss of the picaro to the pressure of social convention. The non-Spanish picaresque novels, on the other hand, typically end happily; the hero manages to remain true to the self and finally basks in the blessings of poetic justice.

A couple of pertinent distinctions need to be made between the line of true picaresque heroes and such characters as Nashe's Jacke Wilton, on the one hand, and Defoe's Moll Flanders on the other. Jacke Wilton's roguish behaviour is not motivated by the dire need that drives the true picaro; Wilton is a rogue for little more than his own amusement—and for that of the reader—in a kind of capriciousness. And Nashe's novel is not particularly interested in exposing and criticizing the mores of a society that is responsible for producing the picaro.[4] That implicit criticism of society is likewise mainly absent from Moll Flanders' narration. Moll does not suffer from the dilemma of the double-bind typical of picaresque heroes. In her case, the techniques necessary for survival are viewed as simply part of the way the world is made; her success in adapting herself to those ways is crowned with the poetic justice of her final peace and comfort. Moll's retrospective moralizing, Bjornson observes, 'obfuscates the real contradiction between her condemnation of criminality and her willingness to enjoy a fortune founded upon the profits of criminal activities' (p. 195).

It is instructive at this point to compare the final moral stance of Gil Blas and Roderick Random: having remained essentially faithful to their moral beings—in spite of whatever roguish vagaries they were guilty of during their adventures—they are worthy of their ultimate rewards. Roderick is much less tolerant of social mores than is Gil Blas, but neither indulges in Moll's moralistic self-justifications.

While the true picaresque hero for the most part accepts the status quo—at the time of his adventures—and devotes his energies to discovering how to fit into society, he does not typically enter into serious dialogue with its representatives; his struggle is not an ideological one—whatever his moral attitude may be (implicitly or explicitly) at the time when he sets down his autobiographical account—his struggle is for mere survival and acceptance.

> . . . the picaroon is always a lone wanderer, a true exile who never achieves authentic dialogue with other men because most of them distrust him and he distrusts them all, once he has acquired a little experience . . . though he deals with everyone and everyone deals with him. . . .[5]

In *Don Quixote* we find a distinct departure from the typical picaresque. In Cervantes' masterpiece the dilemma of the double-bind is significantly replaced by the Quixote-Sancho dialogue. In his 'mad' idealism, the Knight of the Mournful Countenance sets out to do battle with the evils of the world and strike his blows for goodness—in the manner dictated by the rules of behaviour he has found in the chivalric romances. His initial motivation, then, is distinctly different from that of the picaro. There is something of the true picaro's severe practicality in Sancho Panza, however. If Cervantes' novel sets in opposition the high idealism of Don Quixote and the common-sense practicality of Sancho, it is not simply to stage a contest between the two. It has become a commonplace of Cervantian criticism to recognize that in the continuing dialogue between Quixote and Sancho there is a gradual reciprocal modification and transformation of the two—the 'sanchification' of Quixote and the 'quixotification' of Sancho. The novel *tends toward* this necessary compromise (quite like that attempted in Molière's *Le Misanthrope*).

As several astute critics have made clear, at the basis of this Cervantian dialogue lies what Harry Levin has characterized as the conflicting claims of literature and life, and what Leo Spitzer called 'the problem of the book'. 'Cervantes' formula', Levin explains,

> is nothing more nor less than a recognition of the differences between verses and reverses, between words and deeds . . . in short between literary artifice and that real thing which is life itself. But literary artifice is the only means that a writer has at his disposal. How else can he convey his impression of life? Precisely by discrediting those means, by repudiating the air of bookishness in which any book is inevitably wrapped.

Spitzer's comments carry the point a step further:

> . . . that hybrid genre of the novel is born of poetry and of something else, of an extrapoetic factor, of a tendency to encroach upon life, along with an inborn striving toward pure art, a nostalgic yearning back to epic beauty. The older form of narration is everywhere epic poetry, epic poetry that maintains itself in the sphere of pure art, of a stylization of life, without any direct imitation or caricature of life. . . .
>
> But the novel can offer a vicarious life to sap our actual life, and produce an illusion in which the things narrated appear as present, and the lines between romance and reality are blurred. The prosaic form contributes to this illusion, making romance appear as authentic, unaltered reality. . . .[6]

Most critics recognize, finally, that Quixote's 'madness' is confined to regarding the books of chivalric romance as true historical accounts.

In the notes for his lectures on *Don Quixote*, Thornton Wilder was careful to insist that while Cervantes was satirizing Chivalric Romance he was *not* satirizing the ideal of chivalry, and that the 'madness' of Quixote lies in his carrying idealism too far. 'Quixotism', Wilder's notes explain, is making one's behaviour 'conform to rules obviously and joyously against reason'. He offers as examples of Quixotism Father Damien and Jeanne d'Arc but rather oddly adds that of Tom Sawyer freeing Jim.[7]

Since Olin Harris Moore's essay more than sixty years ago, the association of Twain and *Don Quixote* has been solidly if not carefully established.[8] Tom Sawyer, especially in his rôle in *Huckleberry Finn*, is cited as a quixotic figure—following, of course, the clear invitation in Chapter III, where Tom chides Huck for failing to recognize 'the parcel of Spanish merchants and rich A-rabs' with their 'sumter' mules laden with 'di'monds'[9]:

> I said why couldn't we see them, then? He said if I warn't so ignorant, but had read a book called "Don Quixote" I would know without asking.

Tom Sawyer behaves 'by the book', much as Don Quixote does, throughout his appearances in *Huckleberry Finn*; but we ought to remember (1) that that novel is Huck's auto-biography, and (2) that Huck begins his account by referring to *The Adventures of Tom Sawyer*.

In that earlier novel, Tom constantly relies on the various books of romance he has devoured as providing the rules that will effectively guide his behaviour. An important difference, however, is that Don Quixote lives 'by the book' because of his peculiar madness, while Tom does so as a child at play.[10] The fact that Tom's play is consistently a rehearsal for his 'real' action in the novel—romance regularly hardens into reality in *Tom Sawyer*—and thus finally earns him the acclaim of all St. Petersburg, indicates that Tom is meant to be regarded as in no sense mad and his 'play' as something not only serious but important for that society.[11]

Tom, the charming rascal (as Twain certainly regarded him in 1876, and evidently intended his readers to regard him), really has no quarrel with society. In spite of his apparently rebellious behaviour he is really society's darling—and that love is requited. He is 'all boy', a 'regular fellow', just what society wants (and will one day get as president—if it has not already). What qualities of the true picaro Tom seems to have put him in the category of Jacke Wilton or of Moll Flanders. He plays the rogue for the fun of it, not out of any dire need, as the famous whitewashing scene (Chapter II) indicates: his manipulating the boys into doing his chore and bamboozling them into paying for the privilege we regard as a harmless prank—to our shame: the same tendency there exhibited surfaces in the sequel when Tom undertakes to 'free' Jim. As for Moll Flanders, so for Tom there is no double-bind, he really does not need to internalize his society's values, for he has clearly been born already cherishing them.

There is of course the appearance of the quixotesque dialogue in *Tom Sawyer*, carried on between respectable and bookish Tom and 'the juvenile pariah of the village, Huckleberry Finn, son of the town drunkard'. The truly picaresque Huck plays Sancho to Tom's Quixote. The difference here is that Twain's novel does not at all strive toward a reciprocal modification as a result of that dialogue. The Tom-Huck opposition is, in truth, a contest to see whether or not Tom will overcome his regrettable attraction to the juvenile pariah and be able to redeem Huck for society and a civilized life. Of course Tom succeeds in 'saving' Huck, just as he plays a significant symbolic rôle in turning Joe into 'a good Indian'. The heuristic effect of the mythic shape of *The Adventures of Tom Sawyer* establishes Tom as Hero; descent into the lower world (McDougal's Cave) culminates when, on the third day, he arises again to the upper world with his blonde, blue-eyed consort, the $12,000 boon discovered (buried 'under the cross' and to be shared with Huck), the figure of evil (Joe) safely dead, and Huck soon to be a born-again 'regular fellow'—at least for the time being.[12] A distinctly non-Quixotesque ending.

Adventures of Huckleberry Finn exhibits most of the features of the true picaresque form. It is Huck's autobiography and thus has the typical dual-time sequence, although the distinction between the moment of the adventures and the moment of Huck's recording them is emphasized only in the concluding chapter. Huck is the outcast, still at bottom the alien even though he has been momentarily accepted by society as the novel opens. His leaving first the Widow Douglas and then Pap initiates the expression of Huck's double-bind dilemma. Henceforth, Huck's adventures are quite the equivalent of the picaro's attempt to find a place in society. Whether or not the series of adventures ought properly to be called a 'quest', it clearly indicates that Huck is fleeing from a tyranny, represented by both the Widow and Pap, and is seeking a place in society where he can exist free of that tyranny. His goal, thus, is freedom—and is quite the equivalent of Jim's. One would not readily call Huck's struggle with society an ideological one; he is simply seeking—like the typical picaro from Lazarillo onward—the means to survive.

Huck's double-bind is likewise typical; the question is whether or not he will forsake his own integrity and become society's creature. He typically accepts the status quo; he tries to become what society wants, for every alias Huck assumes is tested for society's approval—the Duke and King tell him who he is to be, and the Phelpses finally tell him who he is. Huck occasionally comments that people can be awful cruel to each other, but any moral judgement he makes is against himself—and made according to society's 'moral' standards. He is to that extent the victim of the socializing process, like Lazarillo de Tormes and Guzman de Alfarache. One sees evidence of this in the much discussed crucial scene (in Chapter XXXI) of Huck's decision not to turn in Jim—and the emphasis on the double-bind is quite apparent:

> It was a close place. I took it [the letter to Miss Watson] up, and held it in my hand. I was a-trembling, because I'd got to decide, forever, betwixt two things, and I knowed it. I studied a minute, sort of holding my breath, and then says to myself:
> 'All right, then, I'll *go* to hell'—and tore it up.

That decision prepares exactly for Huck's final decision in the novel—to light out for the Territory.

Huck's story, like that of the typical Spanish picaro, ends unhappily. The difference is that while the Spanish picaro is finally victim of the socializing process and has surrendered whatever 'self' he began with, Huck is 'lost' because he cannot finally be false to himself. Huck's driving independence is truly Emersonian; he must abide by the voice within him (i.e., expressly *not* his conscience—the voice of *learned* duty), which he all too readily admits to be the voice of the Devil but is at last the only voice he knows. Huck's last decision is, then, essentially like that of Edna Pontellier in Kate Chopin's *The Awakening*; he sacrifices his physical self in order to maintain the freedom of his spiritual self.

The events that immediately lead up to and precipitate that

final decision—beginning with the return of Tom to the scene of action—remind us that within the true picaresque form of *Adventures of Huckleberry Finn* is contained something of a quixotesque dialogue, with Tom as a kind of Don Quixote and Huck as Sancho Panza.[13] Here we find the persistence of the very dialogue that lies at the heart of *The Adventures of Tom Sawyer*; the only important difference is that Twain's sympathies have unmistakably shifted. And once again the aim is not to resolve the opposition between Tom and Huck by means of the quixotesque reciprocal modification, but to seek the victory of one of the two over the other. Yet, just as in *Don Quixote*, the crux of the dialogue focuses on the 'problem of the book'.

Much of the social satire in *Huckleberry Finn* (far more bitter satire than the mild and indulgent fun-poking in *Tom Sawyer*) is directed at particular social conventions, and not least at the Southern conventions of chivalry, founded—as Twain professed to believe—on the guidelines of Sir Walter Scott's romances and including, of necessity, the peculiar institution of black slavery. That society, as Susan K. Harris points out, values literacy highly:

> ... even the con men are marginally literate ... while Tom Sawyer, who is often seen as epitomizing the society, is not merely literate but widely read and an active thief of literary ideas for use in his adventures.[14]

In the long drawn out episode of freeing Jim—which James M. Cox wisely calls 'a unique cruelty in a book which depicts so much cruelty'[15]—Tom is once again performing by the book. And if this is play, it is the most deadly and irresponsible and inhumane kind of play; human lives (and particularly Jim's) are at stake. It is play that derives from a more baleful madness than Don Quixote's; and the fact that it is perpetrated by a boy does not mitigate it but makes it all the more chilling.

Huck does not seriously act to deter Tom, for the socialized Huck 'knows' that Tom (like the book-guided society he represents) is 'right'—just as he early knew that the failure to obtain a complete fishing tackle lay not in prayer but in himself ('I couldn't make it work'), would later know that in refusing to inform Miss Watson of the whereabouts of Jim he was condemning himself to Hell, and finally not that society is wrong but that he cannot fit himself into it. The quixotesque dialogue (basically the Cervantian 'problem of the book') nicely matches Huck's double-bind. When the only possible resolution for his dilemma is offered at the Phelpses' farm—where Huck 'becomes' Tom—the preparation is begun for Huck's final decision. That preparation is furthered by Tom's performance in freeing Jim. Huck at last recognizes that the freedom he has been seeking is not to be found—except at the cost of his own integrity and identity. If he does not at last 'reject' society (there is another scholarly quibble over that term), he certainly turns his back most definitely on society—on civilization as he has experienced it. His last words are surely quite lucidly unambiguous (the emphasis is mine):

> I reckon I got to light out for the Territory *ahead of the rest*, because Aunt Sally she's going to adopt me and *sivilize* me and *I can't stand it. I been there before.*

Once again there is no escape for Huck from the double-bind, no escape but continued flight to keep perpetually 'ahead of the rest'; there is no Cervantian compromise—no reciprocal modification—in Twain's version of the quixotesque dialogue. The people of 'the book' have triumphed again; this time, however, Twain makes that triumph tragic.

If *Adventures of Huckleberry Finn* provides a kind of 'clue' to an approach to that novel via Tom's specific mention of *Don Quixote*, there seems to be something tantalizingly similar in the early pages of *A Connecticut Yankee in King Arthur's Court*. In Chapter IV Hank Morgan comments on the earthy language to be heard at King Arthur's court, but explains that it did not surprise him: 'I had read "Tom Jones" and "Roderick Random" and other books of that kind. . . .' The phrase 'books of that kind' quite obviously means, in context, books in which Ladies and Gentlemen speak a racy lingo; but the two examples offered suggest another way of understanding the phrase. *Tom Jones* is of course a novel in the tradition of *Don Quixote*, a fact that Fielding takes pains to encourage his reader to recognize. Smollett's *Roderick Random* is just as clearly in the true picaresque tradition as I have been describing it.[16]

Whether or not Twain consciously intended the pairing to alert us to the traditions in which he was working with *Connecticut Yankee* (which I doubt), the pairing is yet usefully and provocatively there.

Although the novel uses a slight frame, provided by the immediate narrator, 'M.T.', it is principally the autobiography of Hank Morgan (and thus the similarity to Cervantes' *Cipion and Berganza* is worth noting). Here the double time sequence is heavily emphasized, as the adventures of the sixth century are recounted finally to M.T. in the nineteenth century. Numerous critics agree that that device is intended to facilitate nineteenth-century satire of sixth-century England. Hank is obviously an outsider in Arthurian England—not only displaced but dis-timed as well—and must exert himself to find a place in that society or die. He is initially strictly on his own and needs all of his nimble wits and trickery to survive. In order to gain acceptance he does have to learn the ways of that world and make the necessary adaptations to function in it; his ability to out-Merlin Merlin is illustrative of his success in adapting to that society's ways. But for the most part he simply reverses the usual picaresque practice and manages—with considerable success—to change society to suit *him*—or at least the Yankee him, which is after all apparently his more dominant self. The picaresque double-bind is nevertheless an important feature of Hank's career, and it is a clear reflection (at least superficially) of the double time sequence; the dilemma arises from the conflicting demands of the society of Arthurian England, based upon the system of chivalry as Twain found it set down by Malory, on the one hand, and of the individual Hank's personal integrity (apparently)—which is that of the common-sense, technological Yankee of nineteenth-century America.

The best critics of Twain, from Henry Nash Smith and James M. Cox onward, have seen that the opposition between Arthurian chivalry and Yankee common-sense republicanism as presented in *Connecticut Yankee* is really the metaphor for a more profound opposition—one more immediate and personal for Twain—that between the Yankee North and the 'chival-rous' American South:

> The sixth-century Britain of Hank Morgan's adventures shows many points of similarity to the slave-holding Missouri of

Twain's childhood. . . . Most significant of all, perhaps, the landscape of Britain is described by means of words and images identical with those Mark Twain would apply in his *Autobiography* to the Quarles Farm near Hannibal that he had known as a boy.[17]

James M. Cox brings us closer to our present concern by observing that

It is, after all, a tale of the Yankee doing battle with chivalry. Mark Twain himself had made it eminently plain in *Life on the Mississippi* that the South he could not abide was the South which had created itself in the image of Walter Scott and chivalry.[18]

Within the picaresque autobiography of *Connecticut Yankee* there is something of the familiar quixotesque dialogue; and the base of that dialogue—carried on to some extent between King Arthur and Hank on their Cervantian journey—is the important matter of 'the problem of the book'. If that problem is properly recognized in *Connecticut Yankee*, the recognition may clarify for us the basic concern of the novel—or one of the basic concerns, in any case. A further word on Arthurian England as metaphor for the American South (a word accepted by some of the most eminent Twain scholars and critics) explains:

Thus Mark Twain's own observation had deeply impressed upon him the pattern of rapid transition from a backward agrarian society with corrupt institutions and ideals to an industrial society enjoying all the benefits of machine technology and enlightened republican government.[19]

An unintentional note of irony is detectable in that passage: it will be recalled that one of the 'benefits' Sam Clemens 'enjoyed' was the disappearance of the profession of river-boat pilot as he had known it, and that another 'benefit' was associated with the Paige typesetter—one closely connected with *Connecticut Yankee*.

To appreciate the other side of the dialogue we might begin by reviewing the familiar passage in *Life on the Mississippi* (Chapter XLVI: 'Enchantments and Enchanters'), to which Cox refers in the sentences of his quoted above. The condemnation of Southern chivalry, à la Scott, seems pretty obvious:

> Then comes Sir Walter Scott with his enchantments . . . with the sillinesses and emptinesses, sham grandeurs, sham gauds, and sham chivalries of a brainless and worthless long-vanished society. . . . in our South they flourish pretty forcefully still. . . . There the genuine and wholesome civilization of the nineteenth century is seriously commingled with the Walter Scott Middle-Age sham civilization, and so you have practical common sense, progressive ideas, and progressive works, mixed up with the duel, the inflated speech, and the jejune romanticism of an absurd past that is dead and out of charity ought to be buried.

Clear enough. But the repetition of the adjective 'sham' is a curious phenomenon. It may be a redundancy employed for emphasis, or it may be employed to make a nice distinction— i.e., to make clear that the focus of the attack is not grandeurs, gauds and chivalries and the Middle-Age civilization, but rather the *sham* chivalries etc., and the *Walter Scott sham* Middle-Age civilization. That is to say that the attack is directed against belief in the romantic, bookish presentation of those items—an attack very similar to that of Cervantes in *Don Quixote*. Credence is lent to that suggestion by the final paragraph of Chapter XLVI of *Life on the Mississippi*:

> A curious exemplification of the power of a single book for good or harm is shown in the effects wrought by *Don Quixote* and those wrought by *Ivanhoe*. The first swept the world's admiration for the medieval silliness out of existence; and the other restored it. As far as our South is concerned, the good work done by Cervantes is pretty nearly a dead letter, so effectually has Scott's pernicious work undermined it.

One cannot be sure that when he wrote these lines Twain had in mind the distinction between the idea of chivalry and books of chivalric romance; but the unsteadiness of focus in the lines quoted would seem to suggest that something of that distinction was lurking in the back of Twain's mind.

The distinction seems clearly sustained, however, in *Connecticut Yankee*, where the real dialogue involves not only the 'problem of the book'—the opposition of life and literature, of 'verses and reverses' (in Levin's term)—but also the opposition of reason and sentiment (*not* sentimentality), i.e. the Hawthornesque opposition of head and heart. That further opposition is expressed dramatically in the novel in terms of the opposition between the mechanical and the human.

It is usually contended that Twain lost control of his material, lost sight of his intention, as he struggled over a period of nearly five years to bring *Connecticut Yankee* to completion—that he could not, in other words, sustain his Yankee's attack on Southern chivalry through the metaphor of his attack on Arthurian England. I would argue, on the other hand, that if we look again at the evidence afforded by the novel—and keeping in mind the function of the quixotesque dialogue in it—we may discover that while there is some wavering of sympathy, Twain had on the whole rather consistent control of his material. We may discover, that is to say, that while the novel intends to condemn the Southern chivalric life as moulded by Scott's romances, it is at least as concerned with condemnation of Yankee common sense, technology and practicality. The horrid ending of Hank's Arthurian sojourn, with the Battle of the Sand Belt, is anticipated from the very beginning of the novel. We are initially introduced to the curious stranger at Warwick Castle as the man who put the bullet hole in the suit of armour. Almost the first piece of information 'The Stranger's History' gives us introduces the basic terms of the quixotesque dialogue in the novel: 'So I am a Yankee of the Yankees—and practical; yes, and nearly barren of sentiment, I suppose—or poetry, in other words.' There is the opposition, quite distinct. Then he develops his credentials as Yankee: 'I went over to the arms factory and learned my real trade.' He lists the things he can make, and one notices the destructive items that head the list—'guns, revolvers, cannon'—and the often missed irony of its conclusion, 'all sorts of labor-saving machinery'. The next paragraph begins with emphasis it is difficult to miss: 'Well, a man like that is full of fight—that goes without saying.' And he proceeds to explain that a blow on the head received during a fight—at the Colt factory—was responsible for his marvellous translation to sixth-century England.

Hank's nineteenth-century Yankee quality appears, as I have said, to be the more dominant side of his character. Yet the narrative is punctuated with several unforgettable episodes in which his humanitarian (or 'poetic' perhaps) side

167

emerges clearly. Such episodes occur often during his quixotesque journey with the disguised King Arthur. And it is also
during that journey that not only does Hank's sympathy with
the King awaken but also his appreciation of Arthur's man-
liness *as* king. At the end of Chapter XXVIII, when the
knights come wheeling in to save Hank and Arthur from being
hanged, the Boss makes this observation:

> And as he stood apart, there, receiving this homage in his rags,
> I thought to myself, well really there *is* something peculiarly
> grand about the gait and bearing of a king, after all.

By the end of their peregrinations it is hard to escape the
impression that *some* reciprocal modification is going on—the
democratization, or 'Hankification', of Arthur and the
'Arthurification' of Hank. The humanitarian concerns of
Hank cannot, however, be realized in social and political
improvement—perhaps because they can be based only on
'enlightened republicanism' (as Smith terms it) or more nearly
on *outré* liberalism, as Cox suggests.[20] In any case, Hank is
quite unable to establish a political system that will effectively
cure the society of its ills. (This particular dilemma anticipates
that explored by Richard Wright's *Native Son* and given
poignant dramatic expression at the moment Bigger Thomas
turns and walks away from the well-intentioned Max; Bigger
knows that Max, for all his sympathy, is finally not regarding
him as an individual human being but as an item in a social
system.)

Hank's marriage to Sandy and the birth of their daughter,
as Susan K. Harris claims, extend his humanitarian tendency
by personalizing it.[21] But by the time Hank is obliged to move
his family to France because of the illness of his daughter, his
new social programmes are so far developed along Yankee
principles of common sense, technology and practicality that
the holocaust of the suicidal Battle of the Sand Belt is virtually
inevitable; no time remains for the humanizing of his institutions. His group of faithful boys are even victims of Hank's
Yankee insensitivity, as Ms Harris most persuasively reminds
us:

> Aware that they have abandoned the community in which they
> were born and have forfeited their claim to a place in their own

culture, the boys—who no longer even speak the same idiom as their contemporaries—try to articulate the dilemma their new allegiance has posed for them. . . . 'Our minds approve, but our hearts reproach us. . . .'[22]

Again the terms of the basic opposition in the quixotesque dialogue emerge: mind versus heart. It is the equivalent of Hank's earliest statement of the opposition: 'practical . . . nearly barren of sentiment . . . or poetry'.

Twain has clearly enough underlined this dehumanization of Hank's pack of faithful boys by means of a bitter and frivolous joke that is half submerged in the narrative. The joke is set up at that moment when, after killing Sir Sagramore, Hank utters his challenge to all chivalry 'in mass' at the end of Chapter XXIX. He explains that it is a 'bluff':

> At such a time it is sound judgment to put on a bold face and play your hand for a hundred times what it is worth; forty-nine times out of fifty nobody dares to 'call', and you rake in the chips.

The card-playing metaphor alerts us to the *number* of faithful boys Hank and his lieutenant Clarence have to rely on: fifty-two. The exact number of boys is insisted upon, half a dozen times throughout the final two chapters of Hank's autobiography; and Dan Beard's illustration for the beginning of Chapter XLIII is titled 'One of the 52'. The card-playing metaphor is reiterated in the midst of all that when, at the end of Chapter XLII Hank, having decided to move to the offensive, exclaims, 'The *de*fensive isn't my line, and the *off*ensive is. That is, when I hold a fair hand. . . . Oh yes, we'll rise up and strike; that's our game.' The last two references to the specific number drawn up against the Insurgent Chivalry include Hank and Clarence—'we fifty-four were masters of England!'—they are the two Jokers in the pack.

Hank's written challenge to the Commander of the Knights promises, 'we number 54. Fifty-four what? Men? No, *minds*— . . . a force against which mere animal might may no more hope to prevail . . . [etc.].' Hank thus reiterates the opposition of minds and hearts, established much earlier, and emphasizes again that it is the Yankee side of him—the common-sense, practical, technological *mind*—that has created the fiendish conclusion to his career in the sixth century. The other voice of the quixotesque dialogue in the novel—the heart, sentiment, poetry—is represented particularly by Sandy and little Hello-Central.

In the calm hiatus of three years after the defeat of chivalry, Hank explains his marriage and the naming of his daughter. The passage that opens Chapter XLI is full of significant details:

> Sandy . . . was a flawless wife and mother: and yet I had married her for no particular reason. . . . She had . . . resumed her old place at my side. . . . I was a New Englander, and in my opinion this sort of partnership would compromise her, sooner or later. . . . we had a wedding.

The explanation is commonsensical and even practical, and if not strictly 'moral' then at least moralistic—a typical Yankee explanation. Yet Hank refers to himself not as Yankee but as 'New Englander'. And perhaps there is a good reason for the difference, as we can consider in a moment. Hank adds the explanation of his daughter's name:

> In my dreams, along at first, I still wandered thirteen centuries away, and my unsatisfied spirit went calling and harking all up and down the unreplying vacancies of a vanished world. Many a time Sandy heard that imploring cry come from my lips in my sleep.

Susan K. Harris offers the perceptive observation that 'it would appear that his only real intimate had been a telephone operator whom he remembers talking to but never mentions having met face to face.'[23] That concluding clause is important. Ms Harris continues:

> Despite his claim to miss her, her real importance to him may lie in the fact that her response to his call of 'Hello-Central' epitomizes the technological society he has lost.

Here are Hank's words on the matter, at the close of Chapter XV:

> Break—my heart! oh my lost darling! . . . who was so gentle, and lovely, and all the world to me, and whom I shall never see again! How the thought of her carries me back . . . to a vague dim time, a happy time, . . . when I used to wake in the soft summer mornings, out of sweet dreams of her, and say 'Hello, Central!' just to hear her dear voice come melting back to me

with a 'Hello, Hank!' that was music of the spheres to my
enchanted ear.

That is not the speech of 'a Yankee of the Yankees . . . nearly
barren of sentiment . . . or poetry, in other words'. Nor is the
nostalgia focused on the machine of the 'technological society
he has lost'; no, Hank is nostalgic for *the human voice in the
machine* that spoke to his heart, through his 'enchanted ear'.
Whether he did ever see her seems of secondary importance;
what he recalls is the voice.[24] To be sure, the telephone brings
the voice to him, but he does not phone to make a date nor
does the passage quoted focus on the marvels of technology.
The human voice, as contrasted to the dehumanizing and
finally deadly machinery of the technologically expert nineteenth century, is what Hank yearns for. That yearning is
satisfied—the dream of close human contact is realized—in
his sixth-century daughter.

In the 'Final P.S. by M.T.' the delirious Hank believes he
has returned to the sixth century and recovered Sandy. Again,
the passage is full of significant details and important echoes:

> O, Sandy . . . I lost myself a moment . . . such strange and
> awful dreams Sandy! . . . I seemed to be a creature out of a
> strange unborn age, centuries hence, and even *that* was as real
> as the rest! Yes, I seemed to have flown back out of that age into
> this of ours, and then forward to it again, and was set down, a
> stranger, and forlorn in that strange England, with an abyss of
> thirteen centuries yawning between me and you! between me
> and my home and my friends! between me and all that is dear
> to me, all that could make life worth the living! It was awful. . . .

For this Hank, life in 'Arthurian England' means home and all
that makes it worth the living; and it is poignantly contrasted
with 'that strange England'—that nineteenth-century place of
the 'New Englander' who married Sandy for practical, commonsensical, 'moralistic' reasons, at the dictates of head rather
than of heart. The trouble with the Yankee's nineteenth-
century society of common sense, of 'all the benefits of machine
technology and enlightened republican government', is that it
provided so little for the heart, for the basically human; it is a
society without poetry.

James M. Cox has explained most cogently the connection

between Twain's attitude to *Connecticut Yankee* and his hopes for the Paige typesetter, emphasizing the importance of his desire that the machine and the novel be ready for the public on the same day. Yet Cox's suggestion that 'Killing the Yankee was symbolically a crippling of the inventive imagination, as if Mark Twain were driven to maim himself in an effort to survive', somehow rings false, for Cox concludes his comments with the observation that 'writing was at last his [Twain's] life.'[25] It would seem, rather, that Twain was killing the Yankee in order that the other partner in the dialogue— the devoted and loving husband of Sandy and father of Hello-Central—might survive, that in having Hank virtually destroy himself in the Battle of the Sand Belt, Twain was punishing that Yankee side of himself that was 'in love with' the typesetter and that drove him to become a 'machine-driven writer'[26] in the attempt to have the completion of his novel coincide with the completion of the typesetter.

If Twain was, as I believe the evidence of the novel shows, quite able to manage his materials, he was yet unable to manage the quixotesque dialogue those materials so brilliantly set forth. He was never able to fashion that dialogue in the Cervantian manner so that it tended toward the healthy reciprocal modification one finds in *Don Quixote*. He has attempted a fusion of Tom and Huck in the figure of Hank Morgan; and it is in one sense a more effective fusion of opposites than one finds in *The Adventures of Tom Sawyer* (which presents the comic 'Tomification' of Huck) or in *Adventures of Huckleberry Finn* (which presents the tragic failure of the attempt to Tomify Huck). In *Connecticut Yankee* Hank's double-bind matches the quixotesque dialogue, and at the base of that dialogue is 'the problem of the book' in a somewhat different form.

Tom Sawyer's bookishness consists of his reading romances as though they were true, realistic accounts—like history— and his attempt to impose the rules of romance upon real life manages to dehumanize him and to threaten the human existence of those he tries to control. His *mind* has smothered his heart—he has become 'mechanized'. Huck, on the other hand, sees life as real and thus can treat human beings humanely. In spite of his socialized 'conscience' he must finally rely on his 'heart'—he remains the human animal. Tom is the Yankee side of Hank, which claims the importance of the mind—and to which technology is appealing; Huck is that side of Hank which is appealed to not by the written romance of chivalry (the *sham* chivalries Twain condemned in *Life on the Mississippi*) but by the sympathetic humanitarian responsibility of the true ideal of chivalry—the importance of the heart, sentiment, poetry.

The future of picaresque, then, we can see retrospectively, was realized in that series of novels that, following *Lazarillo de Tormes*, employed its original metaphor to give formal expression to the dilemma of the strife between individual integrity and social demands for conformity. On the other hand, the picaresque was fated to be modified by the genius of Cervantes into the masterpiece of *Don Quixote*—a singularly happy fate. There the dilemma is not merely expressed but the resolution is artistically implied. Few have matched Cervantes' achievement; Twain did not, but his success in effectively expressing the dilemma of the individual challenged by society is nonetheless an admirable enough achievement. And perhaps reviewing these works of Twain in the light of 'the future of picaresque'—the true picaresque and the tradition of *Don Quixote*—enables us to understand them more fully.

One might only wish to modify the beginning of *Tom Sawyer* to read: 'You don't know about Tom, without you have read two books by the name of *Adventures of Huckleberry Finn* and *A Connecticut Yankee in King Arthur's Court*, made by Mr. Mark Twain, and he told the truth, mainly. But he didn't really know about Tom, long at first, either.' Without the 'Huckification' of Tom we are lost; Tom really offers so little for the heart.

NOTES

1. Harry Levin, in 'The Example of Cervantes' (1957), calls *Rinconete and Cortadillo* 'a tale endearing to American readers as a Sevillian adumbration of *Tom Sawyer* and *Huckleberry Finn*'; see *Cervantes: A Collection of Critical Essays*, ed. Lowry Nelson, Jr. (Englewood Cliffs, N.J.: Prentice-

Hall, Inc., 1969), p. 41. See also Robert Giddings, *The Tradition of Smollett* (London: Methuen and Co. Ltd., 1967), p. 36: 'Many picaresque novelists are indebted to Cervantes, but to the Cervantes not of *Don Quixote* but *Rinconete y Cortadillo.*'

2. Norton Critical Edition of *Adventures of Huckleberry Finn*, ed. Sculley Bradley, Richmond Croom Beatty, E. Hudson Long and Thomas Cooley, 2nd ed. (New York: W. W. Norton and Co., Inc., 1977), p. 16.

3. *The Picaresque Hero in European Fiction* (Madison, Wisc.: University of Wisconsin Press, 1977), p. 11 and passim.

4. A most useful examination of this distinction is offered in Giddings, ibid., pp. 26–30.

5. Carlos Blanco Aguinaga, 'Cervantes and the Picaresque Mode: Notes on Two Kinds of Realism' (1957), *Cervantes: A Collection*, pp. 138–39.

6. Levin, ibid., p. 36; Leo Spitzer, 'On the Significance of *Don Quixote*' (1962), *Cervantes: A Collection*, p. 88.

7. Wilder's notes (29 May 1930) for his lectures on *Don Quixote* given at the University of Chicago are in the Beinecke Library at Yale University. The reference to Wilder in this connection is really not so far-fetched as it might seem: not only did he give (and repeat) the lectures on Cervantes, but he published his own Quixotesque novel (which he usually referred to as 'picaresque') in 1935, *Heaven's My Destination*; and his last novel, *Theophilus North* (1973), exhibits the fusion of picaresque, utopian, and Gulliverian satire—a fusion approximated in Twain's *Connecticut Yankee*. I am grateful to Dr. David Schoonover, Curator of the Collection of American Literature, in the Beinecke Rare Book and Manuscript Library of Yale University, for permission to use this material.

8. 'Mark Twain and Don Quixote', *P.M.L.A.*, XXXVII (June 1922), 324–46.

9. The reference to sumpter mules is a fascinating 'clue'. When Rincon and Diego Cortado first meet, in *Rinconete and Cortadillo*, and exchange exaggerated accounts of their backgrounds, the term 'sumpter mules' occurs twice in those half-dozen opening pages. One can read quite a distance into *Don Quixote* without coming upon the term. It is worth recalling, furthermore, that the particular *forte* of these young picaroons involves the use of a pack of cards; an echo of that association of picaro and a pack of cards is noted below in the discussion of Hank Morgan's faithful boys.

10. A similar distinction is made by Arturo Serrano-Plaja in his observation that 'Twain was perhaps the first to see how much of the world of children there is in Don Quixote. And so we have [in *The Adventures of Tom Sawyer*] his "correction" of Cervantes' book: A child, doing childish things is much more consistent than an adult who acts like a child.' See *'Magic' Realism in Cervantes: 'Don Quixote' as Seen Through 'Tom Sawyer' and 'The Idiot'* (1967), trans. Robert S. Rudder (Berkeley, Los Angeles, and London: University of California Press, 1970), p. 23.

11. See Lyall H. Powers, 'The Sweet Success of Twain's Tom', *Dalhousie Review*, LIII (Summer 1973), 310–24.

12. For a full development of this idea see Powers, ibid., 318–20.
13. This is an 'inversion' of what we find in Cervantes' *Cipion and Berganza*; the apparently picaresque autobiography of Berganza is actually contained within the dialogue between Berganza and Cipion. See Aguinaga, ibid., p. 143.
14. *Mark Twain's Escape from Time: A Study of Patterns and Images* (Columbia and London: University of Missouri Press, 1982), pp. 61–2.
15. *Mark Twain: the Fate of Humor* (Princeton, N. J.: Princeton University Press, 1966), p. 175; Cox adds: 'All the other cruelties are committed for some "reason". . . . But Tom's cruelty has a purity all its own—it is done solely for the sake of adventure.'
16. See Giddings, ibid., passim.
17. Henry Nash Smith, *Mark Twain's Fable of Progress: Political and Economic Ideas in 'A Connecticut Yankee'* (New Brunswick, N. J.: Rutgers University Press, 1964), p. 83.
18. Cox, ibid., p. 218.
19. Smith, ibid., p. 83.
20. Cox, ibid., pp. 217–18: 'Although he [Hank] sounds and thinks as if he were rebellious, he is quite clearly echoing the sentiments of a society fairly sunk in the complacent and institutionalized "liberalism" which had sponsored the Civil War in 1860–65.'
21. Harris, ibid., pp. 55–7.
22. Ibid., p. 52.
23. Ibid., p. 49.
24. Support for Ms Harris's opinion that Hank did not meet his ideal 'face to face' is given by the initial reference in the novel; Hank interrupts Sandy early in her tale (Chapter XV) to say, 'The humblest hello-girl along ten thousand miles of wire could teach gentleness, patience, modesty, manners, to the highest duchess in Arthur's land.' Hello-Central of the nineteenth century is mainly a *voice*.
25. Cox, ibid., p. 210.
26. Ibid., p. 209.

7

Towards the Absurd: Mark Twain's *A Connecticut Yankee, Pudd'nhead Wilson* and *The Great Dark*[1]

by PETER MESSENT

> I . . . was set down, a stranger and forlorn in that strange
> England, with an abyss of thirteen centuries yawning between
> me and you! between me and my home and my friends! between
> me and all that is dear to me, all that could make life worth the
> living! It was awful—awfuler than you can ever imagine. . . .[2]

Twain's preoccupation with the figure of the stranger in his
later fiction is an accepted fact. This interest leads though, as I
wish to argue, in two closely related directions. First, it suggests
Twain's move towards the Absurd: a fiction of displacement, of
isolation, of restlessness; of lack of centre, lack of firm identity;
of individual constraint, not release; of social reconciliation of
the most empty kind.[3] Secondly, the ontological uncertainty
suggested by the figure of the 'unfurrowed'[4] stranger connects
with that disenchantment with Realism as a literary form which
becomes so clear from *A Connecticut Yankee* onwards; connects,
too, with his move in the direction of Fantasy, a form which,
heavily dependent on *plotting*, allows Twain to disassociate his

characters from a society which enmeshes, and to place them—as aliens, as derelicts completely out of kilter with that universe which surrounds them—in a setting which reinforces his Absurdist leanings.

For images of confusion, meaningless repetition and dereliction abound in Twain's later fantasies. All points of order are untrustworthy. Sudden, inexplicable reversals and transitions occur. In *The Great Dark* Harry Edwards looks through a microscope at a drop of stale water. Moments later he finds himself on shipboard sailing that 'wide circular sea'[5] which that drop becomes when viewed through the microscope. Scientific curiosity translates to experienced nightmare as Edwards finds himself in a chaotic seascape, where all points of known geographical, climatic and astronomical reference have been removed. The mate, Turner, details this confusion to Edwards:

> no Greenland; no Gulf Stream; no day, no proper night; weather that don't jibe with any sample known to the Bureau; animals that would start a panic in any menagerie, chart no more use than a horse-blanket, and the heavenly bodies gone to hell . . . The ship's bewitched.[6]

The twin poles of magic and science (as epitomized by the use of the microscope) form the boundaries of this tale, and it is the world of the fantastic, the unknown, the bewitched, that triumphs. Rational control, or, as will be shown later, most forms of it, collapse.

It is *A Connecticut Yankee in King Arthur's Court* (1889) (written nine years earlier) however—with its themes of dereliction, of uncertainty, of disorder, of lack of centre—that points the way towards the radical uncertainties of both *Pudd'nhead Wilson* and of *The Great Dark*. Hank Morgan in *A Connecticut Yankee* finds himself dislocated, trapped in another world. In his situation, though, he finds initial opportunity for positive action in strong contrast to Edwards' passivity and helplessness in the later story, a contrast which suggests the changing nature of Twain's fictional vision. Hank, too, though, is a realist, associated with a world of common sense, of scientific rationalism, set in opposition to that of Arthurian England— the world of fabulation, of superstition, of magic. As Eric Mottram points out,[7] Hank is a social engineer who transforms

177

a culture through his technological power. Indeed, the relationship between technology, science, social engineering, and personal and political power is insisted on by Twain throughout *A Connecticut Yankee*. Those 'fifty electric suns'[8] which Hank switches on at the end of the novel to illuminate the slaughter which is there to occur, is no casual image. In Notebook 28 (July 1888 to May 1889) Twain is making notes for the novel and his concern over the relationship between natural power and scientific power is already in evidence:

> Hello Exchange!—Gentleman wishes to speak with the Lady of Shalott
> . . . The bicycle.
> Journal items:
> Grayling parties going out.
>   ,,   Relief expeditions.
> $10,000 reward for Boss.
> Search expeditions.
> Journal The Sunburst.
>   Electric Light.[9]

If Thomas Edison, inventor and developer of successful electric lighting, was portrayed in the national press as a 'Wizard',[10] and if Nikola Tesla, working with Edison,[11] invented the first alternating current motor in 1883, then it is interesting to note that Twain, through his association with, and investments in the work of, James W. Paige, was involved in exactly the same kind of area:

> Nov. 1, 1888. I have just seen the drawings & descriptions of an electrical machine lately patented by a Mr. [Teska] Tesla, & sold to the Westinghouse Company, which will revolutionize the whole electrical business of the world. . . . The drawings & descriptions show that this is the *very* machine, in every detail which Paige invented nearly 4 years ago. I furnished $1,000 for the experiments & was to have half of the invention. . . . Tesla . . . tried everything that we tried . . . & he tried one more thing—a thing which we had canvassed—that *alternating* current. *That* solved the difficulty & achieved success.[12]

This concern with invention, with electricity in particular, with power, connects directly of course with the destruction often associated with that power. The relationship between the natural world and the humans living in that world had undergone significant alteration since Franklin first fished for electricity with his kite, as Edison's experiments in the field of electrocution, both of animals and humans, so clearly suggested. The balance between passive recipient and active controller had gone through a 180 degree turn.

So, too, Hank Morgan in *A Connecticut Yankee* abuses the materials at his disposal. Electricity is used not just for illumination but also for purposes of destruction. Engineering is associated with control both of the natural landscape and of the human beings who inhabit it. Hank 'sent an engineer and forty men . . . to turn a mountain brook . . . and bring it . . . under our command . . . that I could make instant use of it'.[13] The 'use' made is to drown those forces attacking his stronghold—the cave, not of adventure and imaginative excitement as in *Tom Sawyer*, but of destruction and defeat (for both parties) here. Electricity runs through the wire fences that surround the cave, an electric power used, again, to slaughter: 'our current was so tremendous that it killed before the victim could cry out . . . our camp was enclosed with a solid wall of the dead'.[14]

The power associated with the figure of scientist/inventor is often, in the popular imagination, linked with destructive potential. In 1892, for example, 'it was rumoured in France that Edison was building an "infernal machine" for the German Emperor "that would destroy the largest cities from a distance of thirty miles and which would annihilate a whole army corps".'[15] Others beside Twain saw that nineteenth-century light-bringers could also be viewed as potential, and actual (in *A Connecticut Yankee*), bringers of darkness.

Although Edison was portrayed nationally as a 'wizard', he himself rejected this rôle:

> A reporter from the New York *Daily Graphic* visited Edison one spring afternoon in 1878 shortly after the appearance of the phonograph—'Aren't you a good deal of a *wizard*, Mr. Edison?' he asked, 'Oh no!' Edison laughed, 'I don't believe much in that sort of thing'.[16]

Hank Morgan, however, in his use of the power which is a result of his late nineteenth-century scientific and technological knowledge, is seen as, and *sees himself as*, a wizard. The worlds of magic and of science overlap both in imagination and effect (as Mary Shelley earlier portrayed in *Frankenstein*). When Hank uses his powers (the ability to make gunpowder) to blow up Merlin's tower and to discredit Merlin himself, he uses the techniques and language of the occult, both to describe and effect his purposes:

> I made about three passes in the air, and then there was an awful crash and that old tower leaped into the sky in chunks, along with a vast volcanic fountain of fire that turned night to noonday, and showed a thousand acres of human beings groveling on the ground in a general collapse of consternation. . . . It was an effective miracle![17]

Hank's democratic front is, this early, being revealed for the fraud that it is, as he actively revels in these *acres* of human beings *groveling*. His power is a form of magic to those who witness it, and is described as such by Hank himself: as 'miracle' (he is later to say, again as a result of a defeat of Merlin, 'everytime the magic of fol-de-rol tried conclusions with the magic of science, the magic of fol-de-rol got left').[18]

In *The Great Dark*, the scientific observer—with his microscope—finds the gap between himself and his observed material swiftly removed. He is translated to a grotesque and fantastic world from which he is unable to escape. The 'fantastic' world in which Hank finds himself is based on historic rather than scientific (a world in a drop of water) actuality. *A Connecticut Yankee* consequently works in the area of historical relativism—a conventional device of utopian/dystopian nineteenth-century fiction—rather than in that of the cosmic relativism of *The Great Dark*. The world of Arthurian England in *A Connecticut Yankee* is more attractive than the nightmarish world of the later work. Indeed, one of Twain's working titles for *Yankee* was *The Lost Land*,[19] indicative of the note of nostalgia and regret which suffuses both this book and so many other of Twain's works. This attractive land is finally closed to Hank not only by Twain's own demands for fictional form[20]; not only by Hank in his rôle of social engineer bringing disaster both on himself and on the human materials he has tried to modify; but also by exactly that 'magic of fol-de-rol' that Hank, and the reader, have scorned throughout the text. The final grim joke of the novel is that Merlin's 'magic' defeats Hank:

> About midnight I [Clarence] awoke, and saw that hag making curious passes in the air about The Boss's head and face.... [She] said with an accent of malicious satisfaction: 'Ye were conquerors; ye are conquered! ... Ye shall all die in this place—every one—except *him*. He sleepeth now—and shall sleep thirteen centuries. I am Merlin!'[21]

Merlin immediately gets his come-uppance as, overtaken by 'a delirium of silly laughter', he reels into one of the electric fences and is electrocuted, still laughing. The important thing is, though, that all our—and Hank's—presumptions concerning the relative effectiveness of different kinds of 'magic' are completely upset.

We *know* science, in the form of the dynamo, the electric fence, gunpowder, *works*. In this ending, where it is old-fashioned magic or wizardry of the *occult* type which excludes Hank from what has come to be his homeland, we fully recognize the pure fictionality and playfulness of Twain's imagination. But nevertheless we—as readers—are left in a position of radical uncertainty as to what our attitude towards the various types of 'magic' introduced in this novel should be. An ambiguous relativism permeates this text.

And this ambiguous relativism points too in the direction of Twain's disenchantment with Realism as a literary technique. From the first, Twain's fiction had committed itself to Realism, to the plumbing of misleading surface to reveal truth beneath. And even as late as *Indiantown* (probably written in 1899) he would describe David Gridley as 'just a piece of honest kitchen furniture transferred from the drawing-room and glorified and masked from view in gorgeous cloth of gold',[22] an image which relates back to his fiction as a whole. Masks and gold trappings are continually being removed to reveal basic essences,[23] essences which in Gridley's case might be plain, but are certainly worthy and 'honest'.

A much earlier example of Twain's realist technique points to the possibility of disenchantment contained within such a technique. In his 1869 sketch 'A Day at Niagara' illusion gives way rapidly to harsher reality:

181

> By and by . . . I came upon a gentle daughter of the aborigines
> in fringed and beaded buckskin moccasins and leggins, seated
> on a bench with her pretty wares about her. . . . I . . . addressed
> her:
> 'Is the heart of the forest maiden heavy? . . . Does she mourn
> over the extinguished council-fires of her race, and the vanished
> glory of her ancestors? . . . Why is my daughter silent? . . .
> The maiden said:
> 'Faix, an' is it Biddy Malone he dare to be callin' names?
> Lave this, or I'll shy your lean carcass over the cataract, ye
> sniveling blaggard!'[24]

Here, Twain's commitment to the removal of romantic veneer,
to reveal truths—however harsh such truths might be—leads
in the direction of disillusionment. As Twain continued
writing his realistic impulse was to lead more and more to the
realization that as veneers and illusions were stripped away,
all that remained was a reality completely *devoid* of either social
or moral worth.

So, in *A Connecticut Yankee*, Twain casts the status of Realism
in doubt. Hank's generally pragmatic and common-sense view
of the world leads only to disaster, to destruction. Science, on
which Realism bases itself, is *not* superior, in terms of its results
at least, to the occult. Equally—and I think this is the
implication of the ending where Merlin's 'magic' finally
defeats Hank—Realism is not allowed superiority over
Fantasy. The two forms, equated with two ways of looking at
the world, of acting—Hank's and Merlin's—are placed in a
highly ambiguous relationship to one another, as is true
throughout this text in fact, a text in which Hank, who—
despite his occult vocabulary—is in fact an arch-realist,
operates throughout within fantastic framework.

But Twain's concern in *A Connecticut Yankee* with radical
uncertainty also points in the direction of what I see to be an
increasing preoccupation with what the modern reader would
call the Absurd in Twain's writing. No certainty exists in
Twain's work from *A Connecticut Yankee* onwards. His
protagonists are caught either between two worlds, as is Hank,
or in nightmarish versions of the everyday world (see the
Dream manuscripts).[25] Dereliction becomes very much of a
norm in his work,[26] and emerges clearly and explicitly as a

theme in *A Connecticut Yankee* with the fictional move therein between two forms of 'magic', two kinds of worlds—industrial and rural, scientific and superstitious, rationalistic and religious, Realistic and Fantastic—in neither of which can Twain, his reader, or his protagonist, rest content.

A Connecticut Yankee is one of the most important of late nineteenth-century fictions in the way it confronts, through fabulist techniques, the problems of a rapidly changing[27] post-Civil War American society. It confronts the problems associated with the rise of, and use of, science and technology in the period; it is a novel about the use and abuse of power of a number of different kinds. It examines, for example, not only the nature and impact of technological power but of political power too and the problems associated with the whole American democratic experiment, as it presents us with Hank who professes belief in democracy but can only put his principles into action from the position he takes as 'The Boss', a position he thoroughly enjoys.

The novel also relates to those speculations about Social Darwinism current at the time (Hank, transplanted to a new environment, his adaptation and survival) and theories of social engineering (another form of power) expounded most notably in the writings of Lester Ward. I have no evidence that Twain had read Ward, but think it interesting and relevant that (in terms of the general philosophical debate in the late nineteenth century concerning evolutionary thought) Ward's 'Mind As A Social Factor' should appear in October 1884,[28] just prior to the writing of *A Connecticut Yankee*. Lester Ward writes:

> The brain is the organ of the mind, its physical seat and cause. Mind is therefore a natural product of evolution, and its achievements are to be classed and studied along with all other natural phenomena.[29]

Hank Morgan comments early in the novel, on finding himself marooned in sixth-century England:

> I saw that I was just another Robinson Crusoe cast away on an uninhabited island, with no society but some more or less tame animals, and if I wanted to make life bearable I must do as he did—invent, contrive, create, reorganize things; set brain and hand to work.[30]

Hank soon adapts to this new environment and survives, indeed flourishes, in it (flourishes, again let it be noted, through his displays of power). As he attains control, so also does Hank speed up the evolutionary process. If Lester Ward tells us, referring to Williams G. Sumner and his school of Social Darwinism, that 'the laissez faire doctrine is a gospel of inaction', that 'man ... *has*, from the very dawn of his intelligence, been transforming the entire surface of the planet he inhabits'[31] through the power of invention, then Hank is such an inventor-transformer: in short, a social engineer. He decisively modifies the evolutionary process, transforming a basically plastic universe through intelligence, will, and invention.

As is evident, Hank does not finally succeed in his attempts to engineer society—perhaps partially because Ward's benevolent impulse ('if nature progresses through the destruction of the weak, man progresses through the *protection* of the weak. This is the essential distinction')[32] is strangely perverted when Hank attempts to follow it. Hank's attempts to speed up the evolutionary process, by putting brain and hand to work, fail both because of his own autocratic leanings, and also—as is made clear in the final stages of the novel—due to the intransigent nature of the human materials with which he is working.[33] Wardian evolutionary dreams of decisively modifying one's social environment by the power of intelligence and invention are shattered in this novel—and indeed any evolutionary philosophy at all is severely questioned in a novel which takes us, in terms of the historical cycle introduced, from darkness to darkness, in terms of social possibilities, from utopia to apocalypse.

A Connecticut Yankee, then, is a central document for the understanding of late nineteenth-century American culture. Twain appears in the novel to be philosophically trapped between two worlds (agrarian and industrial, superstitious and scientific) and between two impulses (evolutionary and anti-evolutionary) neither of which can he finally either celebrate, or indeed even accept. And this kind of entrapment is symptomatic of the feelings of alienation, dereliction and disorder which mark Twain's later manuscripts. A fictional universe is presented in the later Dream Manuscripts most particularly in which man can no longer imaginatively or actually control his physical or metaphysical environment. Despair and futility are the dominant tones of this fiction. The 'comic inadequacy of vision' (Richard Hauck)[34] has now turned tragic as any acceptance of a relativistic and multi-dimensional universe is constantly negated by that sense of terror and anguish felt by Twain's protagonists in a world on which no sense of personal order can be imposed. This is an Absurdist universe, not a comic one.

For Twain's work does not fit easily within the category of black humour; he is not the 'cheerful nihilist' that Richard Hauck would want to make him[35] or, at least, only rarely so. Humour, where it appears, as in *Pudd'nhead Wilson*, is humour of the most ironic kind. That cataclysm which ends *A Connecticut Yankee* suggests that the comic perspective, briefly recaptured in the grim joke with which the main narrative closes, is under serious threat by this stage in Twain's career.

And it is in *Pudd'nhead Wilson* (1894) that Twain moves further in the direction of an Absurdist vision, despite the setting of the novel—back on the Mississippi riverbank, in what is undoubtedly a firm and (superficially at least) ordered community. *Pudd'nhead Wilson* is in effect a novel about identity loss, about alienation. It centres itself around the figure of the outsider. Critics have puzzled over the question of who is the major protagonist, hero or heroine, of this novel.[36] To pursue such an issue is misleading. What Twain does here is base the movement of the narrative around four figures—Wilson, Roxy, Tom, and Valet—each of whom is essentially 'displaced'. Displacement which was finally thematically so important in *A Connecticut Yankee* (*initially* Hank feels he can fit with ease into that new environment which for most of the novel he controls) becomes in *Pudd'nhead Wilson* major theme and emphasis from first to last.

Pudd'nhead Wilson himself shares certain similarities, in terms of the rôle he plays in this novel, with Hank Morgan. For both are essentially alien to the communities they join. Wilson, like Hank, is another outsider, another *progressive* (my stress). Again, irony is writ large in the use of this particular term, an irony reflected in Hank's first challenge to knight-errantry as an institution, in his rôle as 'champion of hard common sense and reason'[37] in Chapter 39 of *A Connecticut Yankee* ('The Yankee's Fight with the Knights'). When he wins that particular day, he comments 'The march of civilization was begun.'[38] The ironical reverberations of that phrase are obvious in terms of the battle of the Sand Belt, civilization's final 'triumph' in that novel.

Pudd'nhead Wilson, scientist, freethinker, experimenter within 'the universe of ideas',[39] enters like Hank, as 'stranger' into a feudal and agrarian world. This world appears well ordered, but is, in fact, both claustrophobic and corrupt, based as it is on that overwhelming fact of slavery which too so tainted Arthur's England. While the reader is encouraged to feel a certain affection for Arthurian England—perhaps *through* Hank's final emotional identification with that environment—Dawson's Landing is held from first to last at emotional arm's length. Illusions of pastoral and domestic innocence may initially predominate:

> Dawson's Landing . . . was a snug little collection of modest . . . frame dwellings whose white-washed exteriors were almost concealed from sight by climbing tangles of rose-vines, honey-suckles, and morning glories. . . . The hamlet's front was washed by the clear waters of the great river.[40]

But such illusions soon give way to reveal the moral squalor which underpins this static and tranquil scenario.

The central irony of *Pudd'nhead Wilson* is that Wilson, when finally the opportunity comes, uses his undoubted 'scientific' talents to expose the barbaric moral reality that lies beneath the idyllic surface of small town American life in the South. And it is here that the lack of meaningful *social or community centre* to which Twain's later fiction so often points is so clearly revealed. But this revealed truth ironically remains blindly ignored by all the members of that community which is implicitly condemned and, indeed, has to remain ignored by Wilson himself—at an official level at least[41]—if he is to survive as *functioning* member of that society of which he is a part. Social reconciliation is the note on which—for Wilson—the novel ends, but it is a note which chimes both ironically and emptily. For Wilson finally uses his powers (and this novel, like *A Connecticut Yankee*, centres itself round various forms of power) to re-establish that morally corrupt social structure (turned topsy-turvy by Roxy) on which the world of Dawson's Landing is based. It is Wilson who reveals that Tom is in fact Valet, and Valet is in fact Tom; that what was taken for white is in fact black, and vice-versa.

The novel is circular, turns back upon itself, in the sense that the social order which was presented initially as fixed and static, is once more operative at the novel's closure. Roxy's subversion of that power set-up had gone undetected until the very end of the novel. Wilson's re-establishment of the status quo is celebrated by the townspeople. The 'real' Tom Driscoll, now 'rich and free', is in 'a most embarrassing situation'[42] as a result of his negro manners, dialect, and bearing. But individual inadequacy can usually be subsumed within, even ignored by, the social and institutional framework within which that individual is contained. Thus, Clarence, in *A Connecticut Yankee* could project an improvement of the monarchical system in England by replacing kings and queens by cats—cheaper to look after, and morally superior to 'the average king'.[43] Systems continue to operate despite the inadequacies of their leaders. The actual point, though, here is that the system itself is, in Dawson's Landing, completely inadequate, both morally and as efficiently functioning social unit, as Wilson reveals. The 'real' Tom becomes an invisible man 'at home and at peace' neither in the white man's parlour or the 'nigger gallery',[44] and despite this living rebuke to a system which operates according to racial schematizations, that very system carries on unaffected in its operations. The Conclusion of the novel commences with a reference to 'The town'[45] and it is this group entity which will now continue to behave, to share the same values, as before, even *despite* the exposed absurdity of those very values.

The four *characters* round which the novel has centred itself are left completely displaced at the conclusion of the narrative. Wilson ends up socially accepted but intellectually distanced; accepted, what is more, by a community whose values, so the Calendar suggests, he despises. Roxy, a muted figure, retreats from an active participation in the novel as warm vernacular figure whose revolt against that dominant culture which has oppressed her and her kind has triggered the narrative action, to bury herself in 'her church and its affairs',[46] a church that will surely obliterate her individuality. Tom and Valet are equally displaced, derelict, the one unable to fit an environment for which his conditioning has unfitted him; the other removed from a community he has lorded it over to be 'sold . . . down the river'[47] as valuable slave, his very identity as murderer, one who has shattered the ordered safety of this community, removed by his status as economic object.

And indeed, the twin central themes of this novel are those of displacement and of the lack of firm identity. The story is actually constructed around these related themes. They take on an importance and a resonance (as regards Twain's later fiction) which is really only hinted at in *A Connecticut Yankee*. The initial plan for this novel is sketched in 'Those Extraordinary Twins', that essential companion piece to *Pudd'nhead Wilson*:[48]

> Originally the story was called 'Those Extraordinary Twins'. . . . I have seen a picture of a youthful Italian 'freak' or 'freaks'[49]— which was—or which were[50]—on exhibition in our cities—a combination consisting of two heads and four arms joined to a single body and a single pair of legs—and I thought I would write an extravagantly fantastic little story with this freak of nature for hero—or heroes. . . .[51]

The tale, as Twain comments, 'changed itself from a farce to a tragedy'[52] as he wrote it and, perhaps unfortunately, he ended up performing 'a kind of literary Caesarean operation'[53] removing the Siamese twins sketch from the main body of the narrative.

His concern with these 'conglomerate twins',[54] though, undoubtedly suggested that theme of conglomerate twinship which was to be dominant in *Pudd'nhead Wilson*. Wilson's own initial joke about the two halves of the same dog,[55] though, met with blank incomprehension by his audience (this book *insists* continually on the fact of two audiences—the Dawson's Landing community and the reader) points again in the direction of the Siamese connection. The whole point, however, about the twins who are to appear in *Pudd'nhead Wilson* is not that they are freaks in accord with Twain's initial plan, but that they are more or less identical: 'One was a little

fairer than the other, but otherwise they were exact dupli-
cates.'[56] And the whole point, in turn, about duplicate twins is
that, though each twin has a distinct and separate identity,
you cannot in fact tell them apart.

This obviously connects with the theme of identity loss
which is central to Twain's developing absurdist vision—a
theme which relates here most directly to Tom Driscoll and
Valet de Chambre. For if the reader asks how Tom and Valet
are to be told apart, how anyone can tell who is Tom and who
is Chambers, the answer is simply, by their fingerprints. There
is absolutely no other way of telling who is who! Identity is
here reduced to its basic essence, the lines on one's skin. There
is no more to it than that.

Identity, so Twain argues, is something that is socially
constructed and always liable to collapse.[57] The idea of the
'self' as fixed, stable and centred in an environment which it
can control is revealed as patent nonsense here, as Twain
questions the very fundamentals of nineteenth-century
novelistic belief.

To expand, if W. D. Howells wrote in *A Hazard of New
Fortunes* that 'conditions *make* character',[58] then that statement
can be applied with few reservations[59] to *Pudd'nhead Wilson*.
Environmental and racial conditioning plays a large part in
the definition of character in this novel and even the reader is
not exempt from such conditioning. We read Roxy's speeches:

> 'Marse Tom, I nussed you when you was a little baby, en I
> raised you all by myself tell you was 'most a young man; en now
> you is young en rich, en I is po' en gitt'n ole, en I come heah
> b'lievin' dat you would he'p de ole mammy 'long down de little
> road dat's left' 'twix' her en de grave, en—.'[60]

and are tempted to see her, to read her character, in a certain
way. Leslie Fiedler comments:

> Roxana ... is no gross, comfortable, placid source of warmth,
> all bosom and grin, but a passionate, complex and beautiful
> mulatto, a truly living woman distinguished from the wooden
> images of virtue and bitchery that pass for females in most
> American novels. She is 'black' only by definition, by social
> convention, though her actual appearance as described by
> Twain, 'majestic ... rosy ... comely', so baffled the platitude-

ridden illustrator of the official edition that he drew in her place a plump and comic Aunt Jemima![61]

It is not, I would contend, the description of Roxana's appearance that confuses, but her language. Her speech patterns conflict with her description ('as white as anybody',[62] 'her attitudes . . . imposing and statuesque, and her gestures and movements distinguished by a noble and stately grace'[63]), and it is this which confuses not just platitude-ridden illustrators, but, I would suggest, any reader. It is difficult to keep a picture of an intelligent, statuesque, white woman in mind when what appears on paper is black slave vernacular, and Twain recognizes this in pointing to the paradox that results from environmental conditioning, as applied to both Roxana and reader: 'From Roxy's manner of speech a stranger[64] would have expected her to be black, but she was not. . . .'[65]

The 'real' Tom is similarly conditioned by his environment as the ending makes clear. A white man, not a white woman, Tom is *entirely* a product of his condition as slave, and lacks the grace and beauty of Roxy (even though he is *officially* 'white' in a way she is not):

> He could neither read nor write, and his speech was the basest dialect of the negro quarter. His gait, his attitudes, his gestures, his bearing, his laugh—all were vulgar and uncouth; his manners were the manners of a slave.[66]

Conditions, to repeat, make character. *Pudd'nhead Wilson* reflects in Twain's use of this theme, the emergence of a Naturalistic fiction in America during this period.

If, then, Tom and Valet are interchangeable; if the only way they can be told apart is by their fingerprints; if both are what their conditioning has made them: then the corollary of this is that the notion of firm identity, of character, as innate more or less disappears. Twain here is launching a fundamental attack on the notion of 'character' as it had previously been accepted by the nineteenth-century novel, and shows his awareness of that instability of identity and social place which lie at the roots of Absurdist fiction.

In *Sister Carrie* identity is something which Carrie *constructs* in the course of the novel, as she shapes a self notable above all for its very plasticity to fit her dominating environment. Here also, though with a very different social and geographical environment, identity is plastic, shaped (for Tom and Valet are not allowed to *negotiate* their environments in the way Carrie can in the fluid, huge, urban world of Dreiser's novel) by the racial and social forces which make up the novel's world. Identity is mainly a result of environment; if a 'cauliflower is nothing but cabbage with a college education' (*Pudd'nhead Wilson's Calendar*),[68] then Twain's world in this novel is one of undifferentiated cabbages, which become different only because grown under different conditions. Identity, individuality, to repeat, can *only* be measured by fingerprinting.

This Naturalistic strain in Twain relates back to my earlier argument regarding Twain's move from Realism to Fantasy. In *Pudd'nhead Wilson*, Twain, having rejected the demythicizations and unmaskings of Realism as leading only in the direction of despair, dips his toe into Naturalist waters: the way in which the individual is enmeshed, and given his identity, by the social structures that surround him. Naturalism, however, most evidently fails to fulfil Twain's imaginative requirements, requirements which lead in the direction of dislocation and disintegration, both personal and social. He is uninterested in *Pudd'nhead Wilson* in the notion of character, in the way identity is constructed by the *negotiation* of an environment. Character here remains necessarily undeveloped as Twain puts all his emphasis not on interiority, but on plot: *plot* as a way of finally upsetting the Naturalist emphasis on a conditioning society. With his manipulation of plot, he manages to shoot his characters out of the edges of society to leave them rootless, nowhere. Tom and Valet's 'conditioning' is finally irrelevant—it is their alienation, their final dereliction, which interests Twain. And this points in the direction of his Absurdist concerns which were most fully realized in his later fantasies (The Dream Manuscripts). Fantasy, to stress, provided the form in which Twain's interest in dislocation and disruption could be most clearly presented.

Twain, then, plots *Pudd'nhead Wilson* to lay stress not just on identity as socially constructed, but more importantly for the future of his fiction, on identity as something which is liable to completely *collapse*. Tom and Valet are left with their identities shattered at the end of this novel, not who they—or anyone else—thought they were, unfurrowed. The possibility of losing one's name, place,[69] and home, losing—moreover—one's world,[70] becomes more and more of a central concern in Twain's fiction as his literary career progressed.

In addition, in *Pudd'nhead Wilson*, Twain moves beyond Naturalism in another way; for him it cannot provide a fully suitable literary form for his fictional concerns. If his four outsiders—Roxy, Wilson, Tom and Valet—are to lesser or greater extent contextualized by that society which surrounds them, then Twain is nevertheless equally interested in the possibility of complete alienation, personal dislocation, disruption: a possibility not easily contained within Naturalism. Moreover, Twain is insistent on seeing society—that society which carries so great a weight in Naturalist fiction generally—as fundamentally lacking in value. Social reconciliation (Wilson's for example) has little worth, can only be read ironically, when the society to which the individual is reconciled, is being so completely rejected—in terms of true moral or social 'worth'—by both reader and author as it is in *Pudd'nhead Wilson*. Twain turns the screw beyond Naturalism in this novel to lead his reader into an Absurdist world.[71]

Twain's fiction, then, from *A Connecticut Yankee* onwards points in the direction both of the Fantastic and of the Absurd. His protagonists are aliens and wanderers. Morgan's brash confidence in *A Connecticut Yankee* modulates through Wilson's ironical self-distancing in *Pudd'nhead Wilson* to a sense in the Dream Manuscripts and beyond, of terror and anguish felt in the face of a world on which no personal order can be imposed, in which the individual is tossed about by forces which he can never fully comprehend.

All firm bearings have been lost in Twain's later work. The confident spirit of *The Innocents Abroad*, where Twain's narrator sets out on the first of those many journeys which, as Jay Martin points out,[72] were to provide a metaphorical centre to his fiction, has given way to that terror which fills his fantasy *The Enchanted Sea Wilderness*, where a 'universal paralysis of life and energy' totally characterizes the region in which the *Adelaide* sails. All firm bearings are now completely lost. The ship's compass no longer provides an accurate pointer but 'whirled and whizzed this way and that, and never rested— never for a moment'.[73] The compass does give a true reading in *The Great Dark*, but this proves totally irrelevant in a world whose shaping physical geography is unknown to ship's captain and crew.

Henry Edwards, Twain's central protagonist in *The Great Dark*, is all at sea metaphorically as well as literally. Humorous elements initially appear in the narrative as when Turner, the second mate, confides to Edwards that 'The Gulf Stream's gone to the devil.' Edwards, in a position of supposed superior knowledge, conscious this whole journey is merely occurring within a dream, is able to appreciate the seaman's remark from a comic point of view. The joke turns sour, however, in the next episode, when the narrator's own certainties are removed with the Superintendent of Dreams' chilling remark: 'Are you quite sure [this journey] is a dream?'[74]

Twain's presented universe is by this stage a universe of radical uncertainty. It is also one of philosophical uncertainty. For that sense of metaphysical confusion, of being caught between two mental stances, which is to be seen so clearly in *A Connecticut Yankee*, is also sharply evidenced at the conclusion of *The Great Dark*. Captain Davis, who commands the boat on which Twain's protagonist is sailing into chaos, makes the following statement to conclude the tale:

> Are we rational men, men who can stand up and face hard luck and . . . say live or die, survive or perish, we are in for it, for good or bad, and we'll stand by the ship if she goes to hell![75]

This speech would seem to lead inescapably in the direction of that statement made by Ralph Ellison's protagonist at the end of *Invisible Man*, a remark echoed in spirit by so much modern American fiction: 'humanity is won by continuing to play in face of certain defeat.'[76] Twain seems to offer his reader a qualified affirmation here; the best man can do is follow Davis's example—stand at his fullest possible stature, to continue deliberately on his set course whatever the difficulties, and to look chaos in the face without in any way flinching.

To say, however, as Richard Hauck does, that Captain

Davis shows 'the courage of Sisyphus'[77] at this narrative point, to suggest that he takes on the rôle of existential hero, is only to mislead. There are no truly existential heroes in Twain's version of Absurdism. Twain, as I suggest, cannot find any point of metaphysical coherence in this fiction. For Twain softens, and indeed undercuts, his abrupt ending to the narrative (a logical ending, though, in philosophic, if not sequential, terms; the narrator's description of a seemingly endless and monstrously confused voyage does in a way need to end with such a statement of human dignity and courage in the face of such cosmic absurdity). He has the captain follow his initial statement of intent with an overwhelming bow in the direction of the conventional pieties: 'this ship is . . . in the hands of God. . . . If it is God's will that we pull through, we pull through.'[78]

The self-contradictory nature of the captain's own statements suggest that metaphysical uncertainty which is so much a mark of Twain's fiction from *A Connecticut Yankee* onwards. Obsessed with notions of order, both as an artist and as a man, in a late nineteenth-century world in which, as Henry Adams recognized, the only law of nature was to be found in Chaos, Twain found himself—and presented his protagonists—more and more as derelicts, homeless, caught between philosophical positions, between worlds (nineteenth- and twentieth-century, black and white), between a series of fixed positions, none of which was finally satisfactory in a universe viewed more and more through Absurdist eyes.

NOTES

1. Part of this article appeared in an earlier form in *Over Here*, a small magazine run by the Midland Branch of the British Association of American Studies: see *Over Here*, Vol. 3, No. 2 (Autumn, 1983), 35–44. I would like to thank David Murray, then editor of that magazine, for his advice and help as I was preparing this article for present publication.

2. *A Connecticut Yankee in King Arthur's Court* (New York and London: Harper & Brothers, 1899), p. 407.

3. I take my terms here from Max F. Schulz's *Black Humor Fiction of the Sixties* (Ohio University Press, 1973). Schulz argues that Black Humour

finds its 'logical home' (p. 7) in dealing with the 'absurdity' that existentialist fiction takes as its subject matter.

4. See Thomas Pynchon, *The Crying of Lot 49* (New York: Bantam Books, Inc., 1967), p. 95.

5. Mark Twain, *The Great Dark*, in John S. Tuckey (ed.), *Mark Twain's Which Was The Dream?* (University of California Press, 1967), p. 104.

6. Ibid., p. 120.

7. Eric Mottram, 'Culture and Technology in America 1850–1900' in *Essays by Eric Mottram and Philip Davies* (Polytechnic of Central London, American Studies Resources Centre, 1978); and *The Location of Dangerous Shoals: American Fictions on the Science of Power*, in *Over Here*, Vol. 3, No. 2 (Autumn, 1983). My argument at this point is a development and expansion of Eric Mottram's comments on Twain.

8. *A Connecticut Yankee*, p. 401.

9. R. P. Browning, M. B. Frank, L. Salamo (eds.), *Mark Twain's Notebooks and Journals Vol. III (1883–1891)* (University of California Press, 1979), p. 418.

10. Mottram, 'Culture and Technology in America 1850–1900', pp. 13–14.

11. Ibid.

12. *Mark Twain's Notebooks and Journals Vol. III*, p. 431.

13. *A Connecticut Yankee*, pp. 394–95.

14. Ibid., pp. 400–1.

15. Wyn Wachhorst, *Thomas Alva Edison: An American Myth* (M.I.T. Press, 1981), pp. 102–3.

16. Ibid., p. 19.

17. *A Connecticut Yankee*, p. 61.

18. Ibid., p. 359.

19. *Mark Twain's Notebooks and Journals Vol. III*, p. 216.

20. In using past history as his subject matter, Twain has no option in terms of the structure of the novel but to operate within a fictional cycle which takes his reader from dark ages to dark ages. The idea of meaningless repetition is thus fundamental as Twain closes the book at the place where, in effect, he began it.

21. *A Connecticut Yankee*, p. 404.

22. *Indiantown* in *Mark Twain's Which Was the Dream?* p. 167.

23. This leads back in turn in the direction of Twain's well-documented debt to south-western frontier humour. To illustrate, see G. W. Harris's 'Parson John Bullen's Lizards' from *Sut Lovingood* (New York: Grove Press, 1954), pp. 79–91. Literally and metaphorically, as the Parson's outer layers (of clothing here) are removed, so his true nature—hidden by the disguise of his profession—lies revealed. This concern with illusion and reality lies at the very heart of the south-western humorous tale.

24. Charles Neider (ed.), *The Complete Short Stories of Mark Twain* (New York: Doubleday & Company, Inc., 1957), pp. 19–20.

25. *Mark Twain's Which Was the Dream?*

26. This theme of being caught between two worlds is by no means new with *Connecticut Yankee* (see Europe and America in *The Innocents Abroad*,

East and West in *Roughing It*). The pessimistic connotations associated with the implied theme of dereliction though become noticeably stronger from this date.

27. See especially Jay Martin, *Harvests of Change: American Literature 1865–1914* (Englewood Cliffs, New Jersey: Prentice-Hall, Inc., 1967).

28. Lester F. Ward, 'Mind As A Social Factor', *Mind*, IX (October, 1884), 563–73.

29. Ibid., p. 563.

30. *A Connecticut Yankee*, pp. 56–7.

31. 'Mind As A Social Factor', p. 568.

32. Ibid., p. 570.

33. 'Did you think you had educated the superstition out of those people?' '. . . Imagine such human muck as this.' *A Connecticut Yankee*, pp. 380 and 389–90.

34. Richard Hauck, *A Cheerful Nihilism* (Indiana University Press, 1971), p. 140.

35. By devoting a chapter to Twain in *A Cheerful Nihilism* Hauck does fully recognize, let it be said, the 'decreasing humorous spirit (p. 157) of Twain's later writings.

36. Leslie Fiedler, for example, in *Love and Death in the American Novel* (New York: Criterion Books, 1960) sees Roxy as standing at 'the center of the motion and the plot' (p. 386). F. R. Leavis is quoted by Richard Chase in *The American Novel and its Tradition* (New York: Doubleday & Company Inc., 1957) as calling Pudd'nhead himself 'the poised and pre-eminently civilized moral center of the drama' (p. 150).

37. *A Connecticut Yankee*, p. 351.

38. Ibid., p. 359.

39. *Pudd'nhead Wilson and Those Extraordinary Twins* (New York and London: Harper & Brothers, 1899), p. 61.

40. Ibid., pp. 11–12.

41. Wilson's Calendar offers evidence of his full realization of the implications of his revelations. His final popularity is thus placed in ironic perspective by the cynical aphorisms which frame it; his own mental alienation from that community which has now for the first time accepted him, thus suggested. Twain comments at the end of the novel, 'he was a made man for good' (p. 223). This could be read two ways: *either* Wilson is 'made' in the sense of his future social and material success; *or* Wilson is now a man *made over* to fill a certain social rôle—if he were to reveal his true thoughts (The Calendar), social as well as intellectual alienation would be reimposed on him.

All this is speculatory. Twain insists on plot to the exclusion of character here. No interiority is allowed. He uses his plot to place a series of figures on the edge of society: we are permitted little or no access to the direct thoughts of those figures to suggest what relationship to their world they see themselves as having. Twain's controlled ironic vision is one which places consistent stress on displacement.

42. *Pudd'nhead Wilson*, p. 224.

43. *A Connecticut Yankee*, p. 363.

44. *Pudd'nhead Wilson*, p. 224.
45. Ibid., p. 223.
46. Ibid., p. 224.
47. Ibid., p. 225.
48. Malcolm Bradbury, in his introduction to the Penguin edition of *Pudd'nhead Wilson* (Harmondsworth, Middlesex, 1969), makes a number of persuasive comments on this novel and on its relationship to *Those Extraordinary Twins*. I develop some of these comments here.
49. See Leslie Fiedler, *Freaks* (New York: Simon & Schuster, 1978), for a study of their popularity with a Victorian audience.
50. Twain's care for grammatical accuracy here and the ambiguity about person(s)—singular or plural—thus reflected, leads in the direction of the ambiguity (philosophically and thematically essential) in *Pudd'nhead Wilson* concerning the nature of identity. One is continually tempted to clarify rôles by talking about the 'real' Tom or the 'false' Tom, whilst recognizing that by the end of the novel—so we, the readers, are conditioned by the conventions and persuasions of narrative—the 'false' Tom has become the only 'Tom' we know and recognize. This ambiguity and confusion is, of course, central to both the argument and the plot of the novel.
51. *Pudd'nhead Wilson and Those Extraordinary Twins*, pp. 230–31.
52. Ibid., p. 230.
53. Ibid., p. 230.
54. Ibid., p. 235.
55. Ibid., p. 16.
56. Ibid., p. 55. In *The Extraordinary Twins*, despite being 'phillipene' (p. 239), the heads of Luigi and Angelo are distinctly different in appearance. Initially, the problem still remains of telling the one brother from the other, 'by their names' at any rate (p. 240).
57. See the constant repetition of this theme in the later Dream Manuscripts. In *Which Was the Dream?* (*Mark Twain's Which Was the Dream*, pp. 31–73), Major General X wakes after his collapse to find his environment changed, his name—now Edward Jacobs—different.
58. *A Hazard of New Fortunes* (Oxford University Press, 1965), p. 396. Howells puts these words into the mouth of Basil March, who, it must be said, is at his most despairing about American society at this point in the novel. That statement, however, could stand as base for any definition of Naturalist literature.
59. Pudd'nhead calls Tom 'degenerate' (p. 126), and Twain mentions his 'native viciousness' (p. 43), the fact that 'he was a bad baby, from the very beginning of his usurpation' (p. 38). The relationship between nature and nurture is muddy at this point, though, as suggested by the final three words of the previous quote. Tom's faults are undoubtedly exaggerated by, if not caused by, his upbringing: 'Tom got all the petting, Chambers got none. Tom got all the delicacies, Chambers got mush and milk, and clabber without sugar. In consequence Tom was . . . "fractious", as Roxy called it, and overbearing: Chambers was meek and docile' (p. 40). In *Indiantown* (pp. 158–62 in particular) and Paul Baender (ed.), *What is*

197

Man? (University of California Press, 1973), Twain would expand his views on the nature-nurture issue.

60. *Pudd'nhead Wilson*, p. 76.
61. Leslie A. Fiedler, *Love and Death in the American Novel*, pp. 386–87.
62. A further irony: blacks obviously do not feature in such a body count!
63. *Pudd'nhead Wilson*, pp. 22–3.
64. The reader as alien?
65. *Pudd'nhead Wilson*, p. 22.
66. Ibid., p. 224.
67. This *despite* the false Tom's 'native viciousness'. What is 'native' here would have been ruthlessly suppressed and exterminated had Tom been brought up as the slave he was born as. His cruelty is allowed to flourish, to exist, as mere extension of that of the class of which he has artificially been made a member, a class which owes its existence to the fact of slavery, that 'daily robb[ery] . . . of an inestimable treasure—[man's] liberty' (pp. 27–8). The irony of the concluding phrase is self-evident.
68. *Pudd'nhead Wilson*, p. 49.
69. See the Dream Manuscripts, especially *Which Was the Dream?*
70. This particular concern looks back to *A Connecticut Yankee*, forward to *The Great Dark*.
71. The stress on fluidity, on openness, on process, in Naturalist thought can also be seen to lead in the direction of the Absurd.
72. See *Harvests of Change*, 'Mark Twain: The Dream of Drift and the Dream of Delight', pp. 165–201.
73. *The Enchanted Sea-Wilderness* in *Mark Twain's Which Was the Dream?* (p. 82). Tony Tanner develops this theme in relation to Henry Adams' writing in 'The Lost America—The Despair of Henry Adams and Mark Twain' in Henry Nash Smith (ed.), *Mark Twain: A Collection of Critical Essays*, (Englewood Cliffs, New Jersey: Prentice-Hall, Inc., 1963), pp. 159–74.
74. *The Great Dark*, pp. 118 and 124.
75. *The Great Dark*, p. 150.
76. *Invisible Man* (Harmondsworth, Middlesex: Penguin Books, 1965), p. 465.
77. *A Cheerful Nihilism*, p. 163.
78. *The Great Dark*, p. 150.

8

Mark Twain and King Leopold of the Belgians

by ROBERT GIDDINGS

> There are many humorous things in the world; among them the
> white man's notion that he is less savage than other savages.
> (Mark Twain, *Following the Equator*, 1897)

1

One evening in Monte Carlo Frank Harris and Lord
Randolph Churchill had a really heart-to-heart talk about
politics. It was after a good dinner at the Hotel de Paris, and
the garrulous Harris found that they were poles apart: 'I
pointed out that just as village communities were superseded
by nations', he recorded, 'so nations now were in process of
being superseded by world empires; already two were being
formed, Russia and the United States, which must soon dwarf
all nations. . . .'[1] The anecdote is not dated by Frank Harris,
but Lord Randolph Churchill died in 1895. Mark Twain lived
and worked during the opening stages of America's rise to
global imperialism and was certainly fascinated by it.[2]

The foundations of the United States' early imperialism
were laid in the immediate post-Civil War period, in the
systematic denial to the Red Indians of the territories they had
inhabited and of the very means by which they had survived.
As Gareth Stedman Jones has so convincingly argued, there
are several significant misconceptions about the historical

development of American imperialism which successfully mask its basic continuity. The fact that in its initial stages it was not territorial or colonial, but was a westward movement across its own continent, involving the destruction of the indigenous population and the conquest of aboriginal territory, has made it seem essentially unlike the British colonization of the West Indies, India, the Antipodes, or the French, Belgian, German or Dutch colonial ventures in Africa and the Far East. U.S. imperialism was initially non-territorial. This has allowed the Land of the Free to pose as a champion of national liberation, whereas the opposite was essentially the case. The national stance is buttressed and supported by the most powerful ideological superstructure:

> . . . the construction of a mythological, non-communist, non-socialist and even non-nationalist road to political independence for the countries of the Third World. To woo aspiring politicians of these new states, the United States has offered the model of the 'American Revolution' of 1776. It was on this basis that Franklin Roosevelt considered that the United States was uniquely equipped to advise India on the road to independence, and it was again on the basis of this claim that Eisenhower felt entitled to ditch his Anglo-French imperialist allies at the time of the Suez crisis in 1956. . . .[3]

The opening up of the West, which occurred after Twain returned from Europe and Palestine (*Innocents Abroad*, 1869) and his marriage and setting up household in Hartford, Connecticut, was the first stage of a rapacious progress which has never felt retiring ebb, but kept due on to the Pacific and beyond. Yet Twain hardly deals with the American Indian in his fiction, except insofar as he features in 'character' rôles from time to time.[4] The great land grab and the massacres which featured as a staple diet in the American press while he experimented with humorous inventions, wrote essays, short stories and published *The Gilded Age* (1873), *A Tramp Abroad* (1880) and *Following the Equator* (1897) seemed hardly to interest him. He told the American press in 1900, after his return from another set of travels: 'I am anti-imperialist. I am opposed to having the eagle put its talons on any other land.' His failures in printing and publishing enterprises had brought him to bankruptcy, and he launched into a world-wide lecturing tour to get himself in funds. What he saw of European imperialism in the South Pacific, Asia and Africa made his blood run cold. These European nations, he argued, did not deserve the term 'civilized'. Of the colonization of Australia, for example, he said:

> We are obliged to believe that a nation that could look on, unmoved, and see starving or freezing women hanged for stealing twenty-six cents' worth of bacon or rags, and boys snatched from their mothers, and men from their families, and sent to the other side of the world for long terms of years for similar trifling offences, was a nation to whom the term 'civilized' could not in any large way be applied. And we must also believe that a nation that knew, during more than forty years, what was happening to those exiles and was still content with it, was not advancing in any slow way toward a higher grade of civilization.[5]

He wrote ironically of the need to annex the Sandwich Islands in order to bring to them the unspeakable benefits of civilization:

> We *must* annex those people. We can afflict them with our wise and beneficent government. We can introduce the novelty of thieves, and all the way up from street-car pickpockets to municipal robbers and government defaulters, and show them how amusing it is to arrest them and try them and then turn them loose—some for cash and some for 'political influence'. We can make them ashamed of their simple and primitive justice. . . . We can give them juries composed entirely of the most simple and charming leatherheads. We can give them railway corporations who will buy their Legislatures like old clothes, and run over their best citizens and complain of the corpses for smearing their unpleasant juices on the track. . . . We can give them Tweed . . . we can furnish them some Jay Goulds who will do away with their old-time notion that stealing is not respectable. . . . And George Francis Train.[6] We can give them lecturers! I will go myself.
>
> We can make that little bunch of sleepy islands the hottest corner on earth, and array it in the moral splendour of our high and holy civilization. Annexation is what the poor islanders need. 'Shall we to men benighted, the lamp of life deny?'[7]

At the time when Mark Twain's creative energies were blooming in a series of works which obviously still retain the power to dazzle the imagination, the Americans were gradually depriving the Red Indians of their land by deceit, slaughter, military might and starvation. The land, once possessed, was soon so abused that the wildlife which had supported generations of numerous Indian tribes[8] was destroyed without hope of regeneration. This is still to a considerable extent a buried part of the nation's consciousness. As John Upton Terrell writes:

> It is incomprehensible to me how a people can benefit by deliberately suppressing and ignoring opprobrious episodes of their past. By what means can they measure their social, economic and cultural progress without taking into account the mistakes, faults and crimes of their ancestors? Persons whose minds are open only to pleasant legends of bygone years are, in effect, condoning the half-truths customarily disseminated by chambers of commerce and advertising agencies and abetting the immoral practices of pseudopatriots and political demagogues.[9]

The curious thing is that Mark Twain seems, on the surface at least, to have done his best to have forgotten it as well. There are moments of outburst, of course, and it would dishonour Twain's memory to deny them. They are so fiery that we should relish them. But they are scattered. For a man who professed and proclaimed his vehement hatred of imperialism, and American imperialism no less than any other proprietary brand, the random nature of his outbursts on behalf of the redskin is very interesting.

2

Mark Twain wrote in his notebook in 1882 that the U.S. government had spent a lot of money killing indians: 'We have killed 200 Indians. What did it cost? $2,000,000. You could have given them a college education for that.' Three years later he urged Grover Cleveland, President of the U.S.A., to protect the Indians in the West from the terrible treatment they were getting both from the private citizenry (settlers and prospectors) and from U.S. government officials: 'You not only have the power to destroy scoundrelism of many kinds in this country, but you have amply proved that you also have the unwavering disposition and purpose to do it.' Enclosed with this letter he sent the President a cutting from the *Southwest Sentinel*, published in Silver City, New Mexico:

$250 REWARD

The above reward will be paid by the Board of County Commissioners of Grant County to any citizens of said county for each and every hostile renegade Apache killed by such citizen, on presentation to said Board of the scalp of such Indian.

By Order of the Board, E. Stine, Clerk[10]

The great humorist was here attempting to swim against a very strong ideological tide.

Social Darwinism was a powerful current in American thinking.[11] The doctrine of the Anglo-Saxon superiority was spread at colleges and universities, where the ideas of such scholars as Edward Augustus Freeman (1823–92)—enshrined in his *Comparative Politics* (1874)—were deeply influential. Freeman asserted that history was a science comparable to the biological sciences, and that

For the purposes of Comparative Politics, a political constitution is a specimen to be studied, classified, and labeled, as a building or an animal is studied, classified, and labeled by those to whom buildings or animals are objects of study.[12]

What is arresting here is the fact that romantic notions of 'nationhood' and the 'manifest destiny' which predate Darwinism (cf. John Mitchell Kemble, *The Saxons in England* (1849) and Charles Kingsley, *The Roman and the Teuton* (1864)) lean on a perverted understanding of biology for their ultimate justification.

As the nineteenth century advanced and manifested European and American nationalism and imperialism— which are among the later stages of the imperatives of capitalism and thus have essentially economic causes[13]— history was distorted to present the justification for favouring certain races over others, by means of a brand of scientific determinism which demonstrated the inevitability of the triumph of certain political and economic systems over others.

203

In other words, the colonial conquest of the West Indies, India, Africa, Asia and the New World by Caucasians was part of God's plan for the world. This was certainly how such matters were in fact taught to those whose happy duty it was to serve the British Empire. J. Fitzgerald Lee, author of a work first published in 1902, but regularly reprinted until the 1930s—recommended to military students and dedicated (with permission) to His Excellency Lord Kitchener—comes right out and says in so many words that the whole thing was God's idea right from the start:

> It is not without some reason, beyond our ken, that the greatest empire in the world, the greatest of the White Race, happens to hold these lands on the other side of the globe, as well as the temperate regions in North America and South Africa. The wonderful growth of the British Empire, from Pole to Pole, has been attributed to various causes: by our friends, to British enterprise and statesmanship; by our enemies, to our alleged qualities of greed and cunning; although recent world-events have proved that these latter characteristics are the monopoly of no one people under the sun. And they cannot be reasonably held to account for such geographical phenomena as the Gulf Stream bearing warm breezes to the British Islands, or the monsoons coming at the right time to water the parching plains of British India. The same inscrutable causes which placed England's geographical position in the centre of the land hemisphere arranged that the great mass of the habitable lands on earth should be in the temperate zone, where men can best live; into these things it is not the business of the geographer to enquire, but only to deal with them as he finds them.[14]

This is the thrust of much influential 'history' produced at this period—cf. John Richard Green, *Short History of the English People* (1874), *The Making of England* (1881) and *The Conquest of England* (1883), and James K. Hosmer, *Short History of Anglo-Saxon Freedom* (1890). These volumes may be seen as more or less respectable history, quite different in kind from the more bizarre products of the racism and imperialism of the time, produced by such pursuasive cranks as Comte Arthur de Gobineau, whose seminal *Essai su l'Inégalité des Races Humaines* was published in 1853–55, and Houston Stewart Chamberlain, whose *Die Grundlagen des neunzehnten Jahrhunderts* (1899) was published in English in 1910. Gobineau's dangerous thesis was that it was only the white races who alone were capable of creating culture and true civilization. Unfortunately, he claimed, they had become enervated as the result of no longer being 'pure'; he put into circulation the idea of the superman and in several respects was the intellectual parent of Nietzsche. Chamberlain, son of an English admiral and public school educated, was a life-long Germanophile and anti-semite. He published a biography of Wagner and married his daughter. During the First World War he became a naturalized German subject and published much anti-British propaganda. For him it was the Germans alone who could produce culture and political organization and stability.[15]

In the mid-nineteenth century when free trade was at its height, even a colonial power such as Britain was actually opposed to territorial expansion. It was almost universally believed that the colonies were an albatross round the national neck and that their ultimate separation and independence from Britain was both desirable and inevitable. That great British imperialist Benjamin Disraeli actually declared in 1852: 'The colonies are a millstone round our necks.'[16] Colonies had been accumulated as the result of various wars, with little thoughts of their development or exploitation as overseas empire.[17] It was not until the second part of the century that the British began in practice to realize the potential of empire—as John George Lambton, Earl of Durham wrote:

> The experiment of keeping colonies and governing them well, ought at least to have a trial, ere we abandon forever the vast dominion [Canada] which might supply the wants of our surplus population, and raise up millions of fresh consumers of our manufactures.

He had been appointed Governor-General of Canada, and his recommendations for reforming the administration of the colony, embodied in the *Durham Report* (1839) are an important staging-post in Britain's development as an imperial nation.[18] The vast accumulation of capital made colonial expansion inescapable.[19] Between 1884 and 1900

Great Britain acquired 3,700,000 square miles of territory and 57,000,000 inhabitants; France got 3,600,000 square miles, with 36,500,000 inhabitants; Germany 1,000,000 square miles and 14,700,000 inhabitants; Belgium 900,000 square miles and 30,000,000 people and Portugal obtained 800,000 square miles and 9,000,000 people.[20] As the Rev. C. S. Dawe so sweetly put it in a little book often given to children as a school prize:

> The British Empire consists not only of the United Kingdom and such large countries as Canada, Australia and India, but it comprises also a host of small settlements dotted about the world, and valuable either for purposes of war or commerce. In consequence of our Empire being world-wide, there is scarcely a month when peace reigns in every part of it. We have generally some little war on hand. . . .[21]

There are few things as strong as ideas at the right time. These ideas gained generous circulation in the U.S.A. at the close of the nineteenth century as the result of their dissemination in educational institutions which turned out so many of the policy-makers of the nation. To take just one example: at Columbia University Theodore Roosevelt was a student of John William Burgess, who had been educated at Amherst, and at Göttingen, Leipzig and Berlin. In 1873 he had been appointed Professor of History and Political Science at Amherst and later became Professor of Political Science and Constitutional Law at Columbia. In his *Political Science and Comparative Constitutional Law* (1890) Burgess argued that he had a new approach to the subject. It was a comparative study which applied the method successful in the natural sciences to political science and jurisprudence. His findings included the demonstration that political capacity was not a gift which was to be found equally distributed among the peoples of the earth. Only a few races had it at all, and of these the Aryan races stood supreme:

> The Teuton really dominates the world by his superior political genius. . . . It is therefore not to be assumed that every nation must become a state. The political subjection or attachment of unpolitical nations to those possessing political endowment appears, if we may judge from history, to be as truly a part of the world's civilization as is the national organization of states.

I do not think that Asia and Africa can ever receive political organization in any other way. . . . The national state is . . . the most modern and complete solution of the whole problem of political organization which the world has yet produced; and the fact that it is the creation of Teutonic political genius stamps the Teutonic nations as the political nations *par excellence*, and authorizes them, in the economy of the world, to assume the leadership in the establishment and administration of states. . . .[22]

The lesson was not wasted on Theodore Roosevelt, whose *The Winning of the West*, published in four volumes (1889–96), portrayed the struggles of the frontiersmen with the Indians as a final working-out of a racial war which was inevitable and in the nature of things. As Richard Hofstadter writes, in Roosevelt's eyes the great expansion of American influence, over the Indians in the West and in extra-territorial American imperialism, was simply the final stages of an expansion to be traced back

many centuries to the days when German tribes went forth to conquest from their marshy forests. American development represents the culminating achievement of this mighty history of racial growth.[23]

In the words of Horace ('Go West, young man, and grow up with the county') Greeley, writing in *An Overland Journey, from New York to San Francisco* (1860):

It needs but little familiarity with the actual, palpable aborigines to convince anyone that the poetic Indian—the Indian of Cooper and Longfellow—is only visible to the poet's eye. To the prosaic observer, the average Indian of the woods and prairies is a being who does little credit to human nature—a slave of appetite and sloth, never emancipated from the tyranny of one animal passion save by the more ravenous demands of another. As I passed over those magnificent bottoms of the Kansas which form the reservations of the Delewares, Potawatamies, etc., constituting the very best corn-lands on earth, and saw their owners sitting around the doors of their lodges at the height of the planting season and in as good, bright planting weather as sun and soil ever made, I could not help saying: 'These people must die out—there is no help for them. God has given this earth to those who will subdue and cultivate it, and it is vain to struggle against his righteous decree.' . . .[24]

But the appalling and horrific scandal of the destruction of the indigenous Indian population of the South West seems to a large extent to be submerged in Twain's writing. He is determined to play down with all his considerable energies the 'noble savage' stereotyping of the Redskin, whom he refused to view—in his own words—'through the mellow moonshine of romance'. Does this mean that so unquestionably a great American writer, who lived through what was, in effect, the colonization of the American West, ignored such human suffering, and that all he had to say about Indians will be found in his portraits of the less attractive side of Indian behaviour?

3

There is ample evidence that Twain found ideas of racial superiority repugnant, and that he had a deep loathing for contemporary European rapaciousness. It is found scattered through his writings, but finds exemplary expression in the extraordinary work, *King Leopold's Soliloquy*, published in Boston in 1905, and in London a year later. It seems to me that he projects his loathing of the criminal treatment of savage people by white colonists and their willing military and government agents in this satiric attack on King Leopold's production of personal wealth from the resources of the Free State of the Congo by a policy of terror, repression, rape and genocide in the guise of a civilizing and christianizing mission to the dark continent.

In the Autumn of 1904 Mark Twain was approached by the English radical and reformer E. D. Morel, head of the Congo Reform Association,[25] who asked him to give his support as a writer to 'the cause of the Congo natives'. The east coast expedition of Verney Lovett Cameron to relieve Livingstone in 1873, which started from Bagamoyo and reached Benguela in November 1875, led to the formation of the Association International Africaine under the auspices of Leopold, King of the Belgians. The proclaimed ambition of the Association was to suppress slavery and civilize Africa. The movement was given considerable impetus by the discoveries of Henry Morton Stanley, who had traced the Congo to the sea. Supported by Leopold he founded the Congo Free State in 1879. This led to the Congo Congress in Berlin in 1884–85, which gave the Free State international status. Before the slave trade could be abolished, war broke out between the Belgians and the Arab slavers under Tippoo Tib. It was this crisis which caused Leopold to adopt the concessional system to exploit the natural resources of the area to recoup the cost of the war. This was the system of obtaining rubber and other materials by exerting terror on the population who were thus compelled to labour in order to produce the supplies for which the country was ransacked.

Leopold had never exhibited the slightest doubt that he knew what colonies were for. He was one of the earliest European statesmen to realize the vast economic advantages to be had from a systematic exploitation of overseas possessions in the tropics. His ideas on this matter predate his acquisition of the Congo Free State in 1885 by over twenty years: witness his famous Letter on the Advantages of Colonization, dated 26 July 1863. Discounting the usefulness of slave colonies, such as Cuba, and bearing in mind the problem which would exist in getting the best out of colonies in cases where the working class in the home European country will not emigrate and the home middle class lack opportunities, he concentrates on the value of 'Colonies inhabited by a numerous native race, which have been made a dependency of some European state'. The native population, he is willing to grant, will have to be 'subordinated to a European people', but the economic advantages to the European country are considerable: 'Such countries are not real colonies but external possessions which are very productive if well chosen. . . .' He admits that 'forced labour' is usually the only way of 'civilizing and imposing moral standards on these lazy and corrupt peoples . . .'. Those who assist the cultivation of the colony properly will one day be able to 'buy back their liberty from the state and become landowners. Taxes will replace labour obligations. . . .' The advantages for the investment of domestic capital are considerable. It is a perfect solution to the vexing problem of capital accumulation, as the colony, if properly selected, will provide investment potential, careers and work, while adding nothing to the budget of the mother country—on the contrary—the colony will support the mother country with an annual bonus of millions, more than paying the costs of government administration and the army and navy needed to run and to police such a scheme.[26] What did it mean for the congo when these theories were put into practice?

On 10 December 1865 Leopold succeeded his father and became Leopold II, King of the Belgians. Ten years later he organized and assumed the presidency of the International Association for the Exploration and Civilization of Central Africa. Henry Morton Stanley had hoped to interest British capital or the British government in developing the lower Congo, but he failed to do so. He was supported by Leopold, who sent him back to Africa to stake claims for the Association. The United States officially recognized the Association as an 'independent state' in 1884, and in 1885 Leopold became King of the Independent State of the Congo.

The Berlin Conference admitted Leopold's claim but supported the idea of free trade, the suppression of the slave trade and the moral well-being of the native population. But, in effect, Leopold was the owner of a million miles of land, with a population of twenty million natives. He sent agents to exploit the resources of the land—mainly rubber and ivory at this stage, before the discovery of the land's vast mineral wealth. The realization of the Congo's economic properties required the people to be dispossessed of their land and put into camps. Their job was to collect rubber, and they were punished if they failed to deliver the required quota. The incentives were the amputation of hands and feet and other barbarities. Within twenty years it was estimated between five and eight million men, women and children died, others surviving as cripples. But the system was efficient. Output increased from $30,000 in 1886 to $8,000,000 in 1900.[27]

From the early 1890s stories of atrocities committed in the Congo began to filter back to Europe and across the Atlantic from missionaries, explorers and reformers. Initially these stories were simply not believed. In 1903 Roger Casement, then British Consul at Boma, in the Belgian Congo, released an official report on the administration of the Congo Free

State. The document was a terrible catalogue of fiendish acts
and told the story of forced labour and coercion—the latter
included the amputation of limbs and genitals, village-burning
and the murder and mutilation of children. Those in charge of
the labour gangs carried baskets full of hands (smoked to
preserve them in the tropical climate) to demonstrate their
authority. Women were raped and sent to the brothels for
Leopold's military or official personnel. The tax system levied
on the native workers ensured they returned whatever miserable wages they actually earned. The entire process was
making Leopold into one of the richest men in the world.

E. D. Morel learned of these atrocities very largely from
Casement's disclosures and was prompted to form the Congo
Reform Association and to contact Mark Twain. But Twain had
the Congo on his mind before this. His correspondence shows
his awareness of Leopold's record in the Congo,[28] and there is
an unpublished *Thanksgiving Sentiment*, which dates from 1904:

> We have much to be thankful for. Our free Republic being the
> official godfather of the Congo Graveyard, first of the Powers to
> recognise its pirate flag & become responsible through silence
> for the prodigious depredations & multitudinous murders
> committed under it upon the helpless natives by King Leopold
> of Belgium in the past twenty years: now therefore let us be
> humbly thankful that this last twelvemonth has seen the King's
> usual annual myriad of murders reduced by nearly one & one
> half per cent; let us be humbly grateful that the good King, our
> pet & protogé, due in hell these sixty-five years, is still spared to
> us to continue his work & ours among the friendless & the
> foresaken; finally let us live in the blessed hope that when in the
> Last Great Day he is confronted with his unoffending millions
> upon millions of robbed, mutilated & massacred men, women
> & children & required to explain, he will be as politely silent
> about us as we have been about him.[29]

In some ways *King Leopold's Soliloquy* is, in effect, like a
vicious parody of a Robert Browning monologue. Twain
seems to have taken Browning's basic ironic method of having
a character, speaking in monologue, attempt to explain or
apologise for his life or career, and in the process actually
condemn himself out of his own mouth, realizing those lines in
Hamlet: 'So full of artless jealousy is guilt,/ It spills itself in

fearing to be spilt.'[30] But Twain pushes the *genre* to the extremes of grotesque self-revelation. It is written as a script for an actor, complete with stage directions. Twain masterfully works in material additional to Leopold's musings—extracts from official reports of activities in the Congo, eye-witness accounts of atrocities and authorial footnotes to add detail. The effect is devastating. The work is beautifully constructed, developing from rather crude knock-about comedy at the opening, through a whole range of brilliant and often moving effects—pathos, bathos, melodrama, comedy and savage irony.

Leopold is placed before us deeply disturbed and anxious at the fact that the truth about the Congo is coming out. He curses and prays by turns:

> In these twenty years I have spent millions to keep the press of the two hemispheres quiet, and still these leaks keep occurring. I have spent other millions on religion and art, and what do I get for it? Nothing. Not a compliment. These generosities are studiously ignored, in print. In print I get nothing but slanders— and slanders again—and still slanders, and slanders on top of slanders! Grant them true, what of it? They are slanders all the same, when uttered against a king.
> Miscreants—they are telling *everything!*[31]

'Everything' turns out to have consisted of Leopold's cunning mixture of hypocrisy, guile and mendacity for his civilizing/ christianizing mission which gave him supremacy in the Congo. He is proud of the way he duped European states and tricked the U.S.A.

> Oh, well, let them blackguard me if they like; it is a deep satisfaction to me to remember that I was a shade too smart for that nation that thinks itself so smart. Yes, I certainly did bunco a Yankee. . . . Pirate flag? Let them call it so. . . . All the same, *they were the first to salute it.*[32]

He goes on to call the American missionaries, British consuls and Belgian officials who have published the truth about the Congo 'pests' who have 'kept back nothing!' Shame should have kept them silent since these exposures place a king in an insufferable light: '. . . they were exposures of a king, a sacred personage and immune from reproach, by right of his selection and appointment to his great office by God himself. . . .'[33]

Twain has now raised our curiosity. What have these pests been saying? Leopold tells us:

> . . . how I levy incredibly burdensome taxes upon the natives—taxes which are a pure theft; taxes which they must satisfy by gathering rubber under hard and constantly harder conditions, and by raising and furnishing food supplies gratis—and it all comes out that, when they fall short of their tasks through hunger, sickness, despair, and ceaseless and exhaustive labour without rest, and forsake their homes and flee to the woods to escape punishment, my black soldiers, drawn from unfriendly tribes, and instigated and directed by my Belgians, hunt them down and butcher them and burn their villages—reserving some of the girls. . . . But they never say . . . that I have laboured in the cause of religion at the same time . . . and have sent missionaries there . . . to teach them the error of their ways and bring them to Him who is all mercy and love. . . .[34]

He goes on to read some of the evidence of these missionaries and meddlers, who work statistics up into offensive kindergarten object lessons, 'whose purpose is to make sentimental people shudder, and prejudice them against me. . . .' He reads out some of these object lessons:

> if the innocent blood shed in the Congo by King Leopold were put in buckets and placed side by side, it would stretch 2,000 miles; if the skeletons of his ten millions of starved and butchered dead could rise up and march in single file, it would take them seven months and four days to pass a given point; if compacted together in a body, they would occupy more ground than St. Louis covers, World's Fair and all. . . .[35]

In order to refute and to minimize the evidence, the King has to read it. This enables us to hear it. He then turns to a pamphlet by the Rev. A. E. Scrivener, a British missionary, which describes a journey made in July, August and September 1903. It is a sickening catalogue of barbarities. The Rev. Scrivener's account ends with his seeing the bones of numerous victims of Leopold's system, and watching the file of rubber collectors coming in:

> with their little baskets under their arms [I] saw them paid their milk tin full of salt . . . saw their trembling timidity, and in fact a great deal that all went to prove the state of terrorism that exists and the virtual slavery in which the people are held.[36]

Leopold is offended at the depths to which his enemies will sink to discredit him—why, Mr. Casement even reprints private diaries and journals not intended for general circulation, which distastefully reveals the mutilation of adults and the killing of children with the butts of rifles. Leopold attempts to excuse 'severing hands, unsexing men etc.' by saying that these were already native customs in which we Europeans simply followed local traditions. And these reformers have the nerve to retort:

> If a Christian King can perceive a saving moral difference between inventing bloody barbarities, and *imitating them from savages*, for charity's sake let him get what comfort he can out of his confession![37]

A report by the Rev. W. H. Sheppard included an interview with a black raider in Leopold's service who describes how he took part in the massacre of between eighty and ninety natives and mutilated their bodies. One victim's skull was made into a tobacco bowl. He saw eighty-one hands (which he counted) being smoked over a fire to preserve them. Leopold turns to the evidence gathered by E. D. Morel and exclaims: 'This Morel is a king's subject, and reverence for monarchy should have restrained him from reflecting upon me with that exposure.'

The climax of Leopold's monologue is his denunciation of the camera—this is the most damaging weapon used against him. It is interesting to note that Twain submitted the *Soliloquy* to American magazines, but none dared to print it. He gave it to the American Congo Reform Association and it was published by the Warren Company of Boston. On Twain's personal advice this edition carried photographs and drawings of mutilated negroes—men, women and children.[38] Leopold now almost begins to despair:

> The kodak has been a sore calamity to us. The most powerful enemy indeed. In the early years we had no trouble in getting the press to 'expose' the tales of mutilations as slanders, lies, inventions . . . and by the press's help we got the Christian nations everywhere to turn an irritated and unbelieving ear to these tales. . . . Yes, all things went harmoniously and pleasantly in those good days, and I was looked up to as the benefactor of a

down-trodden and friendless people. Then all of a sudden came the crash! That is to say, the incorruptible *kodak* and all the harmony went to hell! The only witness I have encountered in my long experience that I couldn't bribe.[39]

How is he going to escape universal condemnation? He reads one last dreadful pamphlet which further summarizes the appalling inhumanities for which he is responsible:

He is *sole* master there; he is absolute. He could have prevented the crimes by his mere command; he could stop them today with a word. He withholds the word. For his pocket's sake.[40]

The end of the *Soliloquy* is a striking example of that cynicism and pessimism which is typical of the mature Twain. Having driven Leopold to the point where there seems no escape, Twain reveals that in human nature itself lies his refuge. The pamphlet the King reads ends with the words:

'We see this awful King, this pitiless and blood-drenched King, this money-crazy King . . . but *we do not wish to look*; for he is a King, and it hurts us, by ancient and inherited instinct it shames us to see a King degraded to this aspect; and we shrink from hearing the particulars of how it happened. *We shudder and turn away* when we come upon them in print.

As Leopold says, this is his salvation: 'Why, certainly, THAT IS MY PROTECTION. And you will continue to do it. I know the human race.'[41]

This work is vintage Twain, the distillation of a lifetime's experience in using words to amuse, pursuade, cajole, moralize, satirize, inform, educate and disturb. In it he combines the skills learned in his long apprenticeship to authorship in the widest sense—*King Leopold's Soliloquy* is a *tour de force* which displays Twain in several aspects of his trade—journalist, lecturer, playwright, preacher, story-teller, and—above all—satirist.

4

The *Soliloquy* did a lot of good. It was a shot in the arm for the American Congo Reform Association. Henry I. Kowalsky, an agent employed by the Belgian government, notified King Leopold in December 1904:

> Mark Twain, or Samuel Clemens (which is his proper name) must certainly have a retainer from the English people. The fight here (in the U.S.A.) is organized as it has never been before. Monster petitions have been circulated and signed; the industry of the opposition is very manifest, and I can assure you that you cannot afford to turn a deaf ear to what I am saying.[42]

The *Soliloquy* had a good press in England and was publicized in the pages of *The Athenaeum, Punch,* the *Bookman* and its author was congratulated by E. D. Morel. Twain gave all his income from this work to the American Congo Reform Association. At this time several leading American capitalists—John Pierpont Morgan, John D. Rockefeller, Thomas Fortune Ryan and Daniel Guggenheim—were negotiating investment in the Congo. The publicity Twain's work had given the Congo was understandably embarrassing, and they spent out large sums to counteract its effects, hiring academics and churchmen to disclaim the atrocity stories. The stakes were very high, for, in the same year which saw the composition of *King Leopold's Soliloquy*, it became clear that the wealth to be made out of the Congo was immense; deposits of copper, zinc, cobalt, cadmium, tungsten and diamonds were discovered.

International tension over the Congo mounted in the light of the condemnation of Leopold. For example, Sir Edward Grey, British Foreign Secretary, declared: 'The Congo state has morally forfeited every right to international recognition.' In February 1908 a British parliamentary paper, *Africa No. 1,* which contained reports from the British Consul at Boma, W. G. Thesiger, further fanned international opinion. In March 1908 Leopold attempted to make the best terms he could, but in August the same year the Belgian government adopted a treaty of cession and the Congo was annexed as a Belgian colony. On 14 November 1908 the Congo Free State ceased to exist.[43] Leopold died the following year.

The Congo horrors remain as fresh now as the time when Mark Twain produced his vehement and effective satire. That this continues to be so underlines the fact that although these personalities and events are historically specific, they nevertheless conform to the depressing and recurring configuration of human experience which constitutes an inescapable ingredient in the paradigm of capitalism—Cuba, the Philippines,

Latin America, Burma, Indo-China, India, the scramble for Africa. . . . The ultimate Twainian irony may be found in the fact that the New World was itself discovered by Christopher Columbus in an earlier version of the same old sordid story. He hoped to capitalize discovery by means of slaves and gold. Slavery proved unprofitable, hundreds of Indians died *en route* to Europe. So it had to be gold. At Hispaniola every man, woman and child was to collect gold for the Spaniards. Every three months they had to bring in a hawk's bell filled with gold dust. Chiefs had to bring in ten times that amount. If they failed, they had their hands chopped off. There were no goldfields. The task was clearly impossible. The wretched natives tried panning for gold, which was fruitless. If they attempted to flee, they were hunted by Spaniards with dogs. Resistance was impossible. Many of them committed mass suicide with casava poison. By 1496 there was clearly no gold left, and the remaining members of the population were used as slave labour on *encomiendas*. By 1540 the entire nation of Arawack Indians had vanished from the face of the earth—totally exterminated.[44] Mark Twain's identification with anti-imperialism was total. He opened his speech at the annual dinner of the New England Society in 1881: 'My first American ancestor, gentlemen, was an Indian, an early Indian. Your ancestors skinned him alive, and I am an orphan.'

NOTES

1. Frank Harris, *My Life and Loves*, edited by John F. Gallagher (New Jersey: Castle Books, 1963), p. 485.
2. See Gareth Stedman Jones, 'The History of U.S. Imperialism' in Robin Blackburn (ed.), *Ideology in Social Science* (Collins, 1973), pp. 207–37.
3. Gareth Stedman Jones, ibid., pp. 207 and following.
4. See Leslie Fiedler, *The Return of the Vanishing American* (Paladin, 1972), pp. 17, 26, 123–28 and 177–78.
5. Mark Twain, *Following the Equator*, quoted in Philip S. Foner, *Mark Twain—Social Critic* (New York: International Publishers, 1975), p. 314.
6. Jay Gould (1836–92): U.S. financier, celebrated for his attempt to corner the gold market. Began life in the leather trade. Entered Wall Street and was a millionaire before he was 21. Lost his fortune in the panic of 1857. Involved in various speculations, investments and deals after the Civil

War, made additional fortunes in railway investments and by 1890 was alleged to own half the mileage in the Southwest. Always suspected of chicanery, bribery and sharp practice. Left over $100,000,000.

William Marcy Tweed (1823–78): 'Boss Tweed', was a New York politician who became the prototype corrupt city boss. When he ran City Hall the aldermen were known as the 'Forty Thieves'; contracts were only accepted after payment of between 10% and 85% to Tweed and his ring. It was estimated that the Thieves took some $30,000,000 to $200,000,000 from the city of New York. Exposed by the *New York Times* and a committee of investigation, Tweed died in jail.

George Francis Train (1829–1904): transport magnate, traveller, millionaire and eccentric, orphaned as a boy in New Orleans, then successively farmworker, grocer's boy, shipping clerk, manager and partner in Train and Company, famous for his clippers and railway construction and tramway systems. Organized French Commune, Marseilles 1870. Train went round the world in 80 days and was the original of Jules Verne's character Phileas Fogg. He ran for the presidency against Grant and Greeley, 1871–72. He styled himself 'Champion Crank'; he was in his day a celebrated lecturer, merchant, promoter, author and character. Went round the world four times in all; the final time (1892) he made it in sixty days.

7. Mark Twain, 'The Sandwich Islands' (1873), in *The Complete Essays of Mark Twain*, edited Charles Neider (New York: Doubleday and Company, 1963), pp. 27–8.

8. Robert Silverberg, *Home of the Red Man* (New York: Washington Square Press, 1973), pp. 101–19; Dee Brown, *Bury My Heart at Wounded Knee: An Indian History of the American West* (Barrie and Jenkins, 1970), pp. 1–12; Thomas R. Detwyler, *Man's Impact on Environment* (New York: McGraw-Hill Book Company, 1971), pp. 515 and 615—see also M. S. Garretson, *The American Bison* (New York Zoological Society, 1938).

9. John Upton Terrell, *Land Grab: The Truth About 'The Winning of the West'* (New York: The Dial Press, 1972), p. vii.

10. Quoted in Foner, op. cit., p. 308.

11. See Richard Hofstadter, *Social Darwinism in American Thought* (Boston: Beacon Press, 1955), pp. 172–200.

12. Edward Augustus Freeman, *Comparative Politics* (New York, 1874), p. 23. Freeman made considerable claims for the Teutonic origins of British institutions—see W. R. Stephens, *The Life and Letters of Edward Augustus Freeman* (1895). Freeman's *The History of the Norman Conquest of England, its Causes and its Results* (1867–76) provides useful insights to late nineteenth-century Anglo-Saxon racial ideology. Freeman was a Fellow of Trinity College, Oxford, where he was later Regius Professor of Modern History from 1884 until his death in 1892.

13. Lenin, *Imperialism, The Highest Stage of Capitalism* (Moscow: Progress Publishers, 1970), pp. 117 and following. See also C. Morris, *The History of Colonization* (New York, 1900), Vol. 2, pp. 88 and following.

14. J. Fitzgerald Lee, *Imperial Military Geography* (William Clowes and Sons Ltd., 1923), p. 16.

15. Emil Ludwig, *The Germans* (Hamish Hamilton, 1942), pp. 306 and following. See also Michael Banton (ed.), *Darwinism and the Study of Society* (1961); Jacques Barzun, *Darwin, Marx and Wagner* (Boston: Little, Brown & Co., 1941) and Carlton J. H. Hayes, *A Generation of Materialism 1871–1900* (New York: Harper and Bros., 1941), pp. 12–13, 246 and 255 and following; cf. General Friedrich von Bernhardi, *Germany and the Next War*, translated by Allen H. Powles (Edward Arnold, 1914), pp. 56 and following.

16. See M. Beer, 'Modern British Imperialism' in *Die Neue Zeit*, Vol. XVI, No. 1 (1898), p. 302.

17. See Edward Grierson, *The Imperial Dream: British Commonwealth and Empire 1775–1969* (Collins, 1972), pp. 55–64.

18. See Gerald S. Graham, *A Concise History of the British Empire* (Thames and Hudson, 1972), pp. 173 and following.

19. E. J. Hobsbawm, *Industry and Empire* (Penguin, 1969), pp. 192 and following; Michael Barratt Brown, *The Economics of Imperialism* (Penguin, 1974), pp. 133–45; Anthony Nutting, *The Scramble for Africa* (Constable, 1970), pp. 15–31; cf. Richard Shannon, *The Crisis of Imperialism 1865–1915* (Paladin, 1974), pp. 105 and following. See also Joseph Schumpeter, 'The Sociology of Imperialism' in *Imperialism and Social Class*, translated by Heinz Norden (New York: Meridian Books, 1971), pp. 3 and following.

20. The figures are from John Atkinson Hobson, *Imperialism* (1902).

21. C. S. Dawe, *Queen Victoria and Her People* (The Educational Supply Association Ltd., 1897), p. 162.

22. John William Burgess, *Political Science and Comparative Constitutional Law* (Boston: Ginn and Company, 1890), Vol. 1, pp. 39, and 44–5.

23. Richard Hofstadter, *Social Darwinism in American Thought* (Boston: Beacon Press, 1955), p. 175.

24. Horace Greeley, *An Overland Journey, From New York to San Francisco* (1860), quoted in *Westward the Way: The Character and Development of the Louisiana Territory as Seen by Artists and Writers of the Nineteenth Century*, edited by Perry T. Rathbone (City Art Museum of St. Louis in Collaboration with the Walker Art Center, Minneapolis 1954), p. 111. The catalogue of this systematic working out of God's will may be perused in the photographic record taken by W. S. Prettyman—see *Indian Territory: A Frontier Record* by W. S. Prettyman, selected and edited by Robert E. Cunningham (University of Oklahoma Press, 1958). William S. Prettyman of Arkansas City, Kansas, took his photographic equipment by wagon and oxen through the Indian territory of Oklahoma in 1880–1909 and made some ten thousand plates which record the historic moment of the opening up of Indian territory to white settlement.

25. E. D. Morel was a well known English radical and reformer, who once described himself as 'one of the best abused men in the British Isles'. The son of a French father and an English mother, he was a life-long campaigner against imperialism and militarism. Before he contacted Twain he had already written extensively about European colonization of Africa—*Affairs of West Africa* (1902), *The British Case in French Congo*

(1903) and *King Leopold's Rule in Africa* (1904). In 1906 he published *Red Rubber: The Story of the Rubber Slave Trade in the Congo* which went through five editions between 1906 and 1908.

26. Leopold, Duke of Brabant (1835–1909), 'Letter on the Advantages of Colonization', 26 July 1863, in *Documents d'histoire précoloniale belge 1861–65*, edited by L. le Febve de Vivy (Brussels: Academie royale des Sciences coloniales, 1955), translated by D. K. Fieldhouse (ed.) *The Theory of Capitalist Imperialism* (Longman, 1967), pp. 46–9.

27. P. T. Moon, *Imperialism and World Politics* (New York: MacMillan and Co., 1926), p. 28.

28. See Foner, op. cit., pp. 384 and following.

29. Quoted in the *Introduction* to Mark Twain, *King Leopold's Soliloquy* (New York: International Publishers, 1971), pp. 16–17.

30. Shakespeare, *Hamlet*, Act IV, scene 5, 19–20. Semantic changes have slightly distorted the meaning of these lines for us—*jealousy* meant for Shakespeare suspicion, or apprehension of evil or mistrust—so the Queen's comment means that guilt is itself so full of suspicion that unskilfully it betrays itself in fearing to be betrayed. See C. T. Onions, *A Shakespeare Glossary* (Oxford: Clarendon Press, 1972), p. 120. The comment suits Twain's portrait of Leopold admirably.

31. Mark Twain, *King Leopold's Soliloquy* (New York: International Publishers, 1971), p. 29.

32. Ibid., p. 31.

33. Ibid., p. 32.

34. Ibid., pp. 33–4.

35. Ibid., p. 36. This is a telling stroke. The Louisiana Purchase Exposition, held in 1904, was still fresh in the public memory. Up to this time it was the greatest world exhibition ever held and covered more ground and offered more exhibits, from more parts of the world, than any other fair. Every state of the U.S.A. was represented, and most major world powers. It incorporated the 1904 Olympic Games. In the seven months of its duration it was visited by 20,000,000 spectators. There was a Belgian exhibition hall but the Congo was not featured. Colonization and imperialism were among the great unmentioned in the exhibition, though the collision of advanced and savage cultures, which is the essence of imperialism, did surface from time to time. The official catalogue describes a group of statuary entitled 'The Destiny of the Red Man' in these words: 'This group, by Adolph Weinmann, is one of the most impressive works of sculpture at the Exposition, expressing forcibly the fate of the aboriginal inhabitants of America. The Indian, with all his trappings and superstitions is departing, along with the bison of the plains. The group expresses the departure of barbarism, driven out by civilizing institutions and influences that are making the Indian self-supporting and fitting him for citizenship.' *The Greatest of Expositions: Official Catalogue of the St. Louis World's Fair 1904* (St. Louis, Missouri: Riverside Press, 1975), p. 144. See Robert Giddings, *St. Louis: Doughnut City*, in *New Society*, 9 September 1976, p. 541.

36. Mark Twain, *King Leopold's Soliloquy*, op. cit., p. 43.

37. Ibid., p. 45.

38. Foner, op. cit., p. 388.

39. Twain, op. cit., p. 68.

40. Ibid., p. 70.

41. Ibid., pp. 70–1.

42. Foner, op. cit., p. 389.

43. See M. Cattier, *Etude sur la situation de l'état indépendent du Congo* (Brussels, 1906) and Neal Ascherson, *The King Incorporated* (1963). The accounts by Roger Casement may be read in *Correspondence and Reports Respecting the Administration of the Free State of the Congo* (H.M.S.O., 1904).

44. See Hans Koning, *Columbus: His Enterprise* (New York: Monthly Review Press, 1976), pp. 85–9. Koning bases his account on the record of a Dominican priest, Batholomé de la Casas, whose eye-witness account, *Devastation of the Indies* (New York: Seabury Press, 1974), in a new English translation, makes a salutary comparison with the account of Columbus's contribution to the history of America in the much acclaimed B.B.C./Time-Life Alistair Cooke version. See Alistair Cooke, *America* (New York: Alfred A. Knopf, 1974), pp. 26–36; cf. Robert Giddings, 'Cooking the Books', in *New Society*, 14 June 1979, pp. 652–53.

9

A Raft Against Washington: Mark Twain's Criticism of America

by ERIC MOTTRAM

The humorist's character, and his constant exposure to audience response of the most dictating kind, makes him peculiarly sensitive to the complexity of his society. But he has none of the false objectivity of the academic sociologist, and attempts to turn Twain into a weapon for Soviet criticism of the United States[1] or into some mystical priest of the American heartlands—notoriously by such as Eliot and Trilling—have failed. No such simplification is possible. He is self-consciously and violently aware of America in its post-Civil War necessities of recovery, but distrusts human action in any society. *The Adventures of Huckleberry Finn* (1885) can be read as subversion of America in so many ways that it is repeatedly banned from libraries and schools. Senator McCarthy himself joined the parade which, in 1957, included the Board of Education of New York City, and in 1982, the Mark Twain Intermediate School, Fairfax County, Virginia.[2] Twain's analysis of hypocrisy is feared by any authority, and his analysis of behaviour without recourse to religious or philosophic authority. His understanding of repressive law, written and unwritten, is penetrating. In an essay on 'The Jewish question' his bases are sardonically expressed enough to antagonize any limited humanist[3]:

222

> I am quite sure that (bar one) I have no race prejudices, and I think I have no colour prejudices nor caste prejudices nor creed prejudices, indeed I know it. I can stand any society. All that I care to know is that a man is a human being—that is enough for me. He can't be any worse.

In old age, his satirical pamphlet entitled *King Leopold's Soliloquy* concerns the wholesale massacre and rape of Congo Africans by Belgians under Leopold II, who posed as a colonial philanthropist and a great Christian. Twain points out that between 1897 and 1907 the population was reduced by 3,000,000 people mutilated or killed in one small region in six months. The American satirist attacked where few others were even aware of an intolerable situation—he has Leopold make what was to be the perpetual complaint of the oppressor in the twentieth century[4]:

> (Studies some photographs of mutilated Negroes—throws them down. Sighs.) The kodak has been a sore calamity to us. . . . In the early years we had no trouble in getting the press to 'expose' the tales of the mutilations as slanders, lies, inventions of busybody American missionaries and exasperated foreigners who had found the 'open door' of the Berlin-Congo charter closed against them when they innocently went out there to trade; and by the press's help we got the Christian nations everywhere to turn an irritated and unbelieving ear to those tales and say hard things about the tellers of them. Yes, all things went harmoniously and pleasantly in those good days. . . . Then all of a sudden came the crash! That is to say, the incorruptible *kodak*—and all the harmony went to hell! The only witness I have encountered in my long experience that I couldn't bribe.

At least in his *public* old age, Twain maintained that the human race could still turn away from atrocities, and that the kodak would be instrumental against the world's Leopolds and their crusades. Huckleberry Finn had already encountered Tom Sawyer's definitions of 'crusader' in *Tom Sawyer Abroad* (1894)—a character already the type of the American trimmer or liberal who can live with the idea that it is 'religious to go and take the land from people that owns it'. 'Bible Teaching and Religious Practice', which only appeared in 1923, exposes the gap between 'human decency' and

223

religious theory and practice among Christians. The exposure of the ludicrous results of taking the Bible literally, *Letters from the Earth*, was written in 1909, the year before his death, but not published until 1962. Twain realized that religion was both tyrannical and unnecessary, that human existence constituted its own hell without inventing another (Jonson's point in *The Devil is an Ass*)—but that it could be dangerous to say so publicly in a society so aggressively, self-righteously orthodox. Penetrating further, at the end of his life, the sheer pettiness of local morality faded for him before the immensity of the godless universe and its facts of death. His vision concerned the monstrosity of life itself. In his story 'The Great Dark', a father buys his children a microscope and wonders what life would be like inside a drop of water placed on a slide the family is examining. They soon find out, suddenly transferred to a ship on those once microscopic waters. Life is reduced to a nightmare of endless voyaging on a dark ocean full of monsters. Instead of a rush towards some hole in the earth's surface, as in Poe's metaphysical imagination, Twain dries the waters and roasts his family under the white glare of the microscope's light—caught in the investigations of the technological. Twain inherited the nineteenth century's horrified fascination with an immanent probability of the end of the world under a cooling sun. Poe's 'MS Found in a Bottle,' O'Brien's 'The Diamond Lens,' and *The Great Dark* are primary American responses to the insane pretensions of religion and the doctrine of progress in America and the West. Earlier, in those days when his exuberance could withstand human nonsense, Twain could make Huck Finn believe he was damned, while the whole text of the novel, with its rejection of a society and contempt for its main behavioural beliefs, surrounds an intense respect for what the boy embodies. Twain's hysteria is just kept under control by his humour. At the end of *A Connecticut Yankee at King Arthur's Court* (1889) it is not, and the limits of the controlling enclosure of humour will preoccupy him for the rest of his writing career. It is therefore appropriate that some of the quotations for the preface to *The Gilded Age* (1873), Twain's first extended work of fiction,[5] are drawn from *The Devil is an Ass* and *Volpone*, since Jonson's satirical comedies expose speculation and fraud enacted as a social programme and a neurosis in both perpetrator and victim, without suggesting revolutionary change, but certainly indicating the parameters of treatment by humour. Like Sherwood Anderson and Flannery O'Connor later, Twain grasps the point at which the warping of social pressures converts behaviour into grotesque eccentricity, a fixity of freakishness which is known as neurosis.

The Gilded Age, whose over-all critical vigour is here taken to be under Twain's major direction, is a narrative panorama of those criticisms which he would continue to quarry in his career. If the consideration that follows includes more para- phrase of plot than would customarily be permitted, it is because it is not a book we are generally familiar with. Twain begins, as he will in *Pudd'nhead Wilson* (1894), by moving on the target of American provinciality, mocking the locals of East Tennessee and their substitutes for loquacity, but in a significant primordial location:

> The speaker bunched his thick lips together like the stem end of a tomato and shot a bumblebee dead that had lit on a weed seven feet away. One after another the several chewers expressed a charge of tobacco-juice and delivered it at the deceased with steady aim and faultless accuracy.

'Squire' Silas Hawkins, who fears he will become one of 'these cattle', owns a double log-cabin store at Obedstown and a huge acreage whose value the coming railroad will increase. But he is in the grip of Colonel Beriah Sellers whose specu- lations have 'crippled' the family once and will again: 'it's always sunrise with that man, and fine and blazing, at that— never gets noon though—leaves off and rises again.' So Hawkins moves his family on by way of the Mississippi riverboat through the American wilderness:

> . . . mile after mile and league after league the vast bends were guarded by unbroken walls of forest, that had never been disturbed by the voice or the footfall of a man or felt the edge of his sacrilegious axe.

Twain's piloting experience also goes into the crucial mad race between the *Amaranth* and the *Boreas*—with the latter using casks of bacon as fuel—which ends in the boats locked together 'under the flooding moonlight'. The wrecked *Amaranth* causes the death of passengers and crew members, and Laura Hawkins loses the man who is her real father. Twain then summarizes this opening pattern of speculation in land and money, technological development at the mercy of greed, and the madness of competitiveness (Volume 1, Chapter 4). The uncoded laws of America once again support the libertarian:

> A jury of inquest was impanelled, and after due deliberation and inquiry they returned a verdict which has been so familiar to our ears all the days of our lives—'NOBODY TO BLAME'.

The boat crash is paralleled by later financial crash, with the concomitant so-called 'trials' of congressmen for irresponsible risk-taking, and the verdict is paralleled by the later verdict on Laura. Under Sellers, Hawkins buys out a Missouri village store, and obtains a new house with a lightning rod, 'store' furniture and white-washed paling fence. Prosperity results from watching the market columns in newspapers—the characteristic capitalist democracy dream of unearned income from gambling. Ten years later—poverty; the younger children are still, however, raised as dependent, the girls untrained as benefits 'a Southern family . . . of good blood'.

Sellers's language is designed to keep them all buoyant within their status fluctuations. Reduced to one candle in one stove, he blarnies on: 'What you want is the *appearance* of heat, not the heat itself—that's the idea.' 'Future riches' will replace 'present poverty'. The ideological assumption is everything—and it is precisely this inherence in American culture that Twain will repeatedly assault. Like the incarnations of the confidence-man on Melville's *Fidele*, Sellers offers his Infallible Imperial Oriental Optic Liniment and Salvation for Sore Eyes as part of a peculiarly American inclination to universal panaceas. And the fake aristocratism of the white upper class in *Pudd'nhead Wilson* is already present in the children's names Washington discovers at the Sellers family luncheon (it is there in the King and the Duke in *Huckleberry Finn* and in the fatally absurd derivations from Scott in the South exposed in *Life on the Mississippi* (1883)): 'To visit such a family, was to find one's self confronted by a congress made up of representatives of the imperial myths and majestic dead of all ages'—Lafayette, Marie Antoinette, and so on. The eternal optimist has them eating 'raw turnips and water', while he talks speculation and dispenses quackery—turnips 'fermenting' in water in the stomach prevent plague and make a man 'feel like a fighting-cock next day'.

Philip Sterling finds law unsatisfying, and then tries journalism—but when he refuses to edit a paper against his principles, he is advised, 'you can't afford a conscience like that' (Chapter 12), so he obtains a job on the railroad, with his friend Henry Brierly. As 'engineers', they travel on 'a causeway of cracked rails and cows, to the West' with a cross-section of speculation types—and inevitably meet Sellers, who is advancing the Stone's Landing project. Through the advent of the railroad, it is to become 'the city of Napoleon in theory and on paper'. But the place is a swamp, and again Twain deflates the pretentious impositions of capitalism on the bases of the country by reverting the present to the wilderness:

> As the sun rose and sent his level beams along the stream, the thin stratum of mist, or malaria, rose also and dispersed, but the light was not able to enliven the dull water nor give any hint of its apparently fathomless depth. Venerable mud-turtles crawled up and roosted upon the old logs in the stream, their backs glistening in the sun, the first inhabitants of the metropolis to begin the active business of the day.

The Civil War barely changes the situation. Laura has become a 'fatal beauty' with the 'power of fascination'. Washington's useless inventions have left him at 30 'without a profession or a permanent occupation'. The nation deteriorates its 'pure products'. Captured by a Federal colonel, Washington is sent back to the Confederates since he can do more damage to his own side there. Sellers, now a captain in the Hawkeye home guards (Twain never could stomach Cooper), invents an air-torpedo which explodes in his shed, and mines the land so densely the inhabitants are too scared to move in their own town (but this is innocuous compared with its version in *A Connecticut Yankee*). After an emotional shock, Laura becomes something of a Beatrice Cenci—but with none of the metaphysics Hawthorne gave to Miriam Schaefer—and fascinates

Brierly, who in turn attracts her to Washington 'where money
or beauty will open any door'. The character of the Capitol is
exemplified by Senator Abner Dillworthy who informs the
Hawkeye citizens of 'the genius of American liberty, walking
with Sunday-school in one hand and Temperance in the other
up the glorified steps of the National Capitol'. Washington
becomes his secretary, promoting his great aim: to link
personal advantage with public good. Laura forwards her
plans between them.

Ruth Bolton, whose father is in the grip of Sellers's pro-
motions, has gone through the Women's Medical College and
tries to achieve both independence and happiness through
employment training. Through her, a more liberal and
altruistic America is inserted into *The Gilded Age*. In the same
field, Philip begins to take engineering seriously. Both are
characters against speculation. But Washington is the primary
target—as it would be for Henry Adams's two novels. The
critical crux appears in Chapter 24:

> Every individual . . . from the highest bureau-chief, clear down
> to the maid who scrubs Department halls, the night watchmen
> of the public buildings and the darky boy who purifies the
> Department spittoons—represents Political Influence.

This is the system of universal control through work control:
'Mere merit, fitness, and capability, are useless baggage to you
without "influence". . . . There is something good and motherly
about Washington, the grand old benevolent National Asylum
for the Helpless.' In this centre of competition, Washington
thrives: 'He had looked upon the President himself, and lived.'
It is 'a world of enchantment . . . the whole atmosphere thick
with speculation . . . he had found paradise at last.'

Ruth, on the other hand, finds Philadelphia, City of
Brotherly Love, 'a house of cards'; her family 'had no idea of
the number of perils that hovered over them, any more than
thousands of families in America have of the business risks and
contingencies upon which their prosperity and luxury hang'.
The text resolves into a mock panegyric on the core of its
motivation—what Galbraith came to excoriate as 'affluence'
and analyse as 'the Crash', and which Melville had already
produced as 'confidence':

Beautiful credit! The foundation of society. Who shall say that this is not the golden age of mutual trust, of unlimited reliance upon human promises? That is a peculiar condition of society which enables a whole nation to instantly recognize point and meaning in the family newspaper anecdote, which puts into the mouth of a distinguished speculator in lands and mines this remark: 'I wasn't worth a cent two years ago, and now I owe two million dollars.'

This is the reason, in location, why Sellers emerges as more than a pathetically amusing clown; he is the type of his society. What then is an American? Colonel Sellers. Now his truly Jonsonian scheme is for 'extracting olive-oil from turnips—if there is any in them'. He comforts his wife in words which anticipate Twain's criticism of the Belgians in the Congo:

Corruptionville, the gaudiest country for early carrots and cauliflowers that ever—good missionary field, too. There ain't another such missionary field outside the jungles of Central Africa. And patriotic?—why, they named it after Congress itself.

The text then supports this with Chapter 28–'How Appropriation Bills Are Carried'—that is, by juggling the figures. Stone's Landing collapses within the fraud of company backers, and returns to the primeval life, in the manner of Gray's 'On Lord Holland's Seat': 'The wary tadpole returned from exile, the bullfrog resumed his ancient song. . . .' The railroad which was intended to provide the future of Stone's Landing is so unsafe that a woman nearly falls to her death between two cars, due to the absence of 'protective grating' and the dangers of speed on curves. Philip, who is travelling to Ilium, Pennsylvania, rescues her, hits the conductor who had insulted her, and finds the whole incident written up comically in the local newspaper. After breaking his arm in a fire alarm panic at a concert, he becomes Ruth's first patient.

In Volume Two, the farce and the exposure shift uneasily—as they will in Twain's later fiction—towards catastrophe which eludes humour. Laura conquers Washington's 'aristocracy' of wealth, with the help of Dillworthy. The enclosure of money renders the terms of value into corruptive ambiguity, just as it does today:

Great wealth gave a man a still higher and nobler place in it than did official position. If this wealth had been acquired by conspicuous ingenuity, with just a little spice of illegality about it, all the better.

The exemplary figure is the Hon. Patrique Oreillé, upgrading himself from Patrick O'Reilley and 'a low rum shop in a foul locality' to 'political influence'. After a scandalous real estate deal, he and a colleague are elected to the New York legislature. Twain again exposes law, and through it an aspect of democracy in America:

> Our admirable jury system enabled the persecuted ex-officials to secure a jury of nine gentlemen from a neighbouring asylum and three graduates from Sing Sing, and presently they walked forth with characters vindicated. The legislature was called upon to spew them forth—a thing which the legislature declined to do. It was like asking children to repudiate their own father. It was a legislature in the modern pattern.

After basking in reflected glory from family wealth, Washington is taunted by Laura into cashing in his father's Tennessee lands—and the novel precipitately writes him off as a success within the success ethic:

> He got up and walked the floor feverishly during two hours; and when sat down he had married Louise, built a house, reared a family, married them off, spent upward of eight hundred thousand dollars on mere luxuries, and died worth twelve millions.

This speed of elimination from the plot signals that the focus is now to be on Laura and Washington. Sellers, in the capital, 'thrives in the air of indefinite expectation', and dreams of being, not President, but 'Grand Lama of the United States'— or 'next to that he would have luxuriated in the irresponsible omniscience of the special correspondent.' He trims his conversation for newspaper report—that is, he lies—and becomes a celebrity, created by the same press that attacks the Knobs Industrial University bill, or the 'Negro University Swindle'— a Dillworthy cause. But the senator welcomes the persecution: 'the great putty-hearted public loves to "gush", and there is no such darling opportunity to gush as a case of persecution affords.'

In a word, Washington is a state of 'lunacy'. The novel carefully exemplifies what historians and sociologists will rarely confront: that such a society's power is irrational to the point of psychosis—the extreme condition of the Shepherd-sons and Grangerfords, and the knights and church in Hank Morgan's Arthurian Britain. Slander rises from the Potomac 'like a miasmic exhalation', and 'love, travel, even death itself, waited on the chances of the dies daily thrown in the two Houses, and the committee rooms there.' In Chapter 14, at the height of uproar, the hypocrisy and manipulation of a particular bill, Sellers is found asleep in the public gallery with his umbrella up: 'The fluctuations of the Washington weather had influenced his dreams, perhaps.'

But the madness reaches Laura disastrously. She murders her old lover, the Confederate colonel Selby, and is imprisoned in the Tombs, while the press has a good time at her expense. Philip buys a tract of land in Ilium 'for a song'; Ruth's father loses more money in speculation; Laura's fate, in Chapter 19, is seen as the last link in a deterministic chain of events; and even Sellers can say to Washington: 'There is no country in the world, sir, that pursues corruption as inveterately as we do.' Washington becomes exhausted with the endless 'dream' of competition and risk.

It is during Laura's trial that the hysteria of the country is most deftly exposed—a configuration of corruption in press, law and religion which anticipates the latter sections of *An American Tragedy* in 1925. The press reports her kindness to fellow prisoners while her defence counsel, Mr. Braham, controls jury selection—'only two could read, one of whom was the foreman, Mr. Braham's friend, the showy contractor.' And again the text demonstrates a deterministic, almost racist belief in 'lower class' degeneracy, partly reflecting common physiognomical theories of the day, and partly a Thoreauvian contempt for the common state of intelligence:

> Low foreheads and heavy faces they all had; some had the look of animal cunning, while the most were only stupid. The entire panel formed that boasted heritage commonly described as the 'bulwark of our liberties'.

Braham suggests hereditary insanity in Laura, aggravated by mental tortures and the facts of being orphaned in the steamboat collision deterministically placed at the outset of Volume One. The father is presented as demented. Sellers himself gabbles on and gives his occupation as 'a gentleman, sir'. Braham stresses the class gap between Selby and the Hawkins family—and puts the court and jury in tears. No one votes for the reintroduction of Dillworthy's bill after a bribery scandal is exposed; Laura is found not guilty; and the women in court kiss Braham—'this beautiful scene is still known in New York as "the kissing of Braham".' But Laura herself is committed to 'the care of the Superintendent of the State Hospital for Insane Criminals'.

Such is the grim logic emerging from the irrational conspiracy—a logic as sardonic and terse as the conclusion of *Pudd'nhead Wilson*. But the text suddenly swerves nervously in on itself, under the effect of the supposed reader's scepticism. 'We beg the reader's pardon' begins a little discourse on history and the novel, fact and fiction—'the novelist who would turn loose upon society an insane murderess could not escape condemnation', and 'the decencies of criminal procedure' demand Laura's incarceration'. But, like Defoe in his preface to *Moll Flanders*, the authors of *The Gilded Age* tease 'the reader' with the complicity of his own position in the society producing the fiction. So the text is wilfully changed, as Dickens provided his alternative to the more accurately brutal conclusion of *Great Expectations*, an earlier novel concerned with the origins of wealth. Laura is freed to 'cheers . . . of popular approval and affection' and her poverty is to be alleviated by a lecture tour, 'that final resort of the disappointed of her sex'. The text further bears down on 'the reader' as the Senate dealing with the Dillworthy case is given as the nation 'leaving the true source of our political power ("the primaries") in the hands of saloon-keepers, dog-fanciers, and hod-carriers'. Only one senator is convinced of Dillworthy's obvious guilt.

Again, the text assaults that reader by bringing Laura down in retribution in spite of the sentimental end of the trial. At her first lecture, she is hustled by the mob, and a stone kills her: 'The jury of inquest found that death had resulted from heart disease, and was instant and painless. That was all. Merely heart disease.'

A Raft Against Washington: Mark Twain's Criticism of America

As Ike McCaslin will years later in *Go Down, Moses*, so Washington, old before his time, decides to relinquish his father's lands as 'a curse'. Appropriately, Sellers takes up law and Philip discovers a coal seam on his plot of land—a piece of 'luck' countered by Ruth's illness. With Philip's support she will live, but her conclusion is distinctly of the period, with a clear sexist context: 'It was new for Ruth to feel this dependence on another's nature, to consciously draw strength of will from the will of another.'

For all its security of fundamental criticism of American capitalism—its carelessness, hypocrisy and downright insanity, together with its sacrificial wearing down of those who try for something other than the financial and speculative—the text is radically uncertain of its readership for such an exposure of hysteria as a thoroughgoing national condition. Thoreau's anarchist wit and self-approval is replaced by a number of strategies of examination—satirical abuse, sardonic revelation and a determinism that confers an inherent pessimism on naturalist fiction. Apart from the buoyancy of hope in Huckleberry Finn and the belated recovery of social status through intelligence in David Wilson, Twain's techniques, including his humour, can barely analyse *and* resist the America whose jester he partly wished to remain. Justin Kaplan's *Mr. Clemens and Mr. Twain* has indicated Twain's doubleness of allegiance as a haunted 'twinship' in a writer who needed to be part of his society and then found himself hiding the critical fictions that damned it and damned the human race. Humour controls the exposure and the repression in his fictions until the point is reached where there can be little repression and less humour. Then Satan speaks in two posthumous works, *The Mysterious Stranger* and *Letters from the Earth*, as the voice of opposition to conformism and hope heard through the masks of the divine realist who offered human beings knowledge rather than comfort and obedience. As Georges Braque once noted: 'It is a mistake to enclose the unconscious in an outline and to situate it at the border of rationality.'[6]

Twain once wrote: 'Every man is a moon, and has a dark side which he never shows to anybody.' In his 1899 sketch 'What Is Man?', his sceptical relativism and sense of the absurd pathos of dogma is clear:

> There are none but temporary Truth-seekers; . . . a permanent
> [truth] is a human impossibility; . . . as soon as the Seeker finds
> what he is thoroughly convinced is Truth, he seeks no further,
> but gives up the rest of his days to hunting junk to patch it and
> caulk it and prop it up with, and make it weatherproof and keep
> it from caving in on him.

Scepticism obviates the easy mind both privately and publicly.
Doubleness of name is matched by duplicity of creative work.
But Twain's is the characteristic unease of the modern writer
whose awareness of hypocrisy and cruelty does not cause him
to retreat entirely into privacy or into suicide, but rather
commits him to a writing of controlled hysteria. Twain was
composing 'Captain Stormfield's Visit to Heaven' as early as
1868, but his wife forbade publication and it did not appear
until after her death in 1907, and then only in extracts. The
story registers a turn-of-the-century experience of the overwhelming immensity of time and space under the pressures of
nineteenth-century analysis of the infinities of a universe
which had become what Henry Adams in 1906 termed a
multiverse. At the end of a century of American developments
in science fiction Twain's captain journeys in space-time to a
Heaven which proves to be a ghastly conventional replica of
Earth societies, confirming, as it were, Huck Finn's worse
intuitions of 'civilization'. Heaven is an aristocratic state, the
eternal hierarchy that human beings are unable to resist as
their ideal—the Washington 'paradise' of *The Gilded Age*.
Sandy McWilliams, the captain's guide, points up the eternal
aristocratism of Christianity, to which, of course, Americans
thoroughly adhered:

> How are you going to have a republic under a king? How are
> you going to have a republic at all, where the head of govern-
> ment is absolute, holds his place forever, and has no parliament,
> no counsel to meddle or make in his affairs, nobody voted for,
> nobody elected, nobody asked to take a hand in its matters, and
> nobody *allowed* to do it? . . . This is Russia—only more so.
> There is no shadow of a republic about it anywhere. There are
> ranks here.

A slight shift and we are in the satirical world of Stanley
Elkin's *The Living Earth* in 1980. But *The Gilded Age* already

indicated Twain's scepticism about the voting and jury systems, and he is by no means consistently against Hank Morgan's industrial labour state imposed on King Arthur's Christian monarchy.

In 'To a Person Sitting in Darkness', which he managed to publish in the liberal and respected *North American Review* in 1901, Twain, like Melville before him, exposed the hypocrisy of Christian colonial aggression, turning from the rottenness of American cities to the international example of cruel exploitation, the greed of missionary organization in China, England's Boer War, the Germans in Africa, and American policy in Cuba. His bitter irony moves into the style of a man under moral pressure, whose sense of outrage is anarchic rather than ideological—the contained anger of a man without 'a permanent truth'. On 30 December 1900, Twain, the celebrated public figure largely assumed to be a humorist and therefore relatively harmless, contributed a New Year greeting to readers of the New York *Herald*, as from the nineteenth to the twentieth century:

> I bring you the stately matron named Christendom, returning bedraggled, besmirched and dishonoured from pirate raids on Kiaou-Chou, Manchuria, South Africa, and the Philippines, with her soul full of meanness, her pocket full of boodle and her mouth full of pious hypocrisies. Give her soap and a towel, but hide the looking-glass.

But why should she not be confronted with her own savage image? Apparently because Twain withdraws from the entropic chaos of the possible results. A year earlier, in 'What Is Man?', Twain proposed—and it is part of that behaviourist materialism which dominates both Theodore Dreiser and B. F. Skinner later in the century—man as a chemical machine, helpless within its determinations. This side of the sketch's polemic is provided by the Old Man, who is opposed by a Young Man with untried optimistic moral assumptions of a vaguely Christian humanist sentimentality. The dialogue is completely biased. The Old Man crushes the Young Man with a model of human existence determined by forces which reduce original ideas and freedom of will in the historically persisted manner of Jonathan Edwards in the eighteenth century and Hemingway, with his 'biological trap', in the twentieth:

> A man's brain is so constructed that it can originate nothing whatever. . . . It has no command over itself, its owner has no command over it. . . . Inestimably valuable is training, influence, education, in right directions—training one's self-approbation to elevate its ideals.

The Young Man protests: What about self-sacrifice?—but when he is challenged can find no instances. A man's impulse is solely to 'content his own spirit . . . and winning its approval'; he loves 'the approval of his neighbours and the public' more than peace. War occurs because 'public opinion could force some men to do anything.' Twain attacks, therefore, the bases of consensus opinion in the controls of democracy in America—and goes further. Emerson's doctrine of self-reliance in America, supported by an overweening transcendentalist optimism, becomes an automatism; men do not create or think, they imitate—'wit-mechanism . . . is automatic in its action', and cannot be manufactured—'men observe and combine, that is all. So does a rat.' Instinct is simply 'petrified thought' and 'fleas can be taught nearly anything that a Congressman can.' The impulse instigating these opinions lies within a statement whose variations may be found throughout Twain's work:

> The fact that man knows right from wrong proves his *intellectual* superiority to the other creatures; but the fact that he can *do* wrong proves his *moral* inferiority to any creature that cannot.

But, says the Old Man, one does not publish such opinions because

> it is a desolating doctrine; it is not inspiring, enthusing, uplifting. It takes the glory out of man, it takes the pride out of him, it takes the heroism out of him, it denies him all personal credit, all applause.

As for nations, they feel rather than think:

> They get their feelings at second-hand through their temperaments, not their brains. A nation can be brought—by force of circumstances, not argument—to reconcile itself to any kind of government or religion that can be devised; in time it wills itself to the required conditions; later, it will prefer them and will fiercely fight for them.

To the Young Man's dismay and alarm, he offers finally: 'Everything has been tried. Without success. I beg you not to be troubled.' It could easily be argued that such a dogmatic enclosure, with its grid fitted tightly over any future, is a spiteful recommendation to endless obedience to Control in all its manifestations against imaginative invention. But within all Twain's work, whatever the strategies of humour, lies this stoic resignation, the melancholy of a non-revolutionary writing after his country's Civil War disaster, and as part of a determinist rejection of the genteel belief in America's self-confidence. 'The Facts Concerning the Recent Carnival of Crime in Connecticut' (1875) probe deeply into the capitalist ethic itself as it seethes in ambivalence at the basis of the American way of life. The narrator is, like one of Melville's self-confident bachelors, vulnerable to any radical aggression on his illusions. But Twain's bachelor becomes a murdering tyrant. The crucial intervention in his life is a 40-year-old two-foot dwarf:

> . . . a vague, general, evenly blended, nicely adjusted deformity [with] a fox-like cunning in the face and the sharp little eyes, and also alertness and malice. And yet, this vile bit of human rubbish seemed to bear a sort of remote and ill-defined resemblance to me!

He obeys the dwarf's authority and listens to his analysis of his most private lies and hypocrisies, tyrannies and irresponsibilities; the list goes back to pushing his younger brother, blindfolded, on to 'a brook thinly glazed with ice'. The creature is in fact the narrator's conscience. When he springs to strangle it, the dwarf floats to the top of a high bookcase in the office. Everything thrown at him misses. Since his conscience is 'as light as a feather', it is out of reach, but still his master and enemy are demanding to be addressed as 'my lord'. This aristocratic vestige of a bygone part of the puritan success ethic confronts a pillar of American society, a two-faced capitalist assailed by a murderous conscience that delights in probing to the point of torture:

> I knew a man . . . who had accidentally crippled a mulatto baby; the news went abroad, and I wish you may never commit another sin if the consciences did not flock from all over the earth

to enjoy the fun and help his master exorcize him. That man walked the floor in torture for forty-eight hours, without eating or sleeping and then blew his brains out. The child was perfectly well again in three weeks. . . . I don't care *what* act you may turn your hand to, I can straightway whisper a word in your ear and make you think you have committed a dreadful meanness. It is my *business*—and my joy—to make you repent of *everything* you do. . . . you used to be conscientious about a great many things; morbidly so, I may say. It was a great many years ago. . . . I kept pelting at you until I rather overdid the matter. You began to rebel. Of course I began to lose ground, then, and shrivel a little.

The dwarf reveals that most of the good and decent men he knows are conscience-racked. But when the narrator's aunt arrives to accuse him of neglecting a poor family he had promised to help, his 'guilt' sharpens into acute suffering and the dwarf falls to the ground. The narrator's behaviour becomes so erratic that his aunt believes he has succumbed to tobacco. He tears the dwarf to shreds and throws the bits into the fire. A free man at last, he turns on his aunt and abuses her out of the office:

Since that day my life is all bliss. . . . I settled all my old outstanding scores, and began the world anew. I killed thirty-eight persons during the first two weeks—all of them on account of ancient grudges. I burned a dwelling that inter-rupted my view. . . . In conclusion, I wish to state by way of advertisement, that medical colleges desiring assorted tramps for scientific purposes, either by the gross, by cord measure-ment, or per ton, will do well to examine the lot in my cellar before purchasing elsewhere, as these were all selected and prepared by myself, and can be had at a low rate, because I wish to clear out my stock and get ready for the spring trade.

In this way he initiates and enjoys the dream and practice of the free enterprise authoritarian state, or the United States of America in its extreme but near-impossible condition: the value-free society, as it will be called in the mid-twentieth century. Twain understands that the sacrificial society depends on the possibility of eliminating the concept of conscience, or any trained built-in moral code of mutual consideration. And he grasps the fact that it is possible by training.

Just over twenty years later, between 1898 and 1900, Twain wrote one of his most accomplished short fictions on the nature of honesty as an assumed value. 'The Man That Corrupted Hadleyburg' essentially dramatizes what Milton called 'a blank virtue'. The town has a reputation for honesty—a social fact of relationship which has to be kept up. Vanity, in characteristic puritan fashion, is disguised as uprightness never put to the extreme test. Practical morality or ethical behaviour appears to cover both selfishness and self-approval. A destitute man was once helped by a Hadleyburg citizen and given twenty dollars—with which he gambles and makes a fortune. Now he wishes to repay the help anonymously, and the citizen can do what he likes with the huge sum of money accumulated from speculation. To the Hadleyburg people it is 'the wages of sin'. Edward Richards turns out to be a man living in the glamour of false reputation for goodness, concealing meanness and profound dishonesty as expediency. Mary Richards prays 'Lead us not into temptation' but only as a superstitious ritual before being tempted. When gold offers itself, Edward says it is the act of Providence whose designs must not be challenged—that would be 'blasphemous presumption'. Where, in 'What Is Man?', the Old Man claimed behaviour is training, and, in *A Connecticut Yankee*, Twain asserted 'Training is everything; training is all there is *to* a person. . . . We have no thoughts of our own, no opinions of our own; they are transmitted to us, trained into us', here Mary Richards rebels against the training with which the town maintains its reputation:

> It's been one everlasting training and training and training in honesty—honesty shielded, from the cradle, against every possible temptation, and so it's artificial honesty, as weak as water when temptation comes, as we have seen this night. . . . Let no man call me honest again—I will not have it.

So the people refuse to be honest in order to save their souls: 'the weakest of all weak things is a virtue which has not been tested in the fire.' Twain reserves his sharpest attack for the man who is not worried by sin unless other people discover his condition and destroy his reputation. His main figure is so corrupted by concealed sin that he becomes half-crazed with its intensity. But the text contains no compassion for human moral dilemma. Twain leaves the town praying 'Lead us into temptation' and thereby, of course, challenging the Lord's Prayer, whose very title is authoritarian and aristocratic and therefore reflected back into Captain Stormfield's Heaven. Twain once remarked that the symbol of man ought to be an axe, 'for every human being has one concealed about him somewhere, and is always seeking the opportunity to grind it.'

In *Innocents Abroad*, the work through which he first received popular approval in 1869, Twain proposes American values of comfort, utility, and progress itself with a dashing confidence, exposing culture-snobs and culture-seekers in Europe and boosting American morale as a post-Civil War journalist. He began, that is, in a period of heavy city development and industrialization, the hypocrisies of Social Darwinism condoning poverty and wealth by natural selection, the domination of high-finance capitalism and those forms of determinism and stoicism which contributed to the naturalist novel in Crane and Dreiser. By 1873 and *The Gilded Age*, Twain—only four years later—is drawn to the Jonsonian exposure of national political and social corruption, the absurdly dangerous visions of horizonless material progress and the urge to irresistible power—the subject of Edmund Wilson's *Patriotic Gore*. Both here and in *The American Claimant* (1892), the figure of Colonel Sellers exemplifies the system barely concealed in a mask of eccentricity. He begins energetic and ends pathetic, a believer in luck, the nineteenth-century goddess who energizes *Our Mutual Friend*, *Daniel Deronda*, Hemingway's fictions and then in the post-war decade, *Death of a Salesman*. Once Sellers's vitality is discarded by the success ethic, he is no longer a comic booster-dreamer, but a ridiculous and irritating old fool, intolerably dangerous as an adviser of youth, because he has maintained the myth beyond its point of exhaustion, a precursor of Lewis's Babbitt. Laura, too, caught in the myths of degradation joins the extended field of Henry Adams's Esther, Crane's Maggie and Dreiser's Carrie, forms of the vulnerable woman in the class-cash-sex nexus. *The Gilded Age* also focuses that theme of exhaustion developed by Dreiser and John Dos Passos, and concentrated by Fitzgerald as the failure of 'the ability to function'.

240

For *A Connecticut Yankee at King Arthur's Court*, sixteen years later, Twain reworks those materials of Arthurian chivalry and medieval church authority—used by writers as diverse as Tennyson, T. S. Eliot and Jean Cocteau—to analyse the technological environment of late nineteenth-century America, accepted uncritically by the mass of Americans. He had already mocked the chivalric pretensions of the Southern ruling classes in *Life on the Mississippi* (1883), a work which also presents the dandy paragon of training, the riverboat pilot Horace Bixby. Now he transfers Hank Morgan, mechanic at the Colt factory in Hartford, Connecticut—a major and highly imitated centre of the American method of manufacture (especially the semi-mechanical assembly of duplicated and replaceable parts)—to feudal Britain. He trains the backward British into a paternalistic technological utopia of Americanism, complete with advertising and advanced weaponry.

Once again, Twain's humour only just controls his exacerbated nerves, his outrage with tyranny and his disgust with human stupidity. Hank is to be the American Franklinite pragmatist of materialism, the kind-hearted Boss. Merlin is cast as magic power over the people by ritual and muddled beliefs. Slaves are those workers and poor stupid enough not to rebel. Hank brings industrialism, the new Grail, wage-labour colonization. Twain's ambivalence is not at all concealed. Hank tells the people: 'I'm going to turn groping and grumbling automata into *men*.' Self-reliance geared into the factory system is intended to create a limited peaceful revolution. Aristocratism is exemplified by the absurd discomforts and impracticability of grotesque suits of armour—a scene both hilarious and painful in Twain's most characteristic manner. But Hank's reformed knights become salesmen advertising soap and toothbrushes, agents of the system Twain elsewhere excoriates.

This novel, like *Huckleberry Finn* and *Pudd'nhead Wilson*, is structured as a dialectic between the cruel and the ridiculous, between degradation and dignity, the pathetic and the stupid, illusion and reality. But Twain transfers the earlier American beliefs in anarchic self-reliance and pragmatic inventiveness at the service of society to an industrial context which drains them of vitality. Hank's factories are 'iron and steel missionaries of future civilization'. He believes revolutions begin in a bloody 'Reign of Terror' and end in technological beneficence. Scepticism directs the plot; Hank may be 'the champion of hard, unsentimental common sense' but he is outwitted by Merlin magic plus the Church. He blows up his technocracy, dynamites and electrocutes 25,000 knights, and kills off his own retinue with the resultant polluted air. Then he leaves these members of 'the damned human race' to fry, as Twain uses his own fictioneer's magic to waft him back to isolationist Hartford.

Hysterical and accurate cynicism also motivates *Pudd'nhead Wilson* (1894), a thorough damnation of social hierarchy and its peculiarly American yearning to imitate European class society, and of the cruel absurdities of racism and slavery. Dawson's Landing is the provincial core of the damned in the heart of America's Mississippi artery lands. The plot articulates ironic despair with the centre of the would-be democratic— Hadleyburg, Eseldorf in *The Mysterious Stranger*, and here a Mississippi small town, a place of overlapping farce and tragedy. The plot's complexities of duplicity constitute the form of the entangled superstition and violence within American small-town hypocrisy and hierarchy, where law is for ever a frontier instability—as it is in the Arkansas town in *Huckleberry Finn* where Colonel Sherburn and Bloggs try to fight it out. The novel is a post-Civil War text on slavery, aristocratism and democratic idiocy. The bloody war had been no lesson, is part of the message. The medievally named pillars of society are exemplified in Pembroke Howard, who lives by the 'code' of Virginia gentlemen, always resorting to duels, and therefore 'very popular with the people' and, of course, 'the judge's dearest friend'. Twain's training obsession is plotted from a white boy—Percy Northumberland Driscoll's son—being reared a black, switched in the cradle with her son by the slave Roxana, so that her boy can escape her fate and be reared as Driscoll's son and heir. Since all three look white, blackness is exposed as a generative myth—absurd but none the less operational. Appearances govern but ancestry governs deeper. Tom, Roxy's son, grows up as Driscoll; she becomes his slave, 'the dupe of her deceptions', 'his chattel now, his convenience, his dog, his cringing and helpless slave, the humble and unresisting victim of his capricious temper and vicious nature.' He becomes, in fact, a ruling-class white, an indolent gambler and drunkard. Chapter 5 is sardonically headed 'Training is everything'. Roxy becomes the heir of 'two centuries of unatoned insult and outrage', but once she gains control over Tom, she too turns tyrant: 'her nature needed something or somebody to rule over, and he was better than nothing.' Twain believes nature will out, in the naturalist convention. Tom's discovery of his blackness demoralizes him completely. He quickly becomes a 'nigger'—that is, the heritage trains a man to know his place in hierarchical racist democracy, and immediately:

> He presently came to have a hunted sense and a haunted look, and then he fled away to the hill-tops and the solitudes. He said to himself that the curse of Ham was upon him.

That is, he accepts the Old Testament myth constantly used by racists throughout the world that Jehovah, later the Christian god, created racism himself.

Twain enables his main white figure, Wilson, to become the exonerated hero through determinism of another kind: not 'the curse of Ham' but the unalterable lines on human hand palms and fingers. The plot turns here again on fixed identity as much as the racist social system, an historically determined process. Wilson turns detective within a world understood, as it is for Poe's Chevalier Dupin, to be fixed in its bases and grasped for control by the man best fitted to manipulate this assumption. (Twain mocks this part of the plot thoroughly in *The Double-Barreled Detective Story*.)

Pudd'nhead Wilson is a black farce composed by a man idealistically defeated by determinism while retaining the ability to turn tyranny and stupidity into critical humour. The complex image of 'blood' fuses the whole crass display—even Roxy traces her ancestry back to Captain John Smith, Pocahontas, and an African king. One of the extracts from Wilson's calendar which head each chapter varies the conclusions of 'What Is Man?': 'If you pick up a starving dog and make him prosperous, he will not bite you. This is a principal difference between a dog and a man.' Law and lawyers are integral to the blood treachery of the text, and therefore, like so many American tales, this one gravitates towards the courthouse. What Poe, in 'Murders in the Rue Morgue', calls 'that moral activity which disentangles' and 'a comprehension of *all* sources of information whence legitimate advantage may be derived', leads here to a scene of grim, legalistic farce. But Chambers, Roxy's real son, is reinstated, and, having learned the meaning of generosity and forgiveness in twenty-three years of slavery, continues her pension. She finds solace in the church, ambiguous as it has shown itself to be.

In a parallel plot, Twain introduces actual twins, the supposed embodiments of European culture the small town sucks up eagerly: a pair of noble Italians who enslave their hosts into infatuated allegiance. Wilson reads Luigi's palm lines as a map of determinism and discovers that, as he has admitted, he killed a man in self-defence and defence of his brother Angelo. When Count Luigi accepts the duel with Tom, the event exposes the shallowness of democracy: 'In [the town's] eyes the principles had reached the summit of human honour. . . . Even the duellists' subordinates came in for a handsome share of the public approbation.' But once the twins become '*too* popular' they lose their election to aldermen. Increasingly, they are loaded with xenophobic blame for events, to the point where their lives parallel those of any person an American small town may decide to hate; they are 'in instant danger of being lynched'. So the two plots meet at the frontier of unwritten law, the point of American chaos. The final chapter heading reads: 'It was wonderful to find America, but it would have been more wonderful to miss it.'

In 1898 Twain produced *The Mysterious Stranger* and hid it. Four years after *Pudd'nhead Wilson* he had reached a chronic division between private writing and public distribution, a schizophrenic separation of private pessimism and public image as comedian. The angel Satan's final words to Theodore Fischer, the narrator, extend 'What Is Man?' into the blackness of *The Great Dark*:

> It is true that which I have revealed to you; there is no God, no universe, no human race, no earthly life, no heaven, no hell. It is all a dream—a grotesque and foolish dream. Nothing exists but you. And you are but a thought, a homeless thought, wandering forlorn among the empty eternities!

Fischer knows he is right, and no Young Man's protest is available. The 1590 Austrian scene is a private and determined hell of Twain's invention, and the plot demonstrates the meaninglessness of moral sense, choice and human dignity. Freedom is to be 'alone in shoreless space, to wander in its limitless solitudes without friend or comrade for ever', and to realize that this *is* the human condition. The angel shows Theodore all history as a brutal competitiveness, a gilded age stretching back into time, in which man's moral sense enables him to choose murder, war and mutual exploitation.

Twain's turn-of-the-century wounded optimism has become a grid of gloom. He is concerned with no systematic philosophic or historical analysis. Once again men are imaged as ants in the control of a superior force—a long American line from Jonathan Edwards to *A Farewell to Arms* and 'Big Two-Hearted River'—and their environment is proposed as a fixture. Community and mutual aid are impossible. Psychology is a pleasure-pain structure of tension and release. In Chapter 7, Twain writes 'God has forsaken us.' But where for Nietzsche contemporaneously, and Camus later, this is a signal to move forwards into a consideration of the existential situation, for Twain it is a signal for despair. His prose begins to lack the energy of his finest fictions and essays, and explicitly, in Chapter 10, man's sense of humour, once a powerful weapon, is now 'lying rusting' because he lacks 'sense and courage':

> Power, money, persuasion, supplication, persecution—these can lift a colossal humbug—push it a little—weaken it a little, century after century, but only laughter can blow it to rags and atoms at a blast. Against the assault of laughter nothing can stand.

That strength has become virtually impossible for Twain; in Chapter 10 he writes:

> No sane man can be happy, for to him life is real and he sees what a fearful thing it is. Only the mad can be happy, and not many of those. . . . Of course, no man is entirely in his own right mind at any time, but I have been referring to the extreme cases.

After Twain, such a delineation became nearly a commonplace—summarized by the great humorist James Thurber in two aphorisms: 'There is no safety in numbers, or in anything else' and 'Run, don't walk, to the nearest exit.' The limits of humour in America were still being pressed hard by the 'black humorists' during the Civil Rights conflict and the imperialism of the 1960s and 1970s, and by the farce and tragedy which destabilize the masterly plot of William Eastlake's *Dancers in the Scalp House*. The beautiful affirmations of *The Adventures of Huckleberry Finn* in 1885 were unique in Twain's career—a 12-year-old uneducated boy's self-reliance and self-release from the society he is trained to inherit and believe: family, religion, law, racism, the system of that civilizated duplicity and its disasters.

Against the Fugitive Slave Law, Huck befriends an adult Negro—and moves in discovery to his crux: 'they're after *us*.' But 'by that time everything we had in the world was on our raft' (Chapter 11). Their very brief raft freedom is betrayed by a king and a duke, the archetypes of Twain's assault on America's aristocratism and lawless competition. Like generations of youths to come, Twain's Huck is kidnapped by adult exploiters. Nigger Jim is saved from final betrayal and supposed return to slavery by Huck's disobedience of Providence: by choosing the freedom of wickedness, by repeatedly 'playing double' (Chapter 31), by contradicting his training, by disguising as a girl and by virtually killing the paternal, the father. The pattern of disobedience itself is written in a rich language which refuses the authority of orthodoxy and transforms the correct into the creative and therefore the subversive. The most moving and wonderful words in the book are Huck's as he tears up the letter to Miss Watson betraying her 'runaway nigger', as by law he should: 'All right, then, I'll *go* to hell.' Survival has to be achieved in a corrupt and hostile society— Huck's hero is a clown acrobat who stands on a galloping horse, shedding seventeen suits before he gracefully bows out (Chapter 22). The raft is an illusory freedom, but the only temporary home possible:

> We said there warn't no home like a raft, after all. Other places do seem so cramped up and smothery, but a raft don't. You feel mighty free and easy and comfortable on a raft.

But that is all. Society, on the contrary, is the head-games of Tom Sawyer's bookish laws and conventions, the training of official America which Huck encounters in his shore expeditions from the voyaging raft which make up most of the text. It is Tom who nearly kills Jim with his final stupidities, what Huck calls 'his bringing-up' (Chapter 42).

Twain's masterpiece poses the aspirations of fugitives against Miss Watson's code of respectability, Huck's honesty and tenderness against criminal legalities. But the boy is only just able to release himself from Tom's world of stereotypes in which Jim is a submissive nigger rather than a companion in revolt. Twain dissolves that murderous exploitive world—Huck's father, Miss Watson, the Grangerfords and Shepherdsons, Colonel Sherburn, the Wilkes brothers, the King and the Duke—the whole pattern of behaviourism and competition called civilization—dissolves it into a futile conflict system. His humour is a highly controlled hysteria edging into sacrificial dangers at each juncture of the narrative but retaining the resistance of art.

But ridicule is not survival. The raft is an impossible ideal, certainly not to be achieved in the United States without bitter isolation: 'What you want, above all things, on a raft, is for everybody to be satisfied, and feel right and kind towards the others.' That ideal is eroded by slavery, feuds, lynching, murder, Christian morality, and white people who eat while a black man is chained up in a nearby hut. A raft simply drifts, relatively unmanoeuvrable on the Mississippi and in danger of being run down by a riverboat in the state of competition of the *Amaranth* and the *Boreas*. Huck's marvellous inventive buoyancy in survival tactics cannot be played back into a reformist, let alone a revolutionary, social action. He rejects the 6,000 dollars and being adopted by Aunt Sally—instances of a civilization he 'can't stand': 'I reckon I got to light out for the Territory ahead of the rest.' The rest, it is implied will inevitably follow—and one day the West will end. Meanwhile, a boy of Huck's ability can at least alienate himself sufficiently for a while—a proposition as precarious as raft freedom in America. In *Europe and Elsewhere* (posthumously, 1923) there is an essay entitled 'The United States of Lynchdom' dealing, in 1900, with the commonplaces of lynching as 'a favorite regulator' of Moral Cowardice, 'this supreme trait of our character'. Perhaps Americans should advertise for brave sheriffs to do their work for them—or better still 'let us import American missionaries from China and send them into the lynching field.'

Twain's image of boyhood revolt is, as F. O. Matthiessen once wrote, compacted both of 'enchanted freedom and haunted terror'. *Huckleberry Finn* remains a major criticism of the frontier elements in American society, reminding us—again in Matthiessen's words, those of a major socialist student of his country, and a great Harvard teacher—'that joy and freedom of the frontier were never long separated from the violence and the cruelty', and the facts which made Nigger Jim Twain's most heroic character. It was Samuel Clemens who lost a fortune in speculation.

NOTES

1. Charles Neider, *Mark Twain and the Russians: An Exchange of Views* (New York: Hill and Wang, 1960).
2. Michael P. Hearn, 'Expelling Huck Finn', *Nation*, 7–14 August 1982, 117.
3. Mark Twain, 'Concerning the Jews' (1899), in *Mark Twain on the Damned Human Race*, ed. Janet Smith (New York: Hill and Wang, 1962). The exception is the French.
4. Ibid.
5. The issues of authorship are succinctly put in a single paragraph of E. Hudson Long's *Mark Twain Handbook* (New York: Hendricks House, 1957), pp. 179–80, the gist of which is that 'although the labours of both Twain and Charles Dudley Warner are evident, they also became inextricable', and Twain felt the work sufficiently his own to consider that 'he was now a novelist, a creator of characters and deviser of plot.'
6. Georges Braque, *Illustrated Notebooks 1917–1955* (New York: Dover Publications, 1971), p. 49.

Notes on Contributors

ROBERT GIDDINGS is a Senior Lecturer in English and Media at Dorset Institute of Higher Education, and author of *The Tradition of Smollett, You Should See Me in Pyjamas* and (with Alan Bold) *True Characters: Real People in Fiction*. He has contributed to *New Society, The Listener, New Statesman* and other journals, and edited *The Changing World of Charles Dickens* and *J. R. R. Tolkien: This Far Land* for the Critical Studies series.

ROBERT GOLDMAN was born in Los Angeles and graduated at Vanderbilt University, and was awarded a Woodrow Wilson Foundation Fellowship to study for his master's degree at Duke University. He has taught in the U.S.A. and in Greece, Spain and Morocco. For six years he was producer/director of the Actors' Repertory Theatre near London, which he founded. He was awarded his Ph.D. from King's College in the University of London, and is currently visiting professor of English at Shimane University, Matsue, Japan.

WILLIAM KAUFMAN grew up in New Jersey and was educated at Montclair State College. His experience includes banjo making in Nashville, music making and teaching, working in graveyards, airports and Wall Street. A Marshall Scholarship took him to the University of Wales, Aberystwyth, to read for his Ph.D. in American Literature.

A. ROBERT LEE teaches American Literature at the University of Kent at Canterbury. He edited the Everyman *Moby Dick* and several volumes in the Critical Studies series—*Black Fiction, Nathaniel Hawthorne: New Critical Essays, Ernest Hemingway: New Critical Essays, Herman Melville: Reassessments*—and has written a B.A.A.S. pamphlet *Black American Fiction Since Richard Wright* (1983) and numerous essays on English and American authors.

PHILIP MELLING is a lecturer in American culture, literature and society and a specialist in the literature of the period 1920–40. He teaches in the Department of Politics at the University College of Swansea.

PETER MESSENT lectures in American Studies at the University of Nottingham. He has also taught at the University of Manchester and California State University. He has written on Kurt Vonnegut in the *Journal of American Studies* and edited *Literature of the Occult* and (with Tom Paulin) *Henry James: Selected Tales*.

ERIC MOTTRAM is Professor of English and American Literature at King's College in the University of London, and the author of books on Kenneth Rexroth, William Faulkner, Allen Ginsberg, Paul Bowles and William S. Borroughs, of *Towards Design in Poetry* and (with Malcolm Bradbury) of *The Penguin Companion to American Literature*. He has published several books of poetry and edited *Poetry Review* 1970–76.

LYALL POWERS is Professor of English at the University of Michigan, Ann Arbor. He was born and educated in Canada, earned his M.A. at Manitoba and his Ph.D. at Indiana. He has taught at universities at Wisconsin, British Columbia, Göttingen, Honolulu. His publications include *Henry James and the Naturalist Movement, Henry James: An Introduction and Interpretation* and *Faulkner's Yoknapatawpha Comedy*, and collections of Henry James's letters.

JOHN S. WHITLEY is Reader in American Studies and Chairman of American Studies at the University of Sussex. He has published books on William Golding and F. Scott Fitzgerald, edited an edition of Dickens's *American Notes* and published essays on various detective story writers. He is currently working on a study of Dashiell Hammett.

Index

Index

Index

Index